Diverse Partnerships for Student Success

Strategies and Tools to Help School Leaders

Larry E. Decker
Virginia A. Decker
Pamela M. Brown

Rowman & Littlefield Education
Lanham, Maryland • Toronto • Oxford
2007

Published in the United States of America
by Rowman & Littlefield Education
A Division of Rowman & Littlefield Publishers, Inc.
A wholly owned subsidiary of The Rowman & Littlefield Publishing Group, Inc.
4501 Forbes Boulevard, Suite 200, Lanham, Maryland 20706
www.rowmaneducation.com

PO Box 317
Oxford
OX2 9RU, UK

British Library Cataloguing in Publication Information Available

Library of Congress Cataloging-in-Publication Data

Decker, Larry E.
  Diverse partnerships for student success : strategies and tools to help school leaders /
Larry E. Decker, Virginia A. Decker, Pamela M. Brown.
    p. cm.
  Includes bibliographical references and index.
  ISBN-13: 978-1-57886-538-3 (hardcover : alk. paper)
  ISBN-13: 978-1-57886-539-0 (pbk. : alk. paper)
  ISBN-10: 1-57886-538-7 (hardcover : alk. paper)
  ISBN-10: 1-57886-539-5 (pbk. : alk. paper)
  1. Community and school—United States. I. Decker, Virginia A. II. Brown,
Pamela M., 1954– III. Title.
  LC221.D42 2007
  371.190973—dc22   2006020718

♾ ™ The paper used in this publication meets the minimum requirements of American
National Standard for Information Sciences—Permanence of Paper for Printed Library
Materials, ANSI/NISO Z39.48-1992. Manufactured in the United States of America.

Contents

Foreword

When Larry Decker asked me to write the foreword for this book, I thought it was a very interesting subject, but wondered about the extent to which it would provide school leaders with the kinds of knowledge and skills necessary to handle the enormous expectations that have changed their roles over the past five years. After reading the book, I was very impressed with its focus on developing school leaders who have the capacity for creating enlightened school visions, building supportive educational partnerships, broadening communication to include active school communities, and becoming strong public relations advocates for their schools. This type of focus for creating politically astute, and public relations savvy, school administrators has been a sorely missing component in traditional higher education preparation programs and in the ongoing professional development of school leaders.

With the advent of the No Child Left Behind (NCLB) legislation, the issue of school choice, and the growth of vouchers, school leaders now must be able to market themselves and their schools in order to remain competitive in today's expanding resource market. The national rush to implement public school reform through high stakes testing too often leaves school administrators with the increasingly difficult task of maximizing resources to improve the performance of all children. The authors remind us that good administrators must know how to establish strong community partnerships in order to develop the comprehensive resources necessary to meet the complex and myriad needs of all children.

I fully recognize the contributions of NCLB in identifying the need for improving disproportionate achievement levels of all various subgroup populations. However, low adequate yearly progress (AYP) results in schools across the nation, and the media hype that has gone with it, have increased the public's perception that public schools are failing. This has led to the serious loss of support for, and belief in, the role of the American public school system. This book will assist principals in learning the skills necessary for creating positive school cultures that welcome, and are inclusive of, the larger community such as parents, community organizations, social service groups, and after-school programs.

I remind the reader that improving the achievement gap is not simply a matter of improved test scores. Mountains of research have demonstrated the detriment to student achievement caused by poverty, inadequate housing, high unemployment, poor health screening, the unavailability of quality health care, and a lack of commitment to universal preschool and Head Start programs. To deny the impact of these conditions on student achievement defies logic and allows our national, state, and local political leaders to blame schools without accepting any responsibilities. Principals and schools cannot hope to combat these problems without the active involvement of and ongoing communication with diverse educational partnerships within communities. The authors make extra effort to encourage school leaders to be strong advocates for their schools and take on leadership roles within their communities to create a vision of learning that will, in fact, improve the learning of all children.

I am optimistic that this book will assist school leaders, aspiring school leaders, and educational administration faculty to understand the newly changing responsibilities of the principalship and the superintendency. To this end, to be successful in today's NCLB "accountability environment," educational leaders must have the knowledge and training to develop a vision of learning for their communities, not just for their schools, that will bring educators, families, and others together. The old African proverb, "It takes a village to educate a child," could not be more true than today. In essence, this proverb frames the context of this timely, instructive, and informative publication. To promote equity and excellence for all students, sustained and coherent collaborative efforts of educators, parents, community groups, and businesses will be required.

A conceptual understanding of the necessity of the changing leadership role is cogently noted by John Kotter, of the Harvard Business School, who wrote, "Successful transformation is 70–90% leadership and only

10–30% management." Arguably, the management responsibilities of a school leader are essential and important (cafeteria supervision, monitoring bus schedules, planning budgets, maintaining facilities, etc.). Today's reality, however, is that these are not the major reasons that administrators fail. While a propensity for careful management may keep existing programs and activities running smoothly, little, if any, transformation takes place. On the other hand, a commitment to leadership helps principals adapt to significantly changing circumstances. It defines what the future should look like, aligns staff with that vision, and inspires them to make it happen. There is a significant difference in the future in both the reward and recognition system for the leader who has the courage and vision to *lead* change, as opposed to *managing* change that is often dictated from a remote policy forum. This type of leadership does not take place in an administrator's office—rather, it requires an inclusive process, continually interacting within a school's broader community and environment.

The words of Herman Melville, written more than a hundred years ago, ring true today in defining the leader's role in a complex and diverse society: "We cannot live only for ourselves. A thousand fibers connect us with our fellow men; and among those fibers, as sympathetic threads, our actions run as causes, and they come back to us as effects." The authors of this book have captured the essence of Melville's cogent message by clearly emphasizing the need for interconnectedness between schools and their communities—stressing the urgency of taking up this timely and necessary challenge. Those administrators who accept this challenge will ultimately engage those "thousand invisible threads," and their actions will allow them to realize the "effects."

Gerald N. Tirozzi, PhD
Executive Director
National Association of Secondary School Principals

Preface

The United States is going through a period of rapid change—demographic shifts, burgeoning multiculturalism, and the effects of a surging global economy. Educators in this dynamic setting are expected to negotiate a complexity of social, economic, and political issues while managing staff shortages, shrinking budgets, diverse school populations, and rigid, often poorly funded state and federal educational mandates and standards. Unfortunately, they must also cope with the fact that the public's faith in its schools appears to be withering and that support for alternatives to public schools, including the charter movement and a voucher system, is growing.

Some educational leaders have responded to this onslaught of challenges by creating schools as closed spaces that have little contact with the outside world, further isolating themselves from potential support. This go-it-alone approach fails to recognize that reaching out to the many stakeholders inside and outside of schools is essential to achieving success in the schools' mission of educating the community's children. As noted by Epstein (2001):

> Educators need to understand the contexts in which students live, work, and play. Without that understanding, educators work alone, not in partnership with other important people in students' lives. Without partnerships, educators segment students into the school child and the home child, ignoring the whole child. (p. 5)

Understanding the context of students' lives requires an understanding of the changing demographics of the nation. A report by the National

Association of State Boards of Education in 2002 asserted that by 2040 no single ethnic group would make up a majority of the population in the United States. Many of our public schools do not reflect this diversity. In fact, in many parts of the country, schools are being resegregated at an alarming rate and those that are most segregated tend to be those with very high poverty rates (Orfield and Lee, 2004). Educational leaders can no longer take the "melting pot" approach to diversity that expects all children to be assimilated into one "American" culture. The challenge for educational leaders is to recognize, respect, and value diversity while promoting the unity, acceptance, and harmony that lead to increasing strength and solidarity for the nation.

Amid the many challenges facing our public schools, educational reform, variously defined, remains the topic of major concern and discussion. Reacting to the political debate that culminated in the passage of the No Child Left Behind Act in 2001, Harkavy and Blank (2002) observe that it would be easy to assume that the only things that matter in education are annual testing in grades 3 through 8, having a qualified teacher in the first four years of school, and allowing parents to move their children out of persistently failing schools. They note that several significant elements of the reauthorized Elementary and Secondary Education Act (ESEA) of 2001 are largely ignored by federal lawmakers and by other leaders and the public at large. Arguing that these ESEA provisions offer a more comprehensive—and realistic—view of what it would take to educate children to their highest potential, Harkavy and Blank point to the provisions that

1. Place a high priority on parental involvement in education.
2. Emphasize the need to coordinate and integrate school services with the support and opportunities from federal, state, and local programs serving youth and families.
3. Support after-school enrichment opportunities—programs in such areas as violence prevention, service learning, family literacy, mentoring, mental health, and others; and services that go beyond a broad focus on academics.
4. Urge an expanded role for community-based organizations that are now directly eligible for federal education funds through the 21st

Century Community Learning Centers Programs and are explicitly encouraged to collaborate with schools. (p. 1)

This book is based on the deep conviction that schools function best in collaboration with the family and the larger community. It offers strategies and tools to help educational leaders create successful educational partnerships in a socioeconomically diverse and multicultural society. The chapters present information on how to identify relevant demographic trends; use outside resources; and create community partnerships to address the educational, cultural, health, lifelong learning, vocational, and recreational needs of students and citizens in a multicultural community. Individual chapters contain material that addresses the applicable National Council for Accreditation of Teacher Education, Educational Leadership Constituent Council, Florida Educational Leadership Examination, Interstate Leaders Licensure Consortium, and Florida Department of Education standards for educational leaders. Most chapters conclude with a listing of websites for more information and links to other relevant sites.

In aggregate, the book offers educational leaders comprehensive, research-based information, concrete program ideas, and numerous Internet sites for additional help in creating and sustaining family and community engagement tailored to the needs of individual communities. It presents ideas and strategies for involving people—individually and collectively in agencies, businesses, and organizations—in order to mobilize the resources of families, community members, and organizations in support of the school's goals.

The goal we share with all educational leaders is to develop, implement, and sustain a comprehensive educational partnership system that helps all children succeed academically, so that they can live productive lives in healthy communities. This ambitious goal has always been an essential part of the American Dream.

REFERENCES

Epstein, J. L. (2001). *School, family, and community partnerships: Preparing educators and improving schools.* Boulder, CO: Westview Press.

Harkavy, I., and Blank, M. (2002). *Community schools: A vision of learning that goes beyond testing.* Retrieved April 10, 2006, from http://www.community schools.org/commentary.html

National Association of State Boards of Education Study Group. (2002). *A more perfect union: Building an educational system that embraces all children.* Alexandria, VA: National State Boards of Education. Retrieved August 12, 2005, from http://www.nasbe.org/Educational_Issues/Reports/More_Perfect _Union.PDF

Orfield, G., and Lee, C. (2004). *Brown at 50: King's dream or Plessy's nightmare?* Cambridge, MA: The Civil Rights Project.

Acknowledgments

We would like to thank Mary Boo for her tireless and sterling work as our editor; Jennifer Sugrhue for her technical editing contributions; and the numerous graduate students at Florida Atlantic University who field-tested the online course that supports this text.

We would also like to express our appreciation to the editor and production staff of Rowman & Littlefield Education who worked with us in bringing this book into print.

Chapter One

Educational Partnerships: Principles and Strategies

Twenty-first-century schools are complex, diverse, and challenging communities. The student base is increasingly multicultural; many languages other than English are spoken at home; and the students represent a wide range of socioeconomic backgrounds. Although the achievement barriers of poverty, language, and foreign culture are often concentrated in a school, school leaders are expected to help meet the demands of a global economy by producing a highly educated and technically adept workforce. Faced with a growing emphasis on academic performance as measured by standardized testing, they must also deal with shrinking school budgets, rising teacher attrition rates, and worries about school safety—including the fear of terrorist attacks. The challenges of these issues can be overwhelming when schools are isolated from the communities they serve.

It has become increasingly important that school leaders reach out to all the stakeholders in their schools to create and nurture supportive networks committed to helping all children succeed. Research shows that effective schools involve families and communities in collaborative relationships that respect cultural differences, address the needs of individual families, and embrace a philosophy of partnership in which power and responsibility are shared (Henderson and Mapp, 2002). Successful schools have in place a comprehensive plan for involving family and community at every level, because educating children in our increasingly diverse society requires "contributions and commitments from everyone in the community" (Dodd and Konzal, 2002, p. 288). Polanyi (2001) asserts that in order to "survive in the world we have transformed, we must learn to think in a new way. As never before, the future of each depends on the good of all" (Statement, para. 1).

THE IMPORTANCE OF FAMILY AND COMMUNITY INVOLVEMENT

When family and community are involved in schools, everyone wins. Research shows that students from families with above-average parental involvement have success rates 30% higher than students from families with below-average parental involvement, as measured by grade point averages, test scores, promotion and retention rates, and teacher ratings (Wherry, 2004). They are also more likely to pass courses, earn credits, attend school regularly, show good behavior, adapt well to school, and be promoted. The benefits of family involvement extend to the schools themselves. In schools in which teachers reported high levels of outreach to parents, test scores improved at a rate 40% higher than test scores in schools reported to have low levels of outreach to parents (Henderson and Mapp, 2002). Such findings have led educators to seek collaboration and partnerships that build on the assets and strengths of families and communities, rather than to emphasize problems. The goals of this collaboration are to create a two-way dialogue between home, school, and community; increase community understanding of the school system; and bring new resources into the learning process. By encouraging community involvement, educators can build a network of allies while increasing student engagement and improving learning outcomes (Mathews and Menna, 2003).

Unfortunately, for many educators, collaboration is not an easy process. Some are reluctant to share power or to delegate certain responsibilities. Others may focus on the loss of control that accompanies shared decision making rather than on the benefits that derive from community input and advice. However, an increasing number of educational policymakers, school leaders, and teachers are discovering that the benefits to be gained from collaboration far outweigh the potential problems. They have learned that a comprehensive educational partnership program increases student achievement and results in greater academic account-ability, better attendance rates, and an improved school climate.

COLLABORATION IN DIVERSE COMMUNITIES

Research by the National Association of State Boards of Education in 2002 projected that by 2040 no ethnic group would constitute a majority in the United States. To meet the educational challenges inevitable in an increasingly diverse school system, school leaders must recognize that all families, regardless of income, race, or ethnicity, are concerned about and want to support their children's education. Recent research shows that students with involved parents, no matter what their ethnic background or socioeconomic status, are more likely to earn higher grades, be promoted, attend school regularly, and go on to postsecondary education (Henderson and Mapp, 2002).

Unfortunately, some families face barriers to parental involvement because of language differences, employment burdens, cultural disparities, and lack of information about how to get involved. They may also encounter a lack of school support for diversity or negative attitudes by school personnel toward families with diverse backgrounds and needs (White-Clark and Lappin, 2005). Although school leaders need to understand these barriers, they should not approach diverse families from a position of trying to remedy deficits but should bring to the relationship the same high expectations they have for all students and families.

RESPONDING TO THE CHALLENGE

When the goal of creating a long-term cooperative relationship is used to guide collaboration and partnership efforts, public schools are operated with a commitment to the idea that they are part of the community. Professional educators and staff receive training to increase their skills in enlisting family and community support. The school curriculum is designed to incorporate a variety of involvement relationships and collab-orative activities among schools, families, students, community members, businesses and industry, and local organizations and agencies. The school culture itself becomes conducive to partnership and collaboration. Ferguson (2005) emphasizes the need to gain the trust of family and community members to facilitate dependable support and interaction. He suggests that school leaders implement initiatives that

1. Help family members feel comfortable in interactions with school staff by creating a welcoming culture.
2. Assist staff to see the value of working with family members and to define what involvement in schools really means.
3. Help staff see the importance of planning involvement strategies.
4. Address barriers to family and community involvement. (p. 3)

Making the decision to create cooperative relationships requires rethinking the roles of school administrators and teachers. School administrators must work conscientiously to create a productive team of staff, parents, students, and other stakeholders. New state and federal standards for the teaching profession hold teachers accountable for engaging families and community members and for creating collaborative partnerships that connect home and school. The Harvard Family Research Project (Caspe, 2001) compiled professional standards of practice related to family and community involvement recommended by professional or certifying organizations. These standards expect teachers to

1. Work with and through parents and families to support children's learning and development.
2. Know the importance of establishing and maintaining a positive collaborative relationship with families to promote academic, social, and emotional growth of children.
3. Propagate communication between home and school that is regular, two-way, and meaningful.
4. Foster relationships with school colleagues, parents, and agencies in the larger community to support students' learning and well-being.
5. Communicate about mathematics goals to help families and other caregivers.
6. Maintain an open, friendly, and cooperative relationship with each

child's family, encourage their involvement in the program, and support the child's relationship with his or her family. (p. 3)

EDUCATIONAL PARTNERSHIP STRATEGIES

The ultimate goal of a comprehensive educational partnership plan is the creation of a responsive support system for collaborative action to address educational concerns, quality-of-life issues of community members, and special needs. The following strategies (Decker and Decker, 2003) provide a framework for developing such a cooperative venture.

Strategy 1: Encourage increased use of community resources and volunteers to augment the curricula. Every community has human, physical, and financial resources that can be used to enrich and expand traditional education programs. Community resources and volunteers have been used to develop programs and expand curricular options, including school volunteer programs, field and study trips, peer tutoring, mentoring, student-based enterprises, and experiential learning.

Strategy 2: Develop educational partnerships between schools and public and private service providers, business and industry, and civic and social service organizations. Complex and interrelated social and economic problems create a broad array of service needs in many communities, and meeting them effectively requires more resources than any single agency or organization can provide. This strategy encourages the development of educational partnerships that cooperate in the use of available resources and avoid unnecessary duplication. Such partnerships might focus on childcare and latchkey programs, drug education and substance abuse efforts, intensive programs to address literacy and other academic competencies, assistance to at-risk youth and minorities, community economic development, internships and work-study programs, and career awareness.

Strategy 3: Use public education facilities as community service centers for meeting the educational, social, health, cultural, and recreational needs of all ages and sectors of the community. The fact that community attitudes and support affect the schools' ability to carry out their mission to educate all children requires educators to consider the needs and the concerns of nonparents. This strategy encourages opening school buildings on a planned, organized basis at hours beyond the regular school day. It takes advantage of the strong support community centers generally receive, as well as the economic benefits of more efficient shared use.

Strategy 4: Develop an environment that fosters lifelong learning. This strategy advocates the promotion of learning as a lifelong process. It recognizes that much learning takes place without formal instruction, both inside and outside the school setting. It encourages the development of lifelong education programs to meet learning needs that change over a lifetime, including the need to acquire new skills and knowledge. Programs and activities might include early childhood education; extended-day and enrichment programs for school-age children; adult education, vocational training, and retraining programs; leisure time activities; and intergenerational programs.

Strategy 5: Establish community involvement processes in educational planning and decision making. The total community has a responsibility to support the mission of educating all community members. Community members, therefore, have a right and a duty to participate in determining community needs, setting priorities, and selecting the most appropriate allocation of resources. This cyclical process, concerned with evaluation and change as well as with initial planning, takes advantage of a basic fact of human behavior: Individuals who participate in planning and decision making develop feelings of ownership in the outcome. Encouraging broad-based involvement capitalizes on another principle: In general, the greater the number and diversity of people involved in the planning, development, implementation, and evaluation of educational opportunities, the greater the likelihood that needs will be met and support for education will be developed and maintained. Involvement opportunities range from participation in ongoing community advisory councils to membership on ad hoc advisory task forces and special study committees.

Strategy 6: Reduce barriers to involvement in diverse communities. Today's school leaders must recognize the many barriers to parent involvement, especially those of time, resources, and language. The task of the school leader is to help level the playing field for diverse families, not just by holding traditional "back-to-school" and other parent evenings, but also by treating families as meaningful partners in their children's education. Actions that may produce results include a personal welcome for all parents, a physical space or room where parents can meet, and the purposeful inclusion of diverse parents on decision-making bodies.

Strategy 7: Provide a responsive, community-based support system for collective action among all educational and community agencies to address both community quality-of-life issues and special needs. This strategy recognizes the complexity of many problems and underscores the fact that their resolution may require cooperative use of resources. Seeking the involvement of other agencies can help schools address such social, health, educational, and economic issues as drug and substance abuse, housing, public safety and crime prevention, at-risk youth, violence and vandalism, teen pregnancy, and racial and minority concerns.

Strategy 8: Develop a system that facilitates home-school-community communication. Research shows that schools that involve all their publics and keep them informed have community support; those that fail to reach beyond parents do not. Effective home-school-community communications go beyond news releases, speeches, newsletters, and open houses to include use of the media, home visitation by teachers and administrators, meet-the-community programs, school displays in the community, and programs conducted away from the school site.

These strategies have overlapping characteristics and functions. Together, they form the outline of an action plan.

CREATING A COMPREHENSIVE EDUCATIONAL PARTNERSHIP PLAN

Creating a truly comprehensive plan involves using the eight strategies in communicating, assessing, planning, and experimenting in an ongoing cyclical process. In a comprehensive partnership plan, schools are no longer isolated providers of a single component—education for children and youth—but active collaborators in a broad community effort. The U.S. Department of Education and the Regional Educational Laboratory Network (2002) examined the changed role of schools in comprehensive partnership strategies:

> As partners, schools have increased cooperation, communication, and interaction with parents, community groups, service providers and agencies,

local policymakers and other stakeholders. School staff share their knowledge and experience with the community beyond the schoolhouse walls—
and return with fresh inspiration to guide policies and practices within the
school. (section 1, Introduction, para. 13)

A guide to creating comprehensive school-linked partnerships, *Putting
the Pieces Together* (U.S. Dept. of Ed., 2002), explains that within these
partnerships:

1. All partners begin to view children as members of families and
   communities, not as isolated individuals. For school staff, understanding the context in which children live helps teachers select the
   most appropriate methods to improve students' learning and
   achievement.
2. By participating in preventive, capacity-building strategies, such as
   early childhood and family support programs, schools and their
   partners can play a major role in building strength and resiliency in
   students, families, and communities.
3. Instead of focusing only on short-term measures—test scores, attendance rates, and disciplinary incidents—school staff can link with
   partner agencies to help families achieve lifelong learning objectives, including adult literacy and job training.

The guide emphasizes that, "as schools incorporate these ideas into
their daily work, all types of staff will collaborate in developing goals,
evaluating program effectiveness, representing the school as a community
partner, and developing successful strategies for working with [families]
and community" (section 1, para. 14).

The chapters that follow address various aspects of a comprehensive
educational partnership plan that reflects the dimensions of diversity in
our schools. They present a rationale for addressing particular areas; relevant research; suggested considerations, examples, and tips; and a list of
helpful references and websites.

REFERENCES

Caspe, M. (2001). *Family-school-community partnerships: A compilation of professional standards of practice for teachers.* Harvard Family Research Project.

Retrieved April 9, 2006, from http://www.gse.harvard.edu/hfrp/projects/fine/resources/standards/

Decker, L. E., and Decker, V. A. (2003). *Home, school, and community partnerships.* Lanham, MD: Scarecrow Press.

Dodd, A. W., and Konzal, J. L. (2002). *How communities build stronger schools.* New York: Palgrave McMillan.

Ferguson, C. (2005). *Organizing family and community connections with schools: How do school staff build meaningful relationships with all stakeholders? A strategy brief of the National Center for Family and Community Connections with Schools.* Austin, TX: Southwest Educational Development Laboratory. Retrieved April 10, 2006, from http://www.sedl.org/connections/resources/rb/b4-REL

Henderson, A., and Mapp, K. (2002). *A new wave of evidence: The impact of school, family and community connections on student achievement.* Austin, TX: Southwest Educational Development Laboratory.

Mathews, D., and Menna, R. (2003, Winter). The importance of parent/school/community collaboration at a time of educational and social change. *Education Canada 43*(1), 20–23.

National Association of State Boards of Education Study Group. (2002). *A more perfect union: Building an educational system that embraces all children.* Alexandria, VA: National State Boards of Education. Retrieved August 12, 2005, from http://www.nasbe.org/Educational_Issues/Reports/More_Perfect_Union.PDF

Polanyi, J. (2001). *Introduction to the Nobel statement.* Retrieved August 14, 2005, from http://www.toronto.edu/jpolanyi/nobelstatement/introduction.html

U.S. Department of Education and the Regional Educational Laboratory Network. (2002). *Putting the pieces together: Comprehensive school-linked strategies for children and families.* Retrieved January 29, 2002, from http://www.ncrel.org/sdrs/areas/issues/envrnmnt/css/ppt/putting

Wherry, J. H. (2004). *Selected parent involvement research.* Fairfax, VA: WestEd. Retrieved August 1, 2005, from http://www.par-inst.com/educator/resources/research/research.php

White-Clark, R., and Lappin, G. (2005). Building home-school partnerships: A way of enhancing reading literacy of diverse learners. *Electronic Magazine of Multicultural Education 7*(1). Retrieved July 20, 2005, from http://www.eastern.edu/publications/emme/2005spring/white-clark_lappin.html

Chapter Two

Understanding the Community and the Status of Families and Youth

The public school and the community are inextricably bound. What happens in a school affects the community, and what happens in the community affects the school. If teachers and school administrators expect to be successful in their primary mission of educating the community's children, they need to know a great deal about the community and the families from which the children come.

That proposition is not as simple as it sounds. For one thing, no two communities are exactly alike. For another, different communities influence schools in different ways. Finally, both communities and families are constantly changing in a variety of ways, some of them highly gratifying and others thoroughly discouraging. The rate of change is increasing with the rapidly multiplying effects of shifts in demographic, multicultural, and diversity factors, and the ever-accelerating demands of a knowledge-based global economy.

The urge for a quick fix is understandable and sometimes irresistible. In a search for easy answers to complex problems, some school critics have been willing to disregard a single undeniable fact: Educational problems reflect community and family problems in all their complexity, diversity, and intractability. Even a brief examination of the demographics of American society at the beginning of the 21st century shows the enormity of the challenges faced by schools.

A DEFINITION OF COMMUNITY

How does a school define its community? A generation ago, an answer to that question was relatively easy. A community is "a population aggregate, inhabiting a contiguous delimitable area, and having a set of basic service institutions; it is conscious of its local unity" (Seay and Crawford, 1954, p. 27). Today this definition would probably be applicable to only small schools in rural areas.

An Internet search produced a variety of definitions of community. LaborLawTalk.com (2005) explains that the word *community* comes from the Latin *minus,* meaning gift, and *cum,* meaning with or together. Thus, "community could be defined as a group of people who share gifts which they provide to all" (para. 2).

WordNet (2005) defines *community* as:

1. A group of people living in a particular area.
2. A group of people having ethnic, cultural, or religious characteristics in common.
3. Common possession (as in, "they share a community of possessions").
4. A group of nations having common interests (as in, "they belong to the UNESCO community").
5. A professional community (as in, "they organize around a learned occupation").
6. Community of interests (as in, "they have shared goals").
7. A residential district or area (a district in which people live, occupied primarily by private residences).

In *Strengthening Community in Education,* Dwyer (1998) defines *community* as "a group of people who are socially interdependent, who participate together in discussion and decision making, and who share certain practices that both define community and are nurtured by it" (section 2, para. 3). He states that within a community there are "generally accepted rules and social norms that protect, respect and please members of the community" and that a "true community requires its participants to engage in the working of a society consensually" (section 2, para. 3). Dwyer points out that membership within a community is about meeting basic needs, each of which is intertwined with the overall purpose of the community.

THE SCHOOL COMMUNITY

Just as educators need to understand the community from which their students come, they must arrive at an understanding of the community that exists within the school itself. Belenardo (2001) emphasizes student effort—as well as teacher and parent effort—may depend greatly on the underlying climate and culture of the school.

McBrien and Brandt (1997) define school climate and culture as "the sum of the values, cultures, safety practices, and organizational structures within a school that cause it to function and react in particular ways. . . . Teaching practices, diversity, and the relationships among administrators, teachers, parents, and students contribute to school climate" (section 1, para. 1). They point out that although the terms *climate* and *culture* are used somewhat interchangeably, school climate refers primarily to the school's effect on students while school culture refers primarily to the way teachers and other staff members work with each other.

Researchers have pointed to the benefits that derive from building a sense of community in schools. Students in schools with a strong sense of community are more likely to be "academically motivated, act ethically and altruistically, develop social and emotional competencies, and to avoid problem behaviors such as drug use and violence" (Schaps, 2003, p. 31). Belenardo (2001), emphasizing the importance of school climate and culture, states that parents, teachers, and students who feel part of a caring and supportive school environment are more likely to respond positively to such schoolwide challenges as the pressure for students to perform well on tests.

Belenardo also points out that even though much has been written about the importance of a sense of community in schools, there is no clear understanding of the organizational elements that contribute to its existence. She reports on research efforts to identify and define elements that indicate whether a sense of community exists in a school. The following six elements provide a comprehensive framework for measuring the presence and the strength of a sense of community in schools. The strength of a school's sense of community may be defined by the degree to which the elements are combined and integrated into a coherent whole.

1. *Shared values.* A cohesive, reinforcing school program is built on a core set of common beliefs and expectations. These shared values underlie the school vision and provide a uniform direction for the development of the instructional program and for behavioral expectations. Indicators of shared values include agreement on instructional expectations and practices, the enforcement of schoolwide discipline standards, high academic standards for all students, and explicit achievement goals.

2. *Commitment.* Commitment is evidenced by a willingness to go beyond the expected participation. The commitment level of members is demonstrated by behaviors and actions that support the group's shared values and beliefs.

3. *Feeling of belonging.* There is a shared emotional connection that provides participants with a sense of being part of something that has a past, present, and future. This feeling of belonging is created by school programs that recognize the positive performance and contributions of individual members; a common agenda of activities and similar experiences that link students, families, teachers, and administrators to the school's traditions; and the acceptance of all members into the group, regardless of individual differences.

4. *Caring.* Caring connects members of the group and results in mutual respect, support, and interest. A feeling of cooperation, rather than competition, is demonstrated through the willingness of adults—educators, families, and community members—to help each other as well as to help students.

5. *Interdependence.* A recognized interrelationship exists among individuals, as well as an understanding that all actions occur in relation to others, rather than in isolation. Cooperative interaction results in ongoing, mutually beneficial skill development and contributes to the collegiality of the school.

6. *Regular contact.* Importance is placed on providing opportunities for all members to meet and communicate. There are regularly scheduled activities that provide ample opportunities for members to interact with one another, develop relationships, and celebrate

their membership in the organization. Established procedures ensure that all members are kept informed of school programs and activities. (Belenardo, 2001)

As our communities become increasingly multicultural and diverse, it is important that educators not only develop an understanding of the demographic and socioeconomic conditions that exist in the communities in which they work, but that they also foster a strong sense of community within the school. Only then can they define their own roles in building the kind of healthy community—in the school and in the larger community—in which learning is valued by all.

HEALTHY COMMUNITIES

Several measures have been used in attempts to define and describe a healthy community. Dwyer (1998) suggests that examining the ways a community provides for individuals' needs yields an understanding of a healthy community as one in which basic needs are purposefully and assertively met in a way that contributes to the functionality of the community itself.

Another way to view the health of a community is in terms of sustainability. *Annex A: Definition and Components of Sustainable Communities* (Local Government Authority, 2005) emphasizes that sustainable communities embody the principles of sustainable development. They "balance and integrate the social, economic, and environment components of their community; meet the needs of existing and future generations; and respect the needs of other communities in the wider region or internationally also to make their communities sustainable" (p. 1). The publication points out that sustainable communities are diverse, reflecting local circumstances, but that they should all be:

1. Active, inclusive, safe, fair, tolerant, and cohesive, with a strong local culture and shared community activities.
2. Well run, with effective and inclusive participation, representation, and leadership.

3. Environmentally sensitive, providing places for people to live that are considerate of the environment.
4. Well designed and built, featuring quality buildings and a pleasant surrounding environment.
5. Well connected, with good transportation services and communication linking people to jobs, schools, health, and other services.
6. Thriving, with a flourishing and diverse local economy.
7. Well served by public, private, community, and voluntary services that are appropriate to people's needs and accessible to all.
8. Fair for everyone, including those in other communities, now and in the future.

Another approach to examining the health of a community is to measure its *social capital*. Popularized by Putnam (2000) in *Bowling Alone: The Collapse and Revival of American Community,* the term *social capital* refers to the individual and communal time and energy available for community improvement, social networking, civic engagement, personal recreation, and other activities that create social bonds between individuals and groups. Social capital researcher Wehlage (Lockwood, 2001) says, "[T]he place-based type of social capital is the old-fashioned notion of community built on trust, shared values and the face-to-face relations of people living in close proximity to one another" (section 2, The Power of Social Capital, para. 3).

According to Putnam (2000), many general benefits accrue to a community from the development of social capital:

1. *Social capital allows citizens to resolve collective problems more easily.* If everyone pitches in, whether it is by taking part in a neighborhood crime watch or helping an older person with lawn work, everyone in the community benefits.
2. *Social capital reduces transaction costs.* Everyday business and social transactions are much less problematic when community networks are in place. Shared responsibilities save money and time.
3. *Growing up in an environment of mutual confidence socializes people to develop benevolence toward others.* Active, reliable connections within the community, between friends and neighbors from

different cultures and backgrounds, creates trust and empathy. Residents learn to appreciate other points of view.

4. *Networks channel helpful information.* Connections within the community increase social and economic opportunities, especially for newcomers.

5. *Social capital improves people's psychological and physical well-being.* Evidence suggests that people whose lives are rich in social capital cope better with traumas and fight illness. (p. 288)

Putnam believes social capital is declining in America, especially in the suburbs. He suggests that the strong sense of community felt by the generation that survived World War II has been replaced by new generations of children used to televisions and electronic entertainment. Other factors working against the community collaboration and cohesion necessary to build social capital include the transition of women into the career-oriented workforce, suburbanization, sprawl, and the pressures of time and money.

Determining whether a community is healthy or not requires an understanding of the various parts of the community that make up the whole. In order to work effectively within a community, educators need information about population data and characteristics: existing cultural groups and their norms, customs, and traditions. They also need information about characteristics and organization of the political system and the power brokers (both formal and informal); communication channels; significant community groups and organizations; economic conditions; patterns of employment and unemployment; social structures, tensions, and problems that affect the learner and the school; community resources and services; school-community relationships; and geographic strengths and weaknesses.

DEMOGRAPHICS AND SOCIOECONOMIC VARIABLES

One way to begin to understand a community is to look at national trends and issues that will have an impact on it over time. For example:

1. *The demographics of the United States are changing rapidly.* By 2050, the Caucasian population will decrease from 74% to between

48% and 53%; the African American population will increase from 13% to 14%; the Hispanic population will increase from 10% to 25%; and the Asian population will increase from 3% to 8% (Peterson, 2004). Currently, 14% of the total U.S. population speaks a language other than English at home; 54% of those speak Spanish (Child Trends, 2005).

2. *America is aging.* According to the 2000 U.S. Census, the ratio of elderly Americans to the total population has jumped from 1 in 25 to 1 in 8. By 2020, there will be 65 million people over age 65 and many will have one year of retirement for every year of work.

3. *Homelessness is increasing.* The Urban Institute (2003) estimates 3.5 million people are likely to experience homelessness in a given year. Families with children are among the fastest growing segment of the homeless population at 40% (The Institute for Children and Poverty, 2004).

4. *The rate of poverty is increasing in many states.* The National Center for Children in Poverty (2004) states that in 2004, 13% of people nationwide were living in poverty, with poverty rates varying widely around the country, from less than 8% in Connecticut and New Hampshire to 22% in Mississippi. Nineteen states had statistically significant increases in poverty rates since 2000; six of those states were located in the Midwest.

5. *The rich are getting richer, and the poor are getting poorer.* Economic Policy Institute (2002) statistics show that in the year 2000, the annual income of the top fifth of U.S. families was 10 times the income of families in the bottom fifth, a 30% increase over 1980. The gap between high-income and middle-income families (defined as consisting of two or more related persons in a household) also increased. In 2000, the income of families in the top fifth income group was three times that of a median-income family, up from a ratio of about 2.3 to 1 in 1980.

THE STATUS OF CHILDREN AND FAMILIES IN AMERICA

The 2000 U.S. Census recorded 39 million family groups with children, up from 30 million in 1970. By one estimate (Policy Institute for Family

Impact Seminars, 2005), only 7% of those families fit the traditional pattern of working father, homemaker mother, and two children. In fact, the whole makeup of the American family is changing. According to the Child Trends Data Bank (2005), between 1970 and 2004, the percentage of children living in mother-only families increased from 11% to 23%, the percentage of children living in father-only families increased from 1% to 5%, and the percentage of children living without either parent (with other relatives or with nonrelatives) stayed fairly constant at about 3% to 4%.

These figures are even more striking when the data are disaggregated by race and ethnicity. Black children are significantly less likely than other children to be living with two married parents. In 2004, 35% of black children were living with two parents, compared with 83% of Asian children, 77% of non-Hispanic white children, and 65% of Hispanic children. In 2004, 9% of all·black children did not live with either parent, compared with 5% of Hispanic children, 3% of non-Hispanic white children, and 3% of Asian children.

Many children rely on their extended families for care. More than 6 million children—approximately 1 in 12—live in households headed by grandparents (4.5 million children) or other relatives (1.5 million children). Data from the 2000 U.S. Census show that 2.4 million grandparents took primary responsibility for their grandchildren's basic needs. Many of these grandparents assumed this responsibility in the absence of the child's parent in the home.

Research confirms that the absence or presence of two parents in the home plays an important role in the growth and development of children. Single mothers are disproportionately poor, and poverty is associated with negative outcomes among children, including increased health issues and lower educational attainment (Vandivere and others, 2004). Single mothers are more likely to work full time, a trend accelerated by welfare reform and its strict work requirements. Under federal law, all mothers on welfare must be working by the child's first birthday, and some state laws require that mothers return to work when children are as young as three months old. Vandivere and others (2004) state that 61% of mothers with children under age three were employed in 2000, compared to 34% in 1975.

Although single-parent families must contend with multiple issues, children in two-parent families in which both parents work may also be at risk for issues related to low income and poverty. More than 16 million children whose parents are employed all year live in families identified as working poor. According to the Family Promise website (2005), a minimum-wage worker would have to work more than 67 hours a week to keep a family of four out of poverty. In addition, young children from low-income families are much less likely to have regular bedtimes and meals; 47% of those with an income below $17,500, compared to 70% for those with incomes over $60,000.

It is a seldom-acknowledged fact that some American children go to bed hungry. According to the National Center for Children in Poverty (2005), in 2003, someone in 3.9 million American households skipped a meal because they could not afford food, and 3.5 million Americans used a charitable food pantry at least once during the year. This report also shows the racial and ethnic quality of hunger. Food insecurity was experienced by 28.5% of African American households and 28.1% of Hispanic households, compared to 11% of white households.

The rapid increase in immigration into the United States over the last half century has been well studied and documented. According to Behrman and Shields (2004), the proportion of students in U.S. schools who are children of immigrants doubled from 10% in 1980 to 20% in 1997. The children of immigrants are more likely to live in a two-parent home, but they are also more likely to have parents who are paid the least, have not graduated from high school, have part-time jobs, and have no private health insurance. A language other than English is spoken at home by 72% of immigrant children.

Looking broadly at the condition of all children in America, the Children's Defense Fund (*Key Facts about American Children,* 2004) reports these sobering facts:

1 in 2 will live in a single-parent family at some point in childhood.
1 in 3 is a year or more behind in school.
1 in 3 is born to unmarried parents.
1 in 4 lives with only one parent.
1 in 5 is born poor.
1 in 6 is born to a mother who did not receive prenatal care in the first three months of pregnancy.
1 in 7 will not graduate from high school.

1 in 8 has no health insurance.
1 in 8 lives in a family that receives food stamps.
1 in 9 is born to a teenage mother.
1 in 14 lives at less than half the poverty level.
1 in 35 lives with grandparents (or other relative) but neither parent.

Annually since 1990, the Annie E. Casey Foundation has presented, in its *Kids Count Data Book,* a broad array of facts intended to illuminate the status of America's children and assess their well-being. *Kids Count* provides ongoing benchmarks against which to evaluate efforts to improve the lives of children. The foundation explains that the 10 measures it uses do not capture the full range of conditions that shape children's lives, but do reflect a wide range of factors that affect their well-being and experiences across a range of developmental stages from birth through early adulthood. Since the data are consistent across states and over time, legitimate comparisons are possible. Each year, the *Kids Count Overview* focuses on a particular topic and the implications of the relevant data.

The 1999 *Kids Count* report focuses on the numbers of youth who are growing up "outside the continuing economic boom, hampered by extraordinarily difficult family conditions that are likely to rob them of their chances of success as adults."

> The futures of 9.2 million American children—one in seven—are at serious risk due to a combination of four or more chronic family conditions. These factors include growing up in a single parent home, having parents with low educational attainment, living in poverty, having parents who are not in the work force, being dependent on welfare, and lacking health insurance. (Press release, para. 2)

The 1999 report emphasizes that of the many complex variables that shape a child's future, none is more important in determining a child's chances in life than the contribution parents are able to make. The "combined disadvantages tend to be mutually reinforcing" and "community conditions can also be powerful subverters of family strength. . . . High levels of crime and violence and concentrated poverty severely undermine family life and make it all the more difficult to change circumstances" (Press release, para. 7).

The 2001 *Kids Count* report shows that over the preceding decade, the well-being of kids had improved on 7 of out 10 key measures. Among the improvements were decreases in the rates of infant mortality, child and teen deaths, and high school dropouts. The child poverty rate fell to 16.9% in 2000 from a decade high of 22.7% in 1993. There was also a steady decline in the rate of teenage births—from 37 per 1,000 teens in 1990 to 30 per 1,000 teens in 1998. There were, however, increases in the rate of low-weight births and the percentage of children living in single-parent families.

The 2001 *Kids Count* report calls attention to a dramatic growth in the number of children under 18 (to more than 72 million), due in large part to immigration. Focusing on the prospects of the nation's young people, the press release quoted Douglas Nelson, president of the Annie E. Casey Foundation:

> Based on the nation's experience with the baby boom of the 1950s, it's clear that this recent rise in America's under-18 population will put heavy new demands on our already struggling public education, child care, and family support systems. If we are going to sustain the recent progress we've seen in conditions affecting kids in the U.S., we will have to do far more to keep pace with the needs of this larger and more diverse generation of American children. . . . Our policy and investment decisions for families in the next few years will determine whether we'll build on the progress of the nineties or see important gains eroded. (Press release, para. 4)

Balancing the Equation, the 2002 *Kids Count* report, focuses on the family incomes of at-risk children. It targets the irregular work schedules of former welfare parents whose absence from home at night and on weekends often leaves children unsupervised and vulnerable or in low-quality childcare. An estimated 8 million children between the ages of 5 and 14 spend some time each week without adult supervision. Many low-income parents also lack such benefits as health insurance and family sick leave. Often parents must choose between taking their child to the doctor or attending a parents evening and keeping their job.

Moving Youth from Risk to Opportunity, the 2004 *Kids Count* report, looks at the children most likely to fail: teens in foster care; youths involved with the juvenile justice system; teens with children of their own;

and youth who did not finish high school. Many of these children enter the adult world dispirited, unsupported, and unprepared. Approximately 3.8 million youth between the ages of 18 and 24 are neither employed nor in school, a 19% increase over 2000. A disproportionately large percentage of these youths come from low-income and minority families.

Kids Count 2004 notes that 16% of the 550,000 children in foster care in 2000 were aged 16 to 18. African Americans are disproportionately represented in foster care, making up more than 40% of the foster care population but less than 20% of the nation's child population. By contrast, white children comprise 31% of the foster care population but 64% of the country's children. African Americans also stay in foster care longer and are least likely to be reunited with their families. Teens in foster care often have overlapping health and mental health problems. Of youths leaving foster care in 2000, 44% had problems obtaining health care most or all of the time. Foster care teens were also behind educationally and had disproportionately greater special education needs.

The 2005 *Kids Count* shows a total of 13 million children living in poverty in the United States in 2003, a half million more children than in 2000. Five out of the 10 child well-being indicators worsened since 2000. The report points out, "These findings are in stark contrast with data in last year's *Kids Count* study that showed eight out of 10 indicators had improved from 1996 to 2001, a period of economic growth and significant expansion of public programs." Focusing on the increase in child poverty, Douglas Nelson, president of the Annie E. Casey Foundation, notes, "The nearly 4 million children living in low-income households where neither their parent(s) nor any other adult in the household worked at all in the past year is an alarming increase of more than 1 million children since 2000" (Press release, p. 1, para. 4).

THE POTENTIAL

Research shows that all children are born ready and willing to learn. The Carnegie Corporation (1996) poignantly describes the potential of children:

> By age three or four, children have the ability to make daring cognitive leaps, to negotiate the slippery slopes of peer relationships, and to manage

the emotional ups and downs that are part of everyday life. If all of us could see their agile minds as easily as we observe their physical agility, perhaps more Americans would believe that every one of these children can learn to levels that surpass any expectations that we might have for them. If we as a nation commit ourselves to their success, if we keep their promise, these children will astonish us. (section 7, para. 23)

Hodgkinson (2006) emphasizes the significant impact of children's environment on their opportunity to develop their potential: "[C]hildren are born with certain physical, cognitive, social and emotional potential. They are *also* born into an environment that will act like a filter, allowing some attributes to be developed and others hidden. They will move through many environments in their lives, some encouraging development and others preventing it" (p. 3). He stresses that "the most permanent factor holding young people back is clearly poverty."

Education and opportunity are central to the promise of America. The sobering reality is that we, as a nation, are not keeping the promise. The Children's Defense Fund Action Council (2002) points out:

Equal educational opportunity is a myth in millennial America. The richest school districts spend 56% more per student than do the poorest. While expenditures are not the sole determinant of educational success, this gaping chasm effectively denies a Head Start to millions of children who happen to live in lower-income school districts. Overall, America's children are not being educated to the high levels they have a right to expect. (p. 2)

The president of the Annie E. Casey Foundation (*Kids Count,* 2004) makes this compelling plea for caring and collaboration by all of the people and agencies involved with high-risk children:

We need parents, residents, schools, colleges, community-based service providers, police, employers, policymakers, funders, and others who are willing to assume ownership and responsibility for seeing that more youth reach adulthood with a good shot at making it, and who are willing to work together to achieve this result. Put more simply, all of us need to respond to this issue with the same tenacity we would employ if our own adolescent sons and daughters, nieces and nephews were at risk. (p. 26)

The challenge to educators is to reconceptualize the role of schools and their relationship to home, community, and the larger society. It is a challenge we can no longer defer.

REFERENCES

Annie E. Casey Foundation. (1999). *Kids count data online.* Retrieved October 14, 2005, from http://www.aecf.org/kidscount/kc1999/news2.htm

Annie E. Casey Foundation. (2001). *Promising progress yet troubling trends face kids in the new millennium.* Retrieved October 14, 2005, from http://www.aecf.org/kidscount/kc2001/kc2001_press

Annie E. Casey Foundation. (2002). *Kids count data book: Balancing the equation.* Retrieved September 15, 2005, from http://www.caseyfoundation.org/kidscount/kc2002/pdfs/essay.pdf

Annie E. Casey Foundation. (2004). *Kids count data book: Moving youth from risk to opportunity.* Retrieved September 15, 2005, from http://www.aecf.org/publications/data/essay_e.pdf

Annie E. Casey Foundation. (2005). *Kids count data book: Helping our most vulnerable families.* Retrieved September 15, 2005, from http://www.aecf.org/kidscount/sld/db05_pdf/entise._db/pdf

Behrman, R. E., and Shields, M. K. (2004). *Children of immigrant families: Analysis and recommendations.* Retrieved November 26, 2005, from http://www.futureofchildren.org/usr_doc/children_of_immigrant_families.pdf

Belenardo, S. J. (2001). Practices and conditions that lead to a sense of community in middle schools. *National Association of Secondary School Principals Bulletin, 85,* 27.

Carnegie Corporation. (1996). *Years of promise.* Retrieved October 14, 2005, from http://www.carnegie.org/sub/pubs/execsum.html

Children's Defense Fund. (2004). *Key facts about American children.* Retrieved October 17, 2005, from http://www.childrensdefense.org/data/keyfacts.aspx

Children's Defense Fund Action Council. (2002). *Stand up for children now.* Retrieved November 26, 2005, from http://www.childrensdefense.org/stand_up_for_children_now.pdf

Child Trends Data Bank. (2005). *Family structure.* Retrieved October 2, 2005, from http://www.childtrendsdatabank.org/indicators/59FamilyStructure.cfm

Dwyer, D. M. (1998). *Strengthening community in education: A handbook for change.* Retrieved October 14, 2005, from http://www.newmaine.com/community/

Economic Policy Institute. (2002). *Despite past boom, income gaps have widened in 45 states over past 20 years.* (Press release). Retrieved November 26, 2005, from http://www.cbpp.org.4–23–02sfp-pr.htm

Family Promise website. (2005). *Fast facts.* Retrieved September 30, 2005, from http://www.familypromise.org/about/faqs.html

Hodgkinson, H. (2006). *The whole child in a fractured world.* Alexandria, VA: American Association for Supervision and Curriculum Development. Retrieved March 27, 2006, from http://www.ascd.org/ASCD/pdf/fractured world.pdf

LaborLawTalk.com. (2005). *Community.* Retrieved October 17, 2005, from http://encyclopedia.laborlawtalk.com/community

Local Government Authority. (2005). *Annex A: Definition and components of sustainable communities.* Retrieved October 17, 2005, from http://www .sustainable-development.gov.uk/

Lockwood, A. T. (2001). Community collaboration and social capital: An interview with Gary G. Wehlage. *Leaders for tomorrow's schools.* Retrieved September 15, 2005, from http://www.ncrel.org/cscd/pubs/lead21/2–1m.htm

McBrien, J. L., and Brandt, R. S. (1997). The definition of school culture and climate. *Education topics.* Retrieved October 17, 2005, from http://www.ascd .org/portal/site/ascd/menuitem.255a4a2dd64a76fddeb3ffdb62108a0c/

National Center for Children in Poverty. (2003). *Living at the edge.* Retrieved August 22, 2005, from http://www.nccp.org/pub_lat.html

National Center for Children in Poverty. (2004). *Basic facts about low income children.* Retrieved August 10, 2005, from http://www.nccp.org/

National Center for Children in Poverty. (2005). *Who are America's poor children?* Retrieved October 1, 2005 from http://www.nccp.org/pub_cpt05b.html

Peterson, A. (2004). *Diversity trends report.* Retrieved November 21, 2005, from http://www.aza.org/AboutAZA/Diversity/Documents/DiversityTrendsReport.pdf

Policy Institute for Family Impact Seminars. (2005). *Family trends.* Retrieved October 20, 2005, from http://familyimpactseminars.org/trends.htm

Putnam, R. D. (2000). *Bowling alone: The collapse and revival of American community.* New York: Simon and Schuster.

Schaps, E. (2003). Creating a school community. *Educational Leadership, 60,* 6.

Seay, M. F., and Crawford, F. N. (1954). *The community school and community self-improvement.* Lansing, MI: Department of Public Instruction.

The Institute for Children and Poverty. (2004). *Miles to go: The flip side of the McKinney-Vento Homeless Assistance Act.* Retrieved September 10, 2005, from http://www.homesforthehomeless.com/index.asp?CID = 3&PID = 25

Urban Institute. (2003). *Assessing the new federalism.* Retrieved October 7, 2005, from http://www.urban.org/Content/Research/NewFederalism/AboutANF/AboutANF.htm

U.S. Census 2000 website. (2000). Retrieved October 10, 2005 from http://www.census.org

Vandivere, S., Gallagher, M., and Anderson Moore, K. (2004). *Changes in children's well-being and family environments.* Retrieved October 1, 2005, from http://www.urban.org/Template.cfm?NavMenuID = 24&template = /Tagged Content/ViewPublication.cfm&PublicationID = 8684

WordNet. (2005). *Community.* Retrieved October 17, 2005, from http://wordnet.princeton.edu/perl/webwn

Websites for More Information and Links to Other Relevant Sites

Annie E. Casey Foundation, http://www.aecf.org
Carnegie Corporation, http://www.carnegie.org
Child Trends, http://www.childtrends.org
Children, Youth and Family Consortium, http://www.cyfc.umn.edu
Children's Defense Fund, http://www.childrensdefense.org
The Future of Children, http://www.futureofchildren.org
Kids Count Data Online, http://www.aecf.org/kidscount
National Center for Education Statistics, http://nces.ed.gov
U.S. Department of Education, Research and Statistics, http://www.ed.gov/stats

Chapter Three

Diversity and Multiculturalism in America

In America, there is an increasingly complex mix of races, cultures, languages, and socioeconomic backgrounds found in a growing number of our schools. Diversity has two clear dimensions, the one that is often biological and has to do with age, gender, race, ethnicity, sexual orientation, and disabilities. The secondary aspect of diversity is sociocultural and invisible. It includes language, education, values, occupation, learning, and style (Noguera, 2003). Although gender, disability, and sexual orientation are important aspects of diversity, they are not the main focus of this chapter. However, some of the approaches offered for creating a more inclusive and equal school environment are transferable across all dimensions of diversity.

Public schools reflect the rapidly changing demographics of our nation and the world. They are just one piece of the kaleidoscope of race, culture, ethnicity, language background, and social class that makes up our increasingly globalized and multicultural society. A 2002 report by the National Association of State Boards of Education (NASBE) predicts that by 2040 no ethnic group will make up a majority of the population of the United States. The social and economic importance of our nation as a global player will depend, to a large extent, on how well schools rise to the challenge of providing a level playing field of educational opportunity for all children, no matter what their social or economic background.

School leaders who are willing to be proactive can reap rich rewards from diverse school populations. Their success will depend to some extent on the recognition of the fact that schools cannot be islands in the local sea of the community. Proactive school leaders will seek community support by building full and equal partnerships with families, businesses, and local agencies to ensure the best possible educational opportunities for their students. "School leaders in positions of authority, such as principals, district administrators and county superintendents, stand in powerful positions from which to influence others. Their policies and practices are highly visible and can shape the ways others perceive human diversity" (Henze and others, 2002, p. 11).

Successful school leaders openly recognize and celebrate differences in their students while promoting unity, reaching out to communities in which many different languages are spoken, and formulating institutional practices that accept and welcome increasingly diverse school communities.

DEFINITIONS

The words *race, ethnicity, culture, diversity, multiculturalism,* and *bilingualism* are among the terms used to help define, order, explain, and clarify responses to multicultural issues within the school system. Although some of the terms are used interchangeably, there are subtle but important differences in their meaning. They may carry different meanings for different audiences or for different ends. In this book:

1. *Race* is defined in the 2000 U.S. Census as one of four groups: white, black, American Indian and Alaska Native, and Asian and Pacific Islander. Although some experts argue that race is a socially constructed concept that has no support in biology (Henze and others, 2002), the term is used here simply to facilitate discussion of census demographics.
2. *Ethnicity* refers not to race, but to selected cultural and sometimes physical characteristics used to classify people into ethnic groups or categories. American ethnic groups include Native Americans, Hispanics, Asian Americans, African Americans, and European Americans, etc. Some ethnic groups are loosely connected, with few common cultural traditions, such as English Americans, German Americans, and Scottish Americans. Other ethnic groups are actu-

ally cultures with shared language and large bodies of tradition (O'Neil, 2004).

3. *Culture* refers to the history, language, customs, values, traditions, and worldview of a particular group at a particular time (Dilg, 1999). Culture is not interchangeable with ethnicity. It is dynamic and changing, dependent on place, time, and the influence of other groups. Successful school leaders understand the important role culture plays in the learning styles and responses of students.

4. *Diversity* is, quite simply, the range of differences that encompass race, ethnicity, gender, social class, ability, and language (Nieto, 2002).

5. *Multiculturalism* has become a value-laden term that has provoked opposition from those who see it as implying a shift from the notion of America as the great melting pot. Multiculturalism can be defined as "a system of beliefs and behaviors that recognizes and respects the presence of all diverse groups in an organization or society, acknowledges and values their socio-cultural differences, and encourages and enables their continued contribution within an inclusive cultural context which empowers all within the organization or society"(Rosado, 1998, What Is Multiculturalism section, para. 2). This definition emphasizes the importance and value of recognizing differences and encouraging the inclusion of other cultural values while still promoting unity.

6. *Multicultural education* is not a curricular approach, but the basic philosophy that permeates all areas of the schools and affirms the diverse nature of the school and community. It recognizes that all students have the right to an equal chance to achieve academically (Banks and Banks, 2001).

7. *Bilingual education* acknowledges the language differences of the estimated one-fifth (9.8 million) of the school population that speaks a language other than English at home (U.S. Census, 2000). As defined in an educational program, it involves the use of two languages of instruction at some point in a student's school career (Nieto, 2002). Students typically take five to seven years to make a successful transition from their native language to English. The bilingual approach to language-minority students is often controversial, prompting charges that it hinders assimilation. However,

research has shown that it is more effective than other programs such as English for speakers of other languages (ESOL) alone in helping with English language development (Collier and Thomas, 2001). A secondary benefit of bilingual education is that it reinforces relationships between language-minority children and their families and encourages more family communication, which is often a casualty of English-only instruction (Nieto, 2002).

THE DIMENSIONS OF DIVERSITY

According to the 2000 U.S. Census, about 75% of the population is non-Hispanic white, and 25% are either black, Hispanic, American Indian, Asian Pacific Islander, or of more than one race. School-age children are 65% non-Hispanic white and 35% are of other racial and ethnic backgrounds. The latter figure is rising steadily. By 2015, fewer than 10 states will have student populations of color that are below 20% (NASBE, 2002). The United States is also becoming more linguistically diverse, partly because of the 13 million immigrants from around the world who came to the country during the 1990s. According to the 2000 Census, about one-fifth (9.8 million) of school-age children speak a language other than English at home, so it is increasingly likely that several languages other than English will be spoken in school.

The 2005 federal poverty level for a family of four is defined as having an income level of $19,350 or less. According to a 2004 report by the National Center for Children in Poverty, racial and ethnic minority children are likely to live in poverty at a far greater rate than white Caucasian children. While 39% (26 million) of all American children live at or below the poverty level, Hispanic children are three times as likely as white Caucasian children to live in poverty and African American children are four times as likely.

One out of four children in poverty lives in an immigrant household. Among the consequences of poverty are inadequate nutrition and increased exposure to environmental toxins. In 2003, the Educational Testing Service reported that 434,000 children under the age of six were found to have dangerously high levels of lead in their blood; and black children may be more than three times more likely than white children to live in older houses where they may be exposed to lead, which has been linked to lower intelligence quotient (IQ) scores in children. Significantly for educators, 20% of the children identified as living at or below the poverty level in 2004 had moved in the previous year.

The number of children living in low-income families, defined as having an income of $37,000 or less for a family of four, is again rising after a downward trend between 1990 and 2000 and is now 8.2 million. Most of these children have parents who work full time, year round. Of the 8.2 million, 62% are Hispanic, 58% are black, and 25% are white (National Center for Children in Poverty, 2004). Many of these children lack such basic necessities as decent housing and adequate food and health care.

RESEGREGATION

Although the U.S. public school system is increasingly diverse, public schools do not uniformly reflect this national diversity. In fact, schools in many regions of the country are becoming resegregated at an alarming rate, and the most segregated schools are also the ones with very high levels of poverty (Orfield and Lee, 2004). The Hispanic population, in particular, has a high rate of segregation by race and poverty, placing many Hispanic children in low-achieving schools with high dropout rates (Orfield, 2001).

Some school resegregation is attributable to growing minority populations, but the trend has a distinctly regional flavor and is not impacting the country uniformly. For African American students, the southern and border states are the least integrated with Florida, North Carolina, Delaware, and Oklahoma showing the largest increases in the number of resegregated schools (Orfield and Lee, 2004). The increase in Hispanic segregation is particularly notable in the West, where there has been a sharp increase in the size of the Hispanic population. The centers of metropolitan areas with large populations—many of which also have concentrated levels of poverty—have intensely segregated school systems. With some notable exceptions, many of these schools reflect the well-documented low-achievement and high dropout rates related to the social impact of poverty (Orfield, 2001).

THE ACHIEVEMENT GAP

Larson and Ovando (2001) use the analogy of an unfair foot race to illustrate the achievement gap in education:

> When children come from privileged homes, they have far greater access to privileged knowledge. Education, then, becomes akin to a grossly unfair race. It is like equipping half of the children with the best running clothes, putting them at the starting line, shooting the gun and allowing them to get half way round the track before allowing the next half, many of whom are burdened with heavy clothing and clunky boots, to begin the race. Not surprisingly, the vast majority of children in the first group appear to have much better running skills than those in the second half. (p. 133)

The term *achievement gap* is used to describe measurable discrepancies in academic achievement, largely along economic, racial, and ethnic lines. The gap is seen on nearly all current school assessments, from the National Assessment of Educational Progress (NAEP) through state tests and tests used by larger school districts. Simply put, there is a measurable gap between the academic performance of students from low-income families and the performance of their more affluent peers, and between minority students, especially African American, Hispanic, and Native American students and their white and Asian American counterparts. Data from the NAEP (National Center for Educational Statistics, 2005) show that, by the end of fourth grade, African American, Hispanic, and low-income students of all races are two years behind students not in these categories. By eighth grade, these students are three years behind and by twelfth grade, poor and minority students are about four years behind. Stated another way, the average 17-year-old African American and Hispanic student is performing at the academic level of a 13-year-old white student (Haycock and others, 2001). While there is some encouraging news—the most recent data from the NAEP, released in July 2005, show elementary school students have improved in reading across the board—there is still much room for improvement.

Unfortunately, the same report shows that overall achievement of 17-year-olds in both reading and math has remained stagnant since the early 1970s. While African American and Hispanic 17-year-olds have made some gains in that time, their reading and math skills today are nearly identical to those of white 13-year-olds.

Educational inequities do not begin in the schoolroom. Some argue that low–birth weight Hispanic and black babies are at a disadvantage from the beginning of life. The gap widens during the preschool years. The Early Childhood Education Longitudinal Study Kindergarten Cohort, a sample of 23,000 kindergartners, shows that black and Hispanic children score substantially below white children at the beginning of kindergarten on math and reading achievement (Haskins and Rouse, 2005). The Family and Child Experiences Survey administered to children as they enter Head Start shows a disproportionate number of minority and low-income children falling 15 points behind the median white children on standard tests of vocabulary, early reading, letter recognition, and early math by ages three and four. Other studies have consistently found that poor and minority children as young as three years old are already performing far below average on tests of school readiness. In *Closing Achievement Gaps,* Haskins and Rouse (2005) make a series of recommendations for addressing these issues. Most relevant to school leaders is their emphasis on involving parents to the maximum degree possible and coordinating preschool programs with public school kindergarten programs.

THE OPPORTUNITY GAP

Clearly, poor and minority students are underachieving in our public schools. Besides falling behind their white peers academically, they are often placed in such pullout programs as Title I, English as a Second Language, and special education. Because these programs often contain less actual classroom instructional time, students enrolled in them can miss the equivalent of a semester or even a year of normal classroom instruction. The fact that nonwhite students, specifically black and Native American, are significantly more likely than white students to be identified as having some kind of a disability exacerbates the effect of less classroom instruction (NASBE, 2002). In 1998, approximately 1.5 million minority children were identified as having mental retardation, emotional disturbance, or a specific learning disability. More than 876,000 of these were black or Native American. In most states, African American children are up to four times more likely to be placed in the categories of mental retardation and emotional disturbance (Losen and Orfield, 2002). It may be that some of this overrepresentation is a result of the low birth weights, poor prenatal care, and exposure to toxins often associated with poverty.

National Association of State Boards of Education research (2002) found that students from minority cultures, especially African Americans and non-English-speaking students, are more likely to be enrolled in high-poverty schools that offer an inadequate curriculum, less-qualified teachers, and fewer resources. They are also more likely to be taught by teachers without even a college minor in the subject they are teaching. These differences are even more pronounced in high schools with predominantly minority enrollments. In high schools with 90% or more minority enrollment, only half the math and science teachers meet the state's minimum requirements to teach those subjects compared to 20% in majority-white schools (Haycock, 2002). These same students are significantly less likely than white students to be in gifted programs, higher level math classes, or advanced placement courses. According to a 2000 study (Gordon and others), in every city where data were available, blacks, Hispanics, or both were underrepresented in gifted programs, and whites were overrepresented. Miami-Dade County in Florida came closest to achieving parity, but even there, African Americans made up 33% of all students, but only 23% of students in advanced placement or gifted classes. By contrast, in Providence, Rhode Island, where blacks were 23% of the student body, they were only 9% of advanced placement students.

Researchers have long pointed to a funding gap between high-poverty and low-poverty schools. In a 2001 study, the Education Trust found that in 42 of 49 states, school districts with the greatest numbers of poor children had less state and local money to spend per student than those with the fewest poor children. The gap, per pupil, varies widely across the North Central Regional Educational Laboratory's region (Haycock and others, 2001). In Illinois, the gap was $1,939; in Indiana, $614; in Iowa, $456; in Michigan, $1,261; in Ohio, $667; and in Wisconsin, $676. The one exception was Minnesota, where the spending for the highest poverty districts actually exceeded that for the lowest by $264 per pupil.

THE CHALLENGES FOR SCHOOL LEADERS

A complex mix of home, community, and school factors creates the achievement and opportunity gaps outlined above. Socioeconomic factors such as unemployment and poor housing and health care all need to be addressed. However, many schools fail to address their own obligation to promote equal access for all students and to prevent discrimination as required by Titles VI and IX of the U.S. Civil Rights Act of 1972. During the last century, many educators held to the "melting pot" belief that all children would eventually be assimilated into one American culture. Obvious differences in race, culture, ethnicity, and religion were either ignored or relegated to special assembly topics. This *institutional silence,* as it came to be known, made blindness to differences a virtue.

As societal institutions, schools have tended to exhibit traditional white values, often developing a *culture of power* that accepts and promotes the dominant white culture and favors students who come from that culture (Henze and others, 2002). However, the rapid growth of diversity in many of our schools has encouraged the development of a new approach, one that recognizes and values differences. Schools become *culturally competent* by encouraging an understanding of differences, fostering high standards for all, and strengthening national ideals that bind rather than divide Americans. The challenge for school leaders is to recognize, respect, and value diversity, while promoting the unity and harmony that lead to increasing strength and solidarity for the nation.

For administrators, successful diversity practices require extensive professional development and staff support (Appelbaum, 2001). School leaders must recognize that the teachers they hire and work with can have a negative or positive impact on issues of diversity within the school. Many studies provide evidence that teachers' expectations of students can become *self-fulfilling prophecies;* some demonstrate that teachers tend to see minority students as low achievers and majority students as high achievers, even when their performance is identical (Ford and Thomas, 1997). Landsman (2004) offers an illustration of how teacher expectations can impact minority children:

> Students in one St. Paul, Minnesota, high school talked about a teacher who asked the white kids in an Advanced Placement class the tough questions

but turned to the few black or Hispanic students when she had an easy question that "anyone could answer." When confronted with this situation, the teacher was stunned. She realized it was true and admitted, "I just assumed you didn't know the answers, and I didn't want to embarrass you." This assumption—that black or Latino students could not possibly know the answers to deep or complex questions—is at the crux of the racism still embedded in many teachers' belief systems. This racism is so subtly expressed that students often cannot put into words what they clearly sense is wrong. (p. 28)

Teacher education programs and in-service professional development can help teachers become more culturally competent. Teachers need to learn how culture influences student learning and develop an understanding of the different experiences of middle-class white and minority and poor children. School personnel should also honestly examine their own prejudices and biases in order to address issues of prejudice in their students.

School leaders can further enhance the cultural competence of their schools by aggressive recruitment of diverse staff. Teachers of color can act as role models, help with cultural and ethnic understanding, and serve as cultural brokers to parents and the larger community. There is much work to be done in this area. In 2001, 90% of schoolteachers in public schools were white, 6% black, and fewer than 5% of other races (National Collaborative for Diversity in the Teaching Force, 2004). The few teachers of color tend to teach in schools with large percentages of their own ethnic and racial groups. Further, while the percentage of students of color is rising, projections for the diversity of teachers are stationary.

MULTICULTURAL EDUCATION

Economic globalization has created an unprecedented need for a workforce that can navigate culturally and linguistically in diverse environments. In the opinion of leading global industrialist Claiborne Smith of DuPont (NASBE, 2002), diversity should be:

Perceived and treated as a business imperative as opposed to the moral or right thing to do. [American] students still remain too isolated from people who are different from them, too insulated in their own culture and languages. They are not learning respect for differences or the cooperative business skills they need to contribute effectively in diverse work teams. (p. 17)

Unfortunately, the whole idea of multicultural education has been highly contentious over the last 30 years, with detractors claiming that its focus on differences has had the effect of dividing rather than uniting. Given the current emphasis on standardized education, there is now an additional fear that multicultural education will take valuable time away from the basic curriculum of math, science, and reading. However, increasing globalization provides strong rationale for school leaders to view multicultural education as essential to an understanding of the increasing diversity of the nation and the world. At their best, multicultural programs help develop critical thinking, examine issues from many different viewpoints, and increase contact among races.

Current multicultural education programs can be divided into three types (NASBE, 2002). *Content-oriented* programs offer information about different cultural groups. At a minimum, they include celebrations of multicultural holidays and heroes. They may also add multicultural themes and materials to the standard curriculum. Their goal is to increase tolerance and reduce bias. *Student-oriented* programs help culturally and linguistically diverse students make transitions into the educational mainstream and include bilingual and bicultural programs taught through research-based cultural learning styles. *Socially oriented* programs seek to reform the cultural and political context of school. They include programs that increase contact among races, encourage the hiring of teachers from diverse cultures, and offer antibias and cooperative learning programs. These socially oriented programs are in line with a transformative approach to school curriculum reform (Banks and Banks, 2001). This approach recommends redefining school culture to embrace a multicultural ethos that broadens student appreciation and understanding of diverse cultures.

SUMMARY

School leaders face enormous challenges as they attempt to prepare the increasingly diverse next generation for constructive roles in the global economy. There is a growing need for a well-educated and globally competitive citizenry, yet many students are attending resegregated schools with low achievement levels and high dropout rates. Schools alone cannot solve the ensuing educational problems, nor can they be held responsible for the social and economic ills endemic to poor communities. However, school leaders do have a role to play in addressing the achievement and opportunity gaps faced by many children. They must understand the underlying causes of these disparities and try to address ensuing educational issues while setting and promoting high standards for all students. School leaders must work to increase the participation of diverse students in rigorous academic courses, invest in teacher professional development, and develop multicultural education programs that help prepare all students for their future lives in a diverse and global society.

REFERENCES

Appelbaum, P. (2001). *Multicultural and diversity education.* Santa Barbara, CA: ABC CLIO.

Banks, J. A., and Banks, C. A. M. (2001). *Multicultural education: Issues and perspectives* (4th ed.). Boston, MA: Allyn and Bacon.

Collier, V. P., and Thomas, W. P. (2001). *A national study of school effectiveness for language minority students' long-term academic achievement final report.* Retrieved August 10, 2005, from http://www.crede.org/research/llaa/1.1_final.html

Dilg, M. (1999). *Race and culture in the classroom: Teaching and learning through multicultural education.* New York: Teachers College Press.

Education Trust. (2001). *The other gap: Poor students receive fewer dollars.* Education Trust Data Bulletin. Retrieved June 13, 2005, from http://www2.edtrust.org/NR/rdonlyres/44CC3286–13BC-41A1-A12E-B1D9B57EA307/0/Edtrustdatabulletin.pdf

Ford, D. Y., and Thomas, A. (1997). *Underachievement among gifted and minority students. ERIC, EDF409660.* Retrieved June 13, 2005, from http://ericec.org/digests/e544.html

Gordon, R., Della Piana, L., and Keleher, T. (2000). *Facing the consequences: An examination of racial discrimination in U.S. public schools.* Retrieved June 27, 2005, from http://www.ARC.org

Haskins, R., and Rouse, C. (2005). *Closing achievement gaps. The future of children.* Princeton, NJ: Brookings.

Haycock, K. (2002). *Closing the achievement gap.* National Association of State Boards of Education. Retrieved September 22, 2005, from http://www.nasbe .org/Standard/8_Winter2002/haycock.pdf

Haycock, K., Jerald, C., and Huang, S. (2001). *Taking on the achievement gap.* North Central Regional Educational Laboratory. Retrieved June 10, 2005, from http://www.ncrel.org/gap/takeon/problem.htm

Henze, R., Katz, A., Norte, E., Sather, S., and Walker, E. (2002). *Leading for diversity: How school leaders promote positive interethnic relations.* Thousand Oaks, CA: Corwin Press.

Landsman, J. (2004). Confronting the racism of low expectations. *Educational Leadership, 62,* 3.

Larson, L. L., and Ovando, C. J. (2001). *The color of bureaucracy.* Toronto, Canada: Wadsworth.

Losen, D. J., and Orfield, G. (2002). *Racial inequity in special education. Executive summary for federal policy makers.* Cambridge, MA: Harvard Education Publishing Group.

National Association of State Boards of Education Study Group (NASBE). (2002). *A more perfect union: Building an educational system that embraces all children.* Alexandria, VA: National Association of State Boards of Education.

National Center for Children in Poverty. (2004). *Basic facts about low income children: Birth to age 18.* Retrieved August 10, 2005, from http://www.nccp .org/pub_lic05

National Center for Education Statistics. (2005). *NAEP 2004 trends in academic progress: Three decades of student performance in reading and mathematics: Findings in brief* (NCES 2005–463). Washington, DC: Government Printing Office.

National Collaborative for Diversity in the Teaching Force. (2004). *Assessment of diversity in America's teaching force: A call to action.* Retrieved July 11, 2005, from http://www.nea.org/teacherquality/images/diversityreport.pdf

Nieto, S. (2002). *Language, culture and teaching: Critical perspectives for a new century.* Mahwah, NJ: Lawrence Erlbaum Associates.

Noguera, P. (2003). *City schools and the American dream.* New York: Teachers College Press.

O'Neil, N. (2004). *Ethnicity and race: An introduction to the nature of social group differentiation and inequality.* Retrieved August 1, 2005, from http:// anthro.palomar.ed/ethnicity/ethnic_htm

Orfield, G. (2001). Schools more separate: Consequences of a decade of resegregation. *Rethinking Schools Online, 16* (1). Retrieved September 14, 2005, from http://www.rethinkingschools.org/archive/16_01/Seg161.shtml

Chapter 3

Orfield, G., and Lee, C. (2004). *Brown at 50: King's dream or Plessy's nightmare?* Cambridge, MA: Harvard University, The Civil Rights Project.

Rosado, C. (1998). *What makes a school multicultural?* Retrieved February 6, 2006, from http://www.edchange.org/multicultural/papers/caleb/multicultural.html

U.S. Census. (2000). Retrieved June 1, 2005, from http://www.census.org

Websites for More Information and Links to Other Relevant Sites

Center for Applied Linguistics, http://www.cal.org

Center for Research on Education, Diversity, and Excellence, http://www.crede.org

Circle of Inclusion Model, http://circleofinclusion.org

Cornucopia of Disability Information, http://codi.buffalo.edu/

Gender, Diversities, and Technology Institute, http://www2.edc.org/GDI/

Multicultural Pavilion, http://www.edchange.org/multicultural/index.html

National Association for Multicultural Education, http://www.nameorg.org/index.html

National Clearinghouse for English Language Acquisition and Language Instruction Educational Programs, http://www.ncela.gwu.edu/

National Dissemination Center for Children with Disabilities, http://www.nichcy.org/

Chapter Four

Essential Role of Communities

Ever since the publication of *A Nation at Risk* (National Commission on Excellence in Education, 1983), the landmark assessment of the condition of American education, public attention has focused as never before on our public school system. As the public came to believe that our schools are deficient and getting worse, blame was often placed on teachers and administrators. Increasingly, however, both professional educators and the public are acknowledging that children who come to the schools from families and communities with severe social problems present over-whelming challenges to educators' ability to teach them. Schools in disad-vantaged communities tend to have, in addition to low student achievement and high student mobility rates, a disproportionate number of inexperienced teachers. A more recent, and much less publicized, report by the Century Foundation, aptly titled *A Notion at Risk*, raises a new alarm "that American education, in some cases, is having the effect of reinforcing existing inequalities," especially in high-poverty schools (Kahlenberg, 2000).

The social and economic issues that impact public schools reflect the increasingly complex multicultural communities in which they are located. Schools and communities impact each other physically, economically, and socially in hundreds of ways. Unfortunately, school administrators and community leaders do not always recognize their interdependence and mutual interests. Educators have launched many initiatives to bring the community into the school, to take school programs and activities into the community, and to create communities of learning within the school itself. What many have failed to do is include the community in the planning and implementation of academic improvement efforts. A potential problem is that, while the community's cooperation and collaboration are essential if improvement is to be made, they may not be easy to get.

REPAIRING THE BOND

Crowson and Boyd (1999) point out that, in spite of a modern legacy of disconnection between U.S. schools and their communities, there is now a growing acknowledgment of the need for schools to be involved in strengthening communities.

> Disturbing social trends have led to the widespread recognition that relationships between schools and their surrounding communities must be strengthened—and, indeed, the communities themselves must be strengthened. Good schooling and the development of children require attention to multiple needs far beyond the narrowly defined educational goals; further, many families now require an active investment by society in improving the "social capital" of neighborhoods to support learning. (p. 3)

David Mathews, chief executive officer for the Kettering Foundation (2000), expresses his concerns based on 10 years of research commissioned by the foundation. "It is not simply that the schools need to be improved; the relationship between the schools and the community needs repair," he notes. Agreeing with Crowson and Boyd about the disconnection between schools and their communities, he writes "[D]espite a long tradition of support for public education, Americans today seem to be halfway out the schoolhouse door." He stresses the need for community building as a way to improve schools. "Strong communities, with people bonded and pulling together, are our last line of defense against the breakdown of families and society. And they are also an essential source of 'social capital,' a necessary form of reinforcement from outside the school that encourages children to learn" (para. 1–2). Mathews (2006) adds: "[T]he schools can't become vibrant, democratic institutions until the public reclaims them as its own. . . . Public ownership [will then express] itself in civic work done on behalf of education" (p. 6).

Over the last 10 years, much of the dialogue about public schools has centered on the concept of accountability. A recent report by the KnowledgeWorks Foundation (2004) suggests that it is time for the American public to be part of a renewed conversation about public education built on the themes of partnership and community renewal. Education is presented as a communitywide task that must be rooted in a "deep and abiding commitment to equity" (para. 15, point 1). The new accountability must go both ways: schools must be open and committed to the community and the community must support the work of public schools.

BUILDING COMMUNITIES FROM THE INSIDE OUT

Economic and social issues—not only in cities but also in suburban and rural areas—complicate the tasks of defining a specific community and delineating ways to improve it. Kretzmann and McKnight (1993) in their definitive work, *Building Communities from the Inside Out,* present a capacity-focused approach to building a healthy community. This model stresses using the assets of each community to build capacity. The authors criticize the traditional needs-driven approach of many community planners and local government representatives because it creates mental images of a needy, problem-ridden community populated by incompetent, deficient people. Thus, problems are addressed through deficiency-oriented programs, and community members begin to think of themselves as incapable of taking charge of either their own lives or their community's future. The authors stress that a fragmented approach to solving intertwined problems leads to policies oriented to maintenance and survival rather than to development, and creates a deepening cycle of dependence on outside resources.

Alternatively, a capacity-focused approach begins with an effort to identify the community's assets and leads to the development of policies and activities based on the capacities, skills, and resources of people and their community. Kretzmann and McKnight point out that two other factors argue for the capacity-focused approach. One is the evidence that significant community development takes place only when community people are committed to the effort; the second is that a community is unlikely to get significant outside help to develop its internal assets.

Kretzmann and McKnight answer the most frequently asked questions on the potential and the limits of a capacity-focused approach:

1. *Will these internally focused strategies really work?* The obvious necessity is for citizens to use every resource at local command to create the future. There is clear evidence in developing societies that domination by outside plans and resources that overwhelm local initiatives and associations cause massive social and economic disasters. The same lesson can be learned about development efforts in the United States where the designs of outsiders have been imposed on local communities.

2. *Is there a danger that local communities and groups won't be inclusive? Aren't parochialism and discrimination problems in many local groups and associations?* Yes. The effort to create open communities has been, and will be, a never-ending struggle.

3. *Aren't there some communities in which there is not much associational life among local citizens? What do you do then?* Communities vary greatly in both the number and the formality of local associations. In some, local citizens may not have had time to create them. In others, there are so many institutions to manage and serve the local residents that associational life may have atrophied for lack of function. Nevertheless, some informal associations may be doing critical community work, even if they do not have a name or officers. Community organizers must find, honor, and enhance the associational relationships already at work. (pp. 373–375)

In *Hidden Treasures,* a new workbook created for the Asset-Based Community Development Institute, Rans (2005) builds on the work of Kretzmann and McKnight by looking specifically at marginalized individuals within communities. She argues that people on welfare, the mentally ill, young people, the disabled, and senior citizens are often made "invisible" by the very services intended to help them. The professionals whose job it is to protect and serve those living on the edges of the community may actually isolate the already marginalized even further. Rans cites five case studies of communities in various parts of the country in which marginalized individuals have been reconnected to the local community through asset-based community building efforts. She points out that, while each community building effort takes a slightly different approach, they all:

1. Center on identifying the gifts and dreams, rather than the needs, of each isolated person.
2. Stress the importance of citizen space—the places where neighbors connect and participate.
3. Rely on "connectors" as keys to the process. Connectors are the people in the community who know everyone and make connections easily and naturally.

The Search Institute of Minneapolis, Minnesota, undertook the challenge of identifying the key factors in community building that enhance the health and well-being of young people. "We have research to suggest that the [developmental] assets make a difference. If our society would invest more in the positive things young people need, then we could expect high yields (in terms of healthier youth) as young people become healthy, contributing members of families, communities, workplaces, and society" (Decker and Decker, 2003, p. 23).

The Search Institute (2005) identified critical influences on young people's growth and development and designated them as either external or internal assets. The four categories of external assets focus on positive experiences provided to young people by individuals and institutions:

1. *Support.* Young people need to experience support, care, and love from their families, neighbors, and many others. They need organizations and institutions that provide positive, supportive environments.
2. *Empowerment.* Young people need to be valued by their community and have opportunities to contribute. For this to occur, they must be safe and feel secure.
3. *Boundaries and expectations.* Young people need to know what is expected of them and whether activities and behaviors are within-bounds or out-of-bounds.
4. *Constructive use of time.* Young people need constructive, enriching

opportunities for growth through creative activities, youth programs, congregational involvement, and quality time at home.
(Search Institute, 2005)

The Search Institute's report also stresses the importance of internal
assets. "There needs to be a similar commitment to nurturing the internal-
ized qualities that guide choices and create a sense of centeredness, purpose, and focus. Indeed, shaping internal dispositions that encourage
wise, responsible, and compassionate judgments is particularly important
in a society that prizes individualism" (Internal Assets, para. 1). Four categories of internal assets were identified:

1. *Commitment to learning.* Young people need to develop a lifelong
   commitment to education and learning.
2. *Positive values.* Young people need to develop strong values that
   guide their choices.
3. *Social competencies.* Young people need skills and competencies
   that equip them to make positive choices, build relationships, and
   succeed in life.
4. *Positive identity.* Young people need a strong sense of their own
   power, purpose, worth, and promise. (Search Institute, 2005)

RULES OF ENGAGEMENT

Warren (2005) argues that if school reform, especially "urban school
reform in the United States is to be successful, it must be linked to the
revitalization of the communities around our schools" (p. 133). He points
out that in the last half of the twentieth century educators and community
developers operated in separate spheres, institutionally and professionally, but he notes hopefully that in many communities across the nation,
community builders and school reformers are beginning to work together
to create effective schools in safe, family friendly neighborhoods. In those
communities, educators are addressing the current emphasis on standardized testing even as they seek to build partnerships with families and community organizations. Community builders are focusing on engaging

residents in a variety of community improvement initiatives, including educational improvement.

In 2001, the Institute for Educational Leadership set out to understand how school reformers and community builders can work together more effectively. Its report, *Education and Community Building: Connecting Two Worlds* (Jehl and others, 2001), recommends the following rules of engagement:

1. Find out about each other's interests and needs.
2. Reach out to potential partners on their own turf with specific offers of assistance.
3. Spell out the purpose and terms of joint efforts, including who will do what by when.
4. Work out the kinks as they arise and change the approach when necessary.
5. Build out from success by sharing positive results and encouraging expanded efforts. (p. 24)

Recent research has explored the use of public schools as tools for community and economic development. In *Using Public Schools as Community Development Tools,* Chung (2002) stresses the importance of a strong link between public schools and neighborhoods. She points out that good public schools attract and retain neighborhood residents partly because they have the power to increase property values. Alternatively, she attributes some of the flight from inner cities to perceived as well as real declines in public school quality.

Chung suggests several strategies for including public schools in community development:

1. Coordination of the development of affordable housing and public schools as a way to concentrate resources, encourage mixed-use development, and reduce the negative effects of involuntary displacement of residents.
2. Development of neighborhood-based public schools as a strategy to develop capacity in disinvested urban areas.
3. Use of public schools as tools for economic development by developing programs for both college preparation and vocational work-

force development, and by building relationships with local businesses.

A SCHOOL SYSTEM FOR A NEW MILLENNIUM

The task of designing a public education system for the new millennium begins with the acceptance of the reality that our educational system in many ways reflects the needs and culture of a bygone era. In *Getting Smarter, Becoming Fairer: A Progressive Education Agenda for a Stronger Nation,* Brown and others (2005) make this point bluntly: "While the No Child Left Behind (NCLB) Act brought needed attention to measuring progress and holding schools accountable, it did not address fundamental challenges facing our education system. It is clear that more is needed if we are to prepare our children for the awesome challenges they will face in this century" (Foreword, para. 2).

Warren (2005) emphasizes that education reform initiatives must address the relationship between school reform and community revitalization, pointing out that it is difficult—and may be impossible—to reform public schools when the communities around them are disintegrating and collapsing. Similarly, community and economic development professionals face great difficulty in revitalizing communities when the schools within their boundaries are failing to educate their students. He recommends viewing the relationship between school and community organizations from the perspective of building social capital, which he defines as "a set of links across institutions" (p. 137) that serve to build relational power and bring diverse groups together to achieve collective ends. Relational power, or the power to accomplish things collectively, is an extension of most theoretical work on social capital, which highlights the benefits of trust, cooperation, and collaboration. Warren believes that the building of relational power is necessary to combat some of the glaring structural inequities in public education often found in poor neighborhoods, although it should not take the place of political and organizational action to address such inequities.

According to Warren, community initiatives can make the following critical contributions to school improvement:

1. Improve the social context of education so that children come to school better able to learn.
2. Foster parental and community participation in the education of children and the work of schools.
3. Work to transform the culture of schools and the practice of schooling and hold school officials accountable for educational gains.
4. Help build a political constituency for public education to support the delivery of greater resources to schools and to address in other ways the profound inequalities that exist in public education. (p. 135)

Michael Timpane, former vice president of the Carnegie Foundation for the Advancement of Teaching, thinks educators should accept a primary role in community reform efforts: "School leadership must be at the head of this parade. No one else can speak with as much legitimacy and effect in every community in the land" (quoted in Decker and Boo, 2001, pp. 3–4).

The American Association of School Administrators (AASA) has led efforts to reconceptualize the role of schools in relation to their communities. In a year-long project, the AASA's Council of 21 initiated a discussion of the kind of school system the nation will need in the future. The resulting report (Withrow, 1999) was designed to stimulate debate in communities about the characteristics of schools and school systems that would be capable of preparing students for a global information age. Paul Houston, AASA executive director, explains that the association does not view the study and its conclusions as the last word, but rather as "a bridge from what our schools and school systems are to what they need to become" (p. v).

The Council of 21, composed of leaders in business, government, education, and other areas, identified 16 characteristics that schools and school systems should have in order to prepare students for a global information age (Withrow, 1999). (The Council notes that the characteristics are not listed in order of priority because all are important.)

1. *The definitions of school, teacher, and learner are reshaped by the digital world.* The term *school* must take on an expanded meaning beyond the physical structure and become more encompassing,

embracing communities of knowledge and learning that are inter-
estwide, communitywide, and worldwide. While there may always
be a school building, a school is likely to resemble a nerve center
that connects teachers, students, and the community to the wealth
of knowledge that exists in the world. "Teachers" must become
orchestrators of learning, moderators, and facilitators, as well as
purveyors of knowledge and subject matter, so that they can help
students turn information into knowledge and knowledge into wisdom. "Learner" needs to be thought of in terms of preparing students for life in the real world. Out of both necessity and curiosity,
lifelong learning must become a reality in people's lives.

2. *All students have equal opportunity for an outstanding education,
   with adequate funding, no matter where they live.* An equal opportunity philosophy must drive everything from funding to the expectations we have for our students. It must apply to individuals with
   disabilities, the disadvantaged, and the legions of children recently
   arrived from other countries.

3. *Educators are driven by high expectations and clear, challenging
   standards that are widely understood by students, families, and
   communities.* Standards and expectations must be high but realistic; schools, teachers, students, families, and other community
   members must be part of the process of developing those standards
   and expectations.

4. *A project-based "curriculum for life" engages students in addressing real-world problems, issues important to humanity, and questions that matter.* Students must be able to connect what they are
   learning with what is happening or may happen in the real world.
   They need to be prepared for responsible citizenship in a democracy. Teachers will be challenged to help students make connections and understand why what they are learning has value.

5. *Teachers and administrators are effectively prepared for the
   global information age.* All teachers and administrators must be
   prepared to make the best possible use of technology, both for student learning and for school and school district efficiency. Ultimately, teachers and administrators must move beyond managing
   time and space to managing for results.

6. *Students, schools, school systems, and communities are connected*

around the clock with each other and with the world through infor-mation-rich, interactive technology. With a concern for equal opportunity, schools and school districts will use technology and electronic networks to get families and the community on the education team.

7. *School systems conduct, consider, and apply significant research in designing programs that lead to constantly improving student achievement.* Schools and school systems must do more research focused on improving student achievement and must use that research as part of the decision-making process. Teachers must take a more active role in research, assisted by training that will help them interpret and apply significant research in the classroom.

8. *Students learn to think, reason, and make sound decisions and demonstrate values inherent in a democracy.* Critical thinking, higher-level thinking, and decision-making skills are basic to a sound education, and those skills must penetrate every area of the curriculum. Schools as well as communities have a responsibility to help students become more civil; understand the importance of being honest, respectful, trustworthy, and caring; understand and become participants in a free and democratic society; understand the consequences of their own actions and how their actions affect others; and understand the need for a code of ethics. Students need to understand rights and exercise responsibilities basic to maintaining those rights.

9. *School facilities provide a safe, secure, stimulating, joyous learning environment that contributes to a lifelong passion for learning and high achievement.* The school should be in touch with the rest of the community and the world. The buildings themselves should be up-to-date, clean, and appropriately lighted, with proper temperature and air-quality controls. They should be places where students want to be.

10. *Leadership is collaborative, and governance is focused on broad issues that affect student learning.* Rather than making major decisions in isolation, administrators must ask the opinions of teachers, families, and others on the staff and in the community; one of the challenges they will face is the management of expectations. However, teachers and principals must have enough flexibility and con-

trol to run their schools and classrooms effectively. What is needed ultimately are communities in which citizens and schools are both willing and able to say, "We're in this together."

11. *Students learn about other cultures, respect and honor diversity, and see the world as an extended neighborhood.* Educators and communities must help students understand and appreciate the beauty of other cultures and respect all people. Students must have a solid grounding in the principles of human rights. They must try to understand people who hold different values and learn to accept dissent and individual differences. Schools must embody the principles of a democratic society and model democratic principles and respect for diversity in the way they are run.

12. *Schools promote creativity and teamwork at all levels, and teachers help students turn information into knowledge and knowledge into wisdom.* We need both individual initiative and the synergy that comes from collaboration. Teamwork involving students, staff, and community must become commonplace, with teams working together face-to-face and electronically. The teacher's role will change dramatically from dispensing information to working alongside students, helping them transform information into knowledge and, eventually, wisdom.

13. *Assessment of student progress is performance-based, taking into account students' individual talents, abilities, and aspirations.* Flexibility is needed in standards and assessments.

14. *A student-centered, collaboratively developed vision provides power and focus for education communitywide.* Educational leaders must develop a vision for education in their communities, and must bring educators, families, and others together to help them do it. School systems and their leaders need to know—through surveys, advisory groups, and just plain listening—what constituents know that they do not know, and what they need to know to give schools their support. Administrators must be open to what staff and community can teach them and must become masters of collaboration, while ensuring the intellectual and moral integrity of the school and school system.

15. *Continuous improvement is a driving force in every school and*

school system. Planning must be a continuous process, and educators must apply the principles of quality management.

16. *Schools are the crossroads and central convening point of the community.* Schools must be around-the-clock hubs for lifelong learning, the connecting point for education and achievement for all who live and work in the community. They will also become centers for health care, housing assistance, social services, and other community services and agencies. School systems must become ever more creative in getting people involved so that everyone in the community is on the education team.

A TESTED METHOD FOR BUILDING COMMUNITY

One proven process for building supportive communities and involving families in the education of their children is community education, usually implemented through community schools. Dryfoos (2002) cites evaluation data gathered by a number of organizations, including the Academy for Educational Development, the Stanford Research Institute, and the Chapin Hall Centers for Children, that demonstrate the positive impact of community schools on student learning, healthy youth development, family well-being, and community life.

For more than six decades, community education advocates have worked to build exceptionally strong ties between public schools and their communities, usually by developing community schools that transform traditional 9 a.m. to 3 p.m. schools into extended-day learning, recreation, and social centers for use by community residents of all ages and needs. In these multipurpose schools, local community residents and professional educators work together to address community problems and needs in partnership with other community agencies and institutions.

Community education offers local residents and community agencies and institutions the opportunity to become active partners in providing enhanced educational opportunities and addressing community concerns. It is based on the following principles (Decker and Decker, 2003):

1. *Lifelong learning.* Education is viewed as a birth-to-death process, and everyone in the community—individuals, businesses, public

and private agencies—shares responsibility for educating all members of the community and providing learning opportunities for residents of all ages, backgrounds, and needs.

2. *Self-determination.* Local people have a right and a responsibility to be involved in determining community needs and identifying community resources that can be used to address those needs.

3. *Self-help.* People are best served when their capacity to help themselves is acknowledged and developed. When people assume responsibility for their own well-being, they build independence and become part of the solution.

4. *Leadership development.* The training of local leaders in such skills as problem solving, decision making, and group process is an essential component of successful self-help and improvement efforts.

5. *Institutional responsiveness.* Public institutions exist to serve the public and are obligated to develop programs and services that address continuously changing public needs and interests.

6. *Maximum use of resources.* The physical, financial, and human resources in every community should be interconnected and used to their fullest to meet the diverse needs and interests of community members.

7. *Integrated delivery of services.* Organizations and agencies that operate for the public good can better meet their own goals and serve the public by collaborating with organizations and agencies with similar goals.

8. *Decentralization.* Services, programs, and other community involvement opportunities that are close to people's homes have the greatest potential for high levels of public participation. Whenever possible, these activities should be available in locations with easy public access.

9. *Inclusiveness.* Community services and programs, and other community involvement opportunities, should be designed to involve the broadest possible cross section of the community and eliminate segregation or isolation of people by age, income, sex, race, ethnicity, religion, or other factors that impede participation and integration.

10. *Access to public information.* Public information is shared across

agency and organizational lines. Community members know more than just the facts; they know what the facts mean in the lives of the diverse people who make up the community. (pp. 40–42)

Using the community education process to design and implement a comprehensive plan for educational and community improvement takes time and the ongoing effort of committed individuals. However, experiences in communities across the nation show that the benefits realized are clearly worth the effort. Community schools, full-service schools, and 21st Century Community Learning Centers are examples of community education in practice.

The Annie E. Casey Foundation (1999) points out:

These and other models represent a move away from education controlled by school boards and central offices toward greater influence (and responsibility) by parents and school-based educators. These approaches can be thought of as "systems of community schools"—systems in which each school has its own staff, mission, and approach to instruction but all are working to improve education and other outcomes for children, parents, and neighborhoods. (p. 4)

COMMUNITY SCHOOLS

A community school is not just another program to be imposed on a school. As Harkavy and Blank (2002) emphasize:

It [the idea of community schools] is a way of thinking and acting that recognizes the historic central role of schools in our communities and the power of working together for a common good. Educating our children, yes, but also strengthening our families and communities, so that they, in turn, can help make schools even stronger and children more successful. . . . Educators are major partners, but not always in the lead role. A capable partner organization—a child- and family-services agency, for example, or a youth-development organization, a college, or a family support center—can serve as the linchpin for the community school, mobilizing and integrating the resources of the community, so that principals and teachers can focus on teaching and learning. In some communities, schools themselves will be best equipped to provide the necessary leadership and coordination. (section 2, para. 3)

Community schools extend the concept of public education beyond the traditional K–12 program. They are not limited by traditional school schedules and roles, focusing instead on current community needs. Community schools are open schools, available for use before and after school for academic, extracurricular, recreation, health, social service, and workforce-preparation programs for people of all ages. They involve a broad range of community members, businesses, public and private organizations, and local, state, and federal agencies. They become places where people gather to learn, to enjoy themselves, and to become involved in community problem solving.

Research confirms that community schools work. Blank and others (2003) report that, although not all evaluations looked at every outcome, the collective results show that community schools make a difference because they improve student learning, promote family engagement with students and schools, help schools function more effectively, and add vitality to communities.

Another reason community schools work is that they provide places and programs in which community members can educate themselves. They involve families and other community members in efforts to improve academic achievement and school climate. They develop public knowledge about the diverse interests and complex interrelationships of a community. They provide a setting for community members to meet, talk through issues, and work together to address problems. They provide opportunities to discover and nurture the public leadership that is needed to sustain a healthy, vibrant community.

Designating schools as community schools is a win-win proposition for both educators and community members. From a problem-solving point of view, a school can be a support center for a whole network of agencies and institutions committed to addressing community needs and expanding learning opportunities for all community members. From an educator's perspective, community schools provide a catalyst and a setting for collaboration with families and communities in the schools' primary mission of educating the community's children.

FULL-SERVICE SCHOOLS

The full-service school meets the need for a communitywide, multi-agency approach to addressing the diverse needs of children and families. Flaxman (2001) explains:

> [The full-service school is] a way to coordinate services through new institutional arrangements in a comprehensive, collaborative, and coherent system for changing youth, families, and the social environment shared by educators; community and business leaders; and health, social services, and mental health practitioners. The school becomes a mechanism for coordinating services that are fragmented among several bureaucracies, training teachers to take a new role in the development of their students, and working cooperatively with families. (p. 9)

A full-service school deals not only with the educational needs of the children who attend but also provides a range of additional services for both the children and their families. Dryfoos (2002) describes the interaction between school authorities and outside agencies in the full-service schools:

> The primary responsibility for high-quality education rests with the school authorities, while the primary responsibility for everything else rests with the outside agencies. The school system pays for education; the other services are supported by an array of non-school sources of funding. It is important to make this distinction clear because some have misinterpreted these community school concepts to mean that the school is asked to provide and to pay for added health and social services or extended hours or parenting education. Quite the contrary, the idea is to divide up the responsibility among a number of agencies, with one set of services devoted to helping children learn and another devoted to helping children and families gain access to the supports they need. The goal is to take some of the burden of rearing and nourishing children off the school system. . . . The services that fall under "everything else" are broadly construed. Experience is showing that almost anything can be provided in a school as long as it meets the needs of the school/community and as long as resources can be identified to bring it in. The most frequently mentioned supports are health, mental health, and social services . . . before- and after-school programs are

almost always included along with mentoring and tutoring. . . . New thinking about old problems can also be worked into the design. (p. 396)

This approach is distinguished by several characteristics (Dryfoos,
2002). Services are provided to children and their families through collaboration among schools, health care providers, and social services agencies. The schools are among the central participants in planning and
governing the collaborative effort. The services are provided at a school
or are coordinated by personnel located at a school or at a site near the
school. The role of school personnel is to identify children and families
who need services and to link them to the services that are available.

AFTER-SCHOOL PROGRAMS

The U.S. Department of Education's 21st Century Community Learning
Centers initiative, begun in 1997, was reauthorized as Title IV, Part B of
the federal No Child Left Behind Act, signed into law by President Bush
on January 8, 2002. The U.S. Department of Education's After-School
initiative falls under this program. This initiative encourages schools to
stay open longer to provide a safe place for homework centers, mentoring
programs, drug and violence prevention counseling, college preparation
courses, and enrichment in core academic subjects.

After-school programs respond to the problems created in many American communities by the fact that parents work longer hours, spend more
time in daily commutes, and have less time for supervising their children
and interacting with their neighbors. Such disconnected communities may
become unsafe, with increased risk of crime and violence. School-based
after-school programs create safe places for children to gather. They help
alleviate parents' concerns about drugs, violence, abuse, traffic, and other
dangers, not just by keeping young people occupied but also by giving
them opportunities to form relationships with reliable adults in the community and encouraging their involvement with their neighborhoods
through service projects (Afterschool Alliance, 2004). According to the
Pew Partnership for Civic Change (2001), children who participate regularly in after-school programs experience more positive outcomes, such
as improved school performance and attendance, improved social skills

and self-confidence, and healthier use of time, than children who have little supervision after school.

Unfortunately, a 2004 national survey by the Afterschool Alliance, *America After 3 PM,* found that the United States is failing to give its children safe, supervised activities during the often-dangerous afternoon hours.

1. Today, 14.3 million children (25%) take care of themselves after the school day ends, including almost 4 million middle school students in grades six through eight.
2. Only 11% of K–12 children (6.5 million) are in after-school programs.
3. Older children are more likely to be unsupervised.
4. African American and Hispanic children are more likely to be unsupervised than other children.
5. Demand for after-school programs is much higher among African American and Hispanic parents; 40% said they would enroll their children in an after-school program if it was available compared to 23% of Caucasian parents.
6. The parents of 30% of children not currently participating in an after-school program said they would enroll their children if one was available. (section 2, Summary of National Findings)

Federal support for after-school programs financed through No Child Left Behind has decreased in keeping with general budget cutting. According to the Afterschool Alliance (2005), society will pay a high price for such cuts. The alliance points to the fact that after-school programs address societally risky and expensive behaviors in youths in two ways: by keeping youth constructively occupied during dangerous hours, and by giving them dependable access to caring adults. A study of California's After School and Education Safety Act of 2002 (Brown and others, 2002) estimated that "each dollar invested in an at-risk child brings a return of $8.92 to $12.90. Most of this remarkable benefit is derived from diverting a relatively small portion of at-risk youngsters from a future path of crime. . . . Even excluding these substantial crime reduction benefits, the Act is cost effective. Non-crime benefits . . . are between $2.99 and $4.05 for every dollar spent" (p. 6).

The Afterschool Alliance (2005) emphasizes that not all benefits of after-school programs can be measured or stated in monetary terms:

> As much as quality afterschool programs are capable of saving money and providing a significant monetary return on investment, many benefits to individual students, teachers, schools, and communities cannot be assigned a dollar value. Time to find a passion or a skill, better self-esteem, teamwork skills, confidence, a greater sense of curiosity, a lifelong love of learning—these things are priceless. (p. 3)

A SOLEMN CONCLUSION AND A WARNING

National polls conducted by the Public Education Network (PEN) in partnership with *Education Week* (PEN, 2005) show that the American public is ready and willing to take responsibility for its public schools, but often feels uncertain about the best way to do it. Wendy Puriefoy, president of PEN (2005), states with urgency the need for public action:

> We as a nation cannot afford to stand by and allow our public schools to become wastelands of mediocrity. We must not allow millions of children to grow up unaware of their rights and responsibilities as citizens, unprepared to support themselves and their families, with little or no stake in society's welfare. We must not accept achievement gaps, tolerate inequitable funding systems, make do with deteriorating buildings and outdated textbooks and defend failing schools and substandard teaching. (para. 6)

Reengaging the public in public schools can begin with the acknowledgment that communities and the schools within their boundaries are inseparable from one another. Schools should be central to the life and learning of the entire community and should embody community values (KnowledgeWorks, 2004). When broken connections between schools and communities are reestablished, schools are more effective and neighborhoods are healthier.

Michael Timpane (quoted in Decker and Boo, 2001), former vice president of the Carnegie Foundation for the Advancement of Teaching, recommends a new way of looking at school-community relationships:

Our schools need new ways to think about and foster parental and community involvement in education. . . . We must develop a new perspective, and it must rest on three challenging propositions:

1. Schools cannot succeed nowadays (or, to put it more strongly, schools will fail) without the collaboration of parents and communities.
2. Troubled families need strong support to become and remain functional.
3. Communities must take charge of all the developmental needs of their children. (pp. 3–4)

Renewing Our Schools, Securing Our Future (Campaign for America's Future, 2005) sums up the challenge involved in the transformation of our educational system.

America today faces both a choice and an opportunity. We cannot pretend that we are ready to meet the challenges of the 21st century if we continue business as usual. The agenda outlined here calls for a marked transformation of our schools. That requires greater commitment, greater accountability, and greater investment. This transformation is essential if we are to provide our children with the education they need and deserve. Our national history is rich with tales of American perseverance, ingenuity, and brainpower rising to take on challenges of each era. We must once again summon the resolve to transform our education system. Our future depends on it. (p. 5)

REFERENCES

Afterschool Alliance. (2004). *America after 3 PM: A household survey on afterschool in America.* Retrieved April 24, 2006, from http://www.afterschoolalliance.org/press_archives/America_3pm/Executive_Summary.pdf

Afterschool Alliance. (2004, January). *Afterschool programs strengthen communities.* Issue Brief No. 18. Retrieved November 30, 2005, from http://www.afterschoolalliance.org/issue_briefs/issue_comm_building_18.pdf

Afterschool Alliance. (2005, November). *Afterschool programs: A wise public investment.* Issue Brief No. 22. Retrieved November 30, 2005, from http://www.afterschoolalliance.org/issue_briefs/issue_costs_22.pdf

Annie E. Casey Foundation. (1999). *Improving community school connections.* Baltimore, MD: Annie E. Casey Foundation.

Blank, M. J., Melaville, A., and Shah, B. P. (2003). *Making the difference: Research and practice in community schools.* Washington, DC: Coalition for Community Schools.

Brown, C. G., Rocha, E., Sharkey, A., and Hadley, E. (2005). *Getting smarter, becoming fairer: A progressive education agenda for a stronger nation.* Retrieved January 10, 2006, from http://www.americanprogress.org/site/pp .asp?c = biJR80VFeb = 994995

Brown, W. O., Frates, S. B., Rudge, I. S., and Tradewell, R. L. (2002). *The costs and benefits of after school programs: The estimated effects of the After School Education and Safety Program Act of 2002.* Retrieved April 24, 2006, from http://rose.claremontmckenna.edu/publications/pdf/after_school.pdf

Campaign for America's Future. (2005). *Renewing our schools, securing our future.* Retrieved April 19, 2006, from http://www.americanprogress.org/atf/ cf/%BE9245FE4–9A2B-43CF-A521–5D6FF2E06E03%7D/ EXEC%20SUMMARY.PDF

Chung, C. (2002). *Using public schools as community development tools: Strategies for developers.* Retrieved April 24, 2006, from http://www.jchs.harvard .edu/publications/communitydevelopment/w02–9_chung.pdf

Crowson, R. L., and Boyd, W. I. (1999). *New roles for community services in educational reform.* Retrieved November 23, 2005, from http://www.temple .edu/lss/pdf/publications/pubs19995.pdf

Decker, L. E., and Boo, M. R. (2001). *Community schools: Serving children, families and communities.* Fairfax, VA: National Community Education Association.

Decker, L. E., and Decker, V. A. (2003). *Home, school, and community partnerships.* Lanham, MD: Scarecrow Press.

Dryfoos, J. G. (2002). Full-service community schools: Creating new institutions. *Phi Delta Kappan, 83,* 5.

Flaxman, E. (2001). The promise of urban community schooling. *ERIC Review, 8,* 2. Retrieved November 29, 2005, from http://permanent.access.gpo.gov/ Dps50000/ERIC%20REVIEW%Archiev/V018n02.pdf

Harkavy, I., and Blank, M. (2002). *Community schools.* Retrieved November 18, 2005, from http://www.communityschools.org/commentary.html

Jehl, J., Blank, M., and McCloud, B. (2001). *Education and community building: Connecting two worlds.* Washington, DC: Institute for Educational Leadership. Retrieved April 20, 2006, from http://www.communityschools.org/combuild .pdf

Kahlenberg, R. D. (Ed.). (2000). A notion at risk: Preserving public education as an engine for social mobility. In *The Century Foundation.* Washington DC: Brookings Press. Retrieved November 29, 2005, from http://www.brookings.edu/press/books/clientpr/priority/notion_at_risk.htm

KnowledgeWorks Foundation. (2004). *Schools as centers of communities.* KnowledgeWorks Foundation Concept Paper. Retrieved April 25, 2006, from http://www.nsbn.org/publications/newsletters/spring2004/knowledgeworks.php

Kretzmann, J. P., and McKnight, J. L. (1993). *Building communities from the inside out: A path toward finding and mobilizing a community's assets.* Evanston, IL: Center for Urban Affairs and Policy Research, Northwestern University.

Mathews, D. (2000). *Putting the public back into public schools.* Retrieved May 1, 2006, from http://www.sedl.org/pubs/sedletter/v14n01/1.html

Mathews, D. (2006). *Reclaiming public education by reclaiming our democracy.* Dayton, OH: Kettering Foundation. Retrieved March 24, 2006, from http://www.reclaimingeducation.org/toc.htm

National Commission on Excellence in Education. (1983). *A nation at risk: The imperative for educational reform.* Washington, DC: U.S. Government Printing Office.

PEN. (2005). *Speaking out on "No Child Left Behind."* Retrieved March 22, 2006, from http://www.publiceducation.org/portals/nclb/national/open_to_the_public.asp

Pew Partnership for Civic Change. (2001). *Wanted, solutions for America: What we know works.* Retrieved November 14, 2005, from http://www.pew-partnership.org/whats_works.html

Puriefoy, W. (2005). *Education: Everyone's responsibility.* Retrieved January 10, 2006, from http://www.forumforeducation.org/news/index.php?id = 93

Rans, S. (2005). *Hidden treasures. A community building workbook: Building community connections by engaging.* Retrieved April 24, 2006, from http://www.northwestern.edu/ipr/abcd/hiddentreasures.pdf

Search Institute. (1998). *Developmental assets: An investment in youth.* Minneapolis, MN.

Search Institute. (2005). *Developmental assets.* Retrieved January 10, 2006, from www.search-institute.org/assets

Warren, M. (2005, Summer). Communities and schools: A new view of urban education reform. *Harvard Education Review, 75,* 2. Retrieved April 24, 2006, from http://gseweb.harvard.edu/~hepg/warren.html

Withrow, F. (with Long, H., and Marx, G.). (1999). *Preparing schools and school systems for the 21st century.* Arlington, VA: American Association of School Administrators.

Websites for More Information and Links to Other Relevant Sites

Afterschool Alliance, http://www.afterschoolalliance.org
Center for Effective Collaboration, http://cecp.air.org
Charles F. Kettering Foundation, http://www.kettering.org
Charles Stewart Mott Foundation, http://www.mott.org
Civic Practices Network, http://www.cpn.org
Coalition for Community Schools, http://www.communityschools.org
National Center for Community Education, http://www.nccenet.org
National Community Education Association, http://www.ncea.com
National Network for Collaboration, http://crs.uvm.edu/nnco/collab/about.html
Northwest Regional Education Laboratory School Community Partnership Team,
    http://www.nwrel.org/partnerships/links/index.html
Search Institute, http://www.search-institute.org

Chapter Five

Home and School as Partners

The generally accepted mission of public schools is to provide an equal education for all children. Historically, geographic barriers, economic inequities, segregation, language and cultural disparities, and other factors have hindered the achievement of this mission. As our school population has become increasingly diverse, achieving the goal of equal opportunity has become even more challenging. Public schools now serve student populations that are a kaleidoscope of race, culture, ethnicity, language background, and social class. Nearly all current school assessments, from the NAEP through state tests, document measurable disparities in academic achievement, largely along economic, racial, and ethnic lines. Closing the achievement gap has been the focus of many educational reform efforts.

Parent and family involvement has become a major component of almost every plan for restructuring schools. Parental roles are specified in the school effectiveness, site-based management, and school choice movements. A growing body of research continues to demonstrate that parent involvement has a significant impact on student achievement. Public opinion agrees with the research findings.

The AASA contracted with professional pollsters in 1999 to find out what the public thinks are the best indicators that schools are providing a high-quality education. Reporting on the results of this poll, Paul Houston (2001), AASA executive director, said:

> The American public believes that "high parental involvement" is the best indicator that a school is providing a high quality education. "Children who

are happy and like school" was the second best indicator. "High scores on statewide tests" was selected as the best indicator by only 18.8% [of those voting]. (e-mail letter)

PROMOTING FAMILY INVOLVEMENT

America 2000: An Education Strategy, an agenda for education reform adopted in 1990 by President George H. W. Bush and the nation's governors, created a national impetus to increase parent and family involvement in school reform and restructuring. The America 2000 strategy was expanded under the Clinton administration and given a new name, Goals 2000. Two goals were added to the 1990 agenda: All teachers will have the opportunity to acquire the knowledge and skills needed to prepare U.S. students for the next century; and every school will promote partnerships that will increase parental involvement and participation in promoting the social, emotional, and academic growth of children (Decker and Decker, 2001).

On January 8, 2002, President George W. Bush signed a new education plan, No Child Left Behind, into law (U.S. Department of Education, 2002). The new law reflected a federal commitment to close the gap between high- and low-achieving students and to ensure that all students, regardless of background, receive a quality education. Although parents are mentioned more than 300 times in various parts of the law (*NCLB Action Briefs,* 2004), promoting parent involvement was not a primary focus. The desktop reference for NCLB (U.S. Department of Education, 2002) states that the law "embodies four key principles—stronger accountability for results; greater flexibility for states, school districts, and schools in the use of federal funds; more choices for parents of children from disadvantaged backgrounds; and an emphasis on teaching methods that have been demonstrated to work" (p. 9).

The passage of NCLB almost immediately raised educators' concerns about what the emphasis on accountability and high-stakes testing would mean to other elements of school restructuring and school reform, particularly in schools serving low-income and minority children. As Harkavy and Blank (2002) observed,

Listening to the recent political debate culminating in the passage of the "No Child Left Behind" Act of 2001, it would be easy to assume that the only things that matter in education are annual testing in grades 3–8, having a qualified teacher in the first four years of schooling, and allowing parents to move their children out of persistently failing schools. (para. 1)

The response of the National Center for Fair and Open Testing (2002) also raised questions about the emphasis on testing:

There is an important role for good assessment of student learning. The public deserves to know how well schools are doing, schools need to use information about student learning to improve teaching, and there should be intervention in schools which are unable to improve even when they have been provided the resources and tools to do so. None of this requires heavy reliance on results from state or commercial standardized tests. (para. 3)

A large percentage of the American public also seems to question the assumption that high test scores correlate with the goal of academic success for all children. Houston (2001) states that in the 1999 AASA poll, "high test scores" was ranked 13th out of 17 possible choices; and in a 2000 AASA poll of registered voters, 63% of the public disagreed with a statement that a student's progress for one school year can be accurately summarized by a single standardized test.

The 33rd annual Phi Delta Kappa/Gallup Poll (Rose and Gallup, 2001) on the public's attitudes toward the public schools confirms the validity of the AASA findings. The poll found that 66% of the public believe that standardized tests should be used to guide instruction; only 30% believe such tests should be used to measure student learning. Additionally, 65% believe student achievement should be measured by classroom work and homework; only 31% would rely on testing. Conclusions of the 37th annual poll (Rose and Gallup, 2005) are unambiguous:

That the public is so strong in its support for closing the achievement gap should send a clear message to policy makers. There is also a message in the conclusions related to NCLB in that they note the public's disagreement with the law's strategies and, at the same time, suggest that there is still time for midcourse corrections. Again, we feel that policy makers would do well to heed the message. (p. 42)

Among the NCLB strategies the 37th annual poll described as "frequently out of step with approaches favored by the public" were these:

1. NCLB uses a single test to determine if a school is in need of improvement; 68% say that a single test cannot give a fair picture.
2. NCLB tests on English and math to determine if a school is in need of improvement; 80% say testing English and math only will not give a fair picture.
3. NCLB gives parents of a child attending a school found to be in need of improvement the chance to transfer their child to a school making "adequate yearly progress"; 79% say they would prefer to have additional help given to their child in his or her own school. (Rose and Gallup, 2005, p. 43)

NCLBGrassroots.org (2005) reports that "the grassroots rebellion against NCLB already has caught on in 47 of the 50 states, with five states—Minnesota, Maine, Nevada, New Jersey, and Virginia—likely to be the biggest anti-NCLB hotspots in 2005–2006." The common threads of the rebellion are:

1. NCLB is an unprecedented federal intrusion into an area historically reserved to states.
2. NCLB's one-size-fits-all approach ignores the realities of good teaching and learning.
3. Under NCLB, valuable class time is diverted to test preparation and away from real teaching and learning.
4. NCLB is too narrow in its substantive focus because students need to master basics such as reading and math, as well as the new basic skills—communication, creative problem solving, collaboration—in order to succeed in the 21st century economy.
5. NCLB relies too heavily on standardized testing to the exclusion of other valuable measures of mastery, such as portfolio reviews and performance.
6. NCLB's punitive approach distracts and undermines educators and administrators using approaches that include incentives and technical assistance . . . [that are] likely to yield positive results over the long term.

7. NCLB is underfunded, placing significant financial strain on states and districts, forcing them to divert funds away from programs that they know work to help struggling students such as smaller class size, early learning and afterschool programs, and others. (para. 6)

NCLBGrassroots.org notes that although the July 2005 NAEP scores showed a narrowing gap in reading and math achievement since the last previous test in 1999, "members of the NAEP governing board cautioned against attributing the closing of the gap to NCLB, noting that the achievement gap began narrowing before 'No Child Left Behind' became law due to a range of efforts in the states" (para. 4).

Many educational experts hope the NCLB rebellion will continue to grow and that educational improvement efforts will include other promising areas, such as the significant link between student achievement and parent involvement. Education Week Research Center (2001) cites one analysis that found that three factors over which parents have enormous control—absenteeism, variety of reading material in the home, and amount of television watched—accounted for nearly 90% of the differences in student test scores. The article also observed:

> If parents have a central role in influencing their children's progress in school, research has shown that schools in turn have an important part to play in determining levels of parent involvement. Research indicates . . . that for parent involvement to flourish, it must be meaningfully integrated with the school's programs and community. (para. 2)

BENEFITS OF FAMILY INVOLVEMENT

The most comprehensive survey of the research on parent and family involvement in education has been reported in a series of publications developed over the last two decades by Henderson and Berla: *Parent Participation–Student Involvement* (1981); *The Evidence Continues to Grow* (1987); and *A New Generation of Evidence: The Family Is Critical to Student Achievement* (1994). In an annual synthesis, Henderson and Mapp (2002) state:

> The evidence is consistent, positive, and convincing: families have a major influence on their children's achievement in school and through life. . . .

When schools, families, and community groups work together to support learning, children tend to do better in school, stay in school longer, and like school more. (p. 7)

Studies cited also show that family involvement has positive effects on school quality and program design.

Effects on Student Success

1. When parents are involved, students achieve more, regardless of socioeconomic status, ethnic/racial background, or parents' education level.
2. The more extensive the family involvement, the higher the student achievement.
3. Students whose families are involved have higher grades and test scores, have better attendance records, and complete their homework more consistently.
4. When parents and families are involved, students display more positive attitudes and behavior.
5. Students whose families are involved have higher graduation rates and higher enrollment rates in postsecondary education.
6. Different involvement levels produce different gains. To produce long-lasting gains for students, the parent and family involvement activities must be well planned, inclusive, and comprehensive.
7. Educators have higher expectations of students whose parents and families collaborate with teachers. They also have higher opinions of those parents and families.
8. In programs designed to involve parents and families in full partnerships, the achievement of disadvantaged children improves, sometimes dramatically, with the children farthest behind making the greatest gains.
9. Children from diverse cultural backgrounds tend to do better when families and professionals collaborate to bridge the gap between the home culture and the school culture.
10. Antisocial student behaviors, such as alcohol use and violence, decrease as family involvement increases.
11. The benefits of involving parents and families are significant at all ages and grade levels. Middle and high school students whose par-

ents and families remain involved make better transitions, maintain the quality of their work, develop realistic plans for the future, and are less likely to drop out.

The most accurate predictor of a student's success in school is not income or social status, but the extent to which the student's family is able to (1) create a home environment that encourages learning; (2) communicate high, yet reasonable, expectations for achievement and future careers; and (3) become involved in their children's education at school and in the community.

Effects on School Quality

1. Schools that work well with families have better teacher morale and higher ratings of teachers by parents.
2. Schools in which families are involved have more support from families and better reputations in the community.
3. School programs that involve parents and families outperform identical programs without such involvement.
4. Schools in which children are failing improve dramatically when parents and families are enabled to become partners with teachers.
5. Schools' efforts to inform and involve parents and families are stronger determinants of whether inner-city parents will be involved in their children's education than are the level of parent education, family size, marital status, or student grade level.

Effects on Program Design

1. The more the relationship between parents and educators approaches a comprehensive, well-planned partnership, the higher the student achievement.
2. For low-income families, programs offering home visits are more successful in involving parents and families than programs requiring parents to visit the school.
3. When families receive frequent and effective communication from the school or program, their involvement increases, their overall evaluation of educators is higher, and their attitudes toward the program are more positive. Parents and families are much more likely to become involved when educators encourage and assist them in helping their children with schoolwork.

4. When parents and families are treated as partners and given relevant information by people with whom they are comfortable, they put into practice the involvement strategies they already know are effective but have been hesitant to use.
5. Collaboration with families is an essential component of a reform strategy, but it is not a substitute for high-quality education programs or comprehensive school improvement.

Moles and D'Angelo (1993) and Wherry (2004) report on other teacher, administrator, school, and community benefits of successful home-school involvement. When parent involvement is a goal, teachers receive in-service training on how to work with families from diverse backgrounds; get more support from principals for their work with families; have more respect for, and better appreciation of, parents' time and ability to reinforce learning; and maximize time and resources by sharing knowledge, skills, and resources cooperatively. Administrators benefit from better communication between school and home, fewer family complaints about inconsistent and inappropriate course content and homework, and improved school climate as children see parents and teachers as partners. Schools and communities benefit from improved teacher morale, higher ratings of teachers by families, decreased teacher turnover, more school support from families and community members, and improved school climate and reputation.

STANDARDS AND MODELS OF PARENT INVOLVEMENT

There are many models for involving parents in the education of their children. Two frequently cited models were developed by Joyce Epstein of Johns Hopkins University in Baltimore and Susan Swap of Wheelock College in Boston. The National Standards for Parent/Family Involvement Programs developed by the National PTA (1998) in cooperation with education and parent involvement professionals through the National Coalition for Parent Involvement in Education closely follow the Epstein model. There are six standards, each with quality indicators. The first five relate to parent and family involvement, the sixth to collaboration with the community at large. The National PTA (2004) explains, "[T]hese standards, together with their corresponding quality indicators, were created to be used in conjunction with other national standards and reform initiatives in support of children's learning and success" (p. 10).

Another program, the Parent Involvement Schools of Excellence certification program, provides schools with tools to assess and enhance their commitment to parent involvement based on the PTA's National Standards for Parent and Family Involvement. The standards and quality indicators used in the Parent Involvement Schools of Excellence certification process are listed below:

Standard I. Communicating

Communication between home and school is regular, two-way, and meaningful.

Quality Indicators. Effective programs:

1. Communicate with parents in a variety of ways (i.e., newsletter, e-mail, home visits, and phone calls).
2. Provide information to parents in a language and format parents can understand.
3. Conduct conferences with parents that accommodate needs such as the varied schedules, language translations, and childcare.
4. Encourage parents and educators to share such information as student strengths and learning preferences during parent-teacher conferences.
5. Provide clear information regarding school policies and procedures.
6. Discuss student report cards with parents.
7. Disseminate information on topics such as school reforms, policies, disciplinary procedures, assessment tools, and school goals.
8. Encourage immediate contact between home and teachers when concerns arise.
9. Distribute student work for parental review on a regular basis.
10. Communicate with parents regarding positive student behavior and achievement as well as misbehavior or failure.
11. Promote informal activities at which families, staff, and community members may interact.

12. Provide staff development regarding effective communication techniques and the importance of regular two-way communication between school and family.
13. Use technology (i.e., telephone hotline, translation equipment, e-mail, website) to foster communication with parents.

Standard II. Parenting

Parenting skills are promoted and supported.

Quality Indicators. Effective programs:

1. Communicate the importance of a positive relationship between parents and their children.
2. Link parents and families to supportive services and resources in the community.
3. Share information on parenting issues with all families by including information on the school's website, hotline, and/or newspaper.
4. Establish school policies that recognize and respect families' cultural and religious differences.
5. Provide an accessible parent/family information and resource center.
6. Work with PTAs, parent educators, and other community groups to host on-site meetings and classes on parenting.

Standard III. Student Learning

Parents and families play an integral role in assisting student learning.

Quality Indicators. Effective programs:

1. Provide clear information regarding the expectations for students in each subject at each grade level, as well as information regarding student placement, student services, and optional programs.
2. Regularly assign homework that requires students to discuss and interact with their parents about what they are learning.
3. Assist parents in understanding how students can improve skills, get help when needed, meet class expectations, and perform well on assessments.
4. Involve parents in setting student goals for each school year.

5. Involve parents in planning for transition to middle school, high school, or postsecondary education and careers.
6. Provide opportunities for professional staff to learn about successful ways to engage families in children's education.

Standard IV. Volunteering

Families are welcome in the school, and their support and assistance are sought.

Quality Indicators. Effective programs:

1. Ensure that greeting by office staff, signage near entrances, and other interactions with families create a climate in which parents and family members feel valued and welcome.
2. Survey families regarding their interests, talents, and availability to volunteer.
3. Ensure that family members who are unable to volunteer in the school building are given options for helping in other ways (i.e., at home or in places of employment).
4. Provide ample training on volunteer procedures and school protocol.
5. Develop a system for contacting parents to ask them to volunteer throughout the school year.
6. Show appreciation for parent participation and contributions.
7. Educate and assist teachers to effectively use volunteer resources.
8. Match volunteer activities with volunteer interests and abilities.
9. Track volunteer hours throughout the school year.
10. Include parent involvement activities on the school's report card.

Standard V. School Decision Making and Advocacy

Families are full partners in the decisions that affect children and families.

Quality Indicators. Effective programs:

1. Provide workshops for parents that teach them how to influence decisions, raise issues and concerns, and resolve problems.

2. Encourage the formation of local PTAs or other parent groups that respond to issues of interest to families.
3. Include and give equal representation to parents on decision-making and advisory committees.
4. Provide families with current information regarding school policies and practices and both student and school performance data.
5. Encourage and facilitate active parent participation in the decisions that affect students (i.e., student placement, course selection, and individualized education plans).
6. Treat family concerns with respect and demonstrate genuine interest in developing solutions.
7. Promote family participation on school district, state, and national committees that focus on education issues.
8. Provide training for staff and families on how to be collaborative partners and share decision making in areas such as policy, curriculum, budget, school reform, safety, and personnel issues.
9. Provide parents with opportunities to participate in professional development activities (i.e., workshops, technology training). (National PTA, 1998, pp. 10–20)

Swap (1993) examines home-school involvement in terms of the mutuality of interaction between home and school. She identifies four models that reflect a continuum of increasing involvement: protective, school-to-home transmission, curriculum enrichment, and partnership. For each model, she discusses the goal, the assumptions on which the model is based, and the model's advantages and disadvantages.

WHY ARE THERE SO FEW COMPREHENSIVE PROGRAMS?

Summarizing almost 25 years of research, Henderson and Mapp (2002) state:

When parents talk to their children about school, expect them to do well, help them plan for college, and make sure that out-of-school activities are constructive, their children do better in school. When schools engage fami-

Table 5.1. Swap's Home-School Involvement Model

	Protective Model	*School-to-Home Transmission Model*	*Curriculum Enrichment Model*	*Partnership Model*
Goal	To reduce conflict between parents and educators, primarily through the separation of parents' and educators' functions, and to protect the school from interference by parents.	To enlist parents in supporting objectives of the school.	To expand and extend school's curriculum by incorporating families' contributions.	For parents and educators to work together to accomplish a common mission generally, for all children in school to achieve success.
Assumptions	Parents delegate to the school the responsibility for educating their children. Parents hold school personnel accountable for results. Educators accept this delegation of responsibility.	Children's achievement is fostered by continuity of expectations and values between home and school. School personnel should identify the values and practices outside the school that contribute to student success. Parents should endorse the importance of schooling, reinforce school expectations at home, provide conditions at home that nurture development and support school success, and ensure that the child meets minimum academic and social requirements.	Continuity of learning between home and school is critically important to children's learning. The values and cultural histories of many children are omitted from the standard curriculum, leading to a discontinuity of culture between home and school, and often to reduced motivation, status, and achievement. The omission of cultural values distorts the curriculum, leading to a less accurate and less comprehensive understanding of events and achievements, and to a perpetuation of damaging beliefs and attitudes about minorities. Parents and educators should work together to enrich curriculum objectives and content. Relationships between home and school are based on mutual respect, and both parents and teachers are seen as experts and resources in the process of discovery.	Accomplishing the joint mission requires a re-visioning of the school environment and the discovery of new policies, practices, structures, roles, relationships, and attitudes in order to realize the vision. Accomplishing the joint mission demands collaboration among parents, community representatives, and educators. Because the task is highly challenging and requires many resources, no single group acting alone can accomplish it.

Advantages	Generally effective at achieving its goal of protecting the school against parental intrusion.	Programs based on this model have increased children's school success. Parents seek clear direction from the school about the social and academic skills needed for children's success and about the parents' role in supporting the development of those skills. Parents welcome clear transmission of information, particularly when they have not had access to the social mainstream and seek such access for their children.	Model offers an attractive approach for incorporating parent involvement into children's learning. Drawing on the knowledge and expertise of parents increases the resources available to the school and provides rich opportunities for adults to learn from each other. The contributions of minorities who have not traditionally participated in schools are especially welcomed.	A true partnership requires a transforming vision of school culture based on collegiality, experimentation, mutual support, and joint problem solving.
Disadvantages	Exacerbates many conflicts between home and school by failing to create structures or predictable opportunities for preventive problem solving. Ignores the potential of home-school collaboration for improving school achievement. Rejects rich resources for enrichment and school support that could be available to the school from families and other members of the community.	Programs built on this model often contain components that reflect an unwillingness to consider parents as equal partners with important strengths. Some conditions such as dangerous housing, poor health, or stringent employment demands may limit some parents' ability to devote time and energy to parent involvement activities. Schools may find it difficult to draft clear boundaries between the roles of school and home in formal education. There is a danger of demeaning the value and importance of the family's culture in an effort to transmit the values and goals of the school. Differences in class or educational background can make teachers and parents uncomfortable; turf concerns may have to be addressed and negotiated.	Creating continuity between home and school demands a significant investment of parents' and educators' time and resources. The number of different cultures represented in some classrooms may make curriculum adoption very complex. Debate still rages about what the school's mission should be in educating children from diverse backgrounds: Should a "majority" culture be taught to all, or should curriculum reflect the diversity of the children? Differences in class or educational background can make teachers and parents uncomfortable; turf concerns must be addressed and negotiated.	This model is difficult to implement. It requires exchanging the traditional solitary role of the educator for a collaborative role, and the development of new patterns of scheduling and interaction to support this new role.

lies in ways that are linked to improving learning, students make greater gains. When schools build partnerships with families that respond to their concerns and honor their contributions, they are successful in sustaining connections that are aimed at improving student achievement. And when families and communities organize to hold poorly performing schools accountable, studies suggest that school districts make positive changes in policy, practice, and resources. (p. 8)

In the face of this evidence, an obvious question is why so few schools have implemented comprehensive family involvement programs.

Part of the answer is simple. Many educators—teachers and administrators—receive little or no training in how to involve families. The Harvard Family Research Project (Lynn, 1997) analyzed teaching certification requirements of all 50 states and found that only 22 even mentioned family involvement. "Even when it was mentioned, often it wasn't defined in clear and precise terms. . . . Phrases such 'parent involvement,' 'home-school relations,' and 'working with parents' often appeared without any explanation or examples of what they meant. . . . The conclusion was that these issues were not a high priority in state certification" (Lack of Specifics section, para. 1).

The researchers also examined the 60 teacher-education programs in the 22 states that did mention family involvement and found little substantial coursework. Only nine teacher-education programs that focused on family involvement as an important concept engaged students in hands-on activities and promoted a broad concept of family involvement that recognized the value of home-school collaboration.

Representatives of more than 40 organizations and institutions involved in school reform, parent involvement, education improvement, youth development, and research met in Del Mar, California, in 1997, to examine several issues related to the achievement of low-income students, including the fact that despite persuasive research showing a close connection between parent involvement and improved student achievement, few school reform efforts were making serious attempts to include low-income families (Lewis and Henderson 1997). The Del Mar conference participants candidly acknowledged that in many low-income schools, the most formidable barrier to parent involvement was racism and agreed that racism in personal attitudes and in public policy should be put on the table for public discussion. The report noted that parents interviewed for a Title I study of parent involvement often defined what they wanted from school in one word: respect.

Another explanation for the apparent lack of parent involvement programs is the changing definition of family. By one estimate (Policy Institute for Family Impact Seminars, 2005), only 7% of U.S. families fit the traditional image of a working father, homemaker mother, and two children. "Family" now includes single mothers and children, single fathers and children, grandparents raising children, foster parents, foster grandparents, and older siblings responsible for childcare. Educators need to change the way they think about children's support systems and devise ways to work with all kinds of families.

Part of the explanation for the lack of programs undoubtedly resides with educational priorities. Pressures on school leaders and staff come from many sources. For many schools, the mandates for accountability, the focus on high-stakes testing, safety concerns, and inadequate physical, personnel, and financial resources have profoundly affected educational priorities. Other matters have taken priority over investments in professional development that supports family involvement, creating time for staff to work with parents, supplying necessary resources, designing innovative strategies to meet the needs of diverse families, and providing useful information to families on how they can contribute to their children's learning. Ultimately, however, the most influential factor determining the degree of emphasis placed on family involvement is the resolve of each school system's administrators. As Funkhouser and Gonzales (1997) conclude:

> Schools, under the leadership of principals, possess the primary responsibility for initiating school-family partnerships. . . . Once schools initiate the dialogue and bring parents in as full partners, families are typically ready and willing to assume an equal responsibility for the success of their children. (p. 31)

CHARACTERISTICS OF SUCCESSFUL PARTNERSHIPS

There is no single blueprint for a partnership school—a school that collaborates effectively with families. Because schools are so different, there is no single model; no single set of practices defines a partnership school. In recognition of this diversity, the U.S. Department of Education published *Family Involvement in Children's Education—Successful Local Approaches: An Idea Book* (Funkhouser and Gonzales, 1997), which reports on selected local approaches. The department's Office of Educational Research and Improvement published a condensed version in 2001. In general, researchers found that schools that are successful in involving large numbers of parents and other family members use a team approach in which each partner assumes responsibility for the success of the partnership. The researchers concluded that, although the most appropriate strategies for a particular community depend on local interests, needs, and resources, successful approaches share an emphasis on innovation and flexibility.

The experiences of local schools and districts led to the development of the following guidelines (Funkhouser and Gonzales, 1997):

1. *There is no one-size-fits-all approach to partnership.* Build on what works well locally. Begin the school-family partnership by identifying—with families—the strengths, interests, and needs of families, students, and school staff and design strategies that respond to identified strengths, interests, and needs.
2. *Training and staff development is an essential investment.* Strengthen the school-family partnership with professional development and training for all school staff, as well as for parents and other family members. Both school staff and families need the knowledge and skills that will enable them to work with one another and with the larger community to support children's learning.
3. *Communication is the foundation of effective partnerships.* Plan strategies that accommodate the varied language and cultural needs, as well as the lifestyles and work schedules of school staff and families. Even the best-planned school-family partnerships will fail if the participants cannot communicate effectively.
4. *Flexibility and diversity are key.* Recognize that effective parent involvement takes many forms that may not necessarily require parents' or other family members' presence at a workshop, meeting, or the school. The emphasis should be on families helping children

learn, and this can happen in schools, homes, or elsewhere in a community.

5. *Projects need to take advantage of the training, assistance, and funding offered by sources external to schools.* These external sources may include school districts, community organizations and public agencies, local colleges and universities, state education agencies, and regional assistance centers.

6. *Change takes time.* Recognize that developing a successful school-family partnership requires continued effort over time, and that solving one problem often creates new challenges. Further, a successful partnership requires the involvement of many stakeholders, not just a few.

7. *Projects need to regularly assess the effects of the partnership using multiple indicators.* The indicators may include levels of family, staff, and community participation in, and satisfaction with, school-related activities. They may also include measures of the quality of school-family interactions and varied indicators of student academic progress.

FRAMEWORK FOR FAMILY INVOLVEMENT PARTNERSHIPS

The National Coalition for Parent Involvement in Education (NCPIE, 2005) believes that a comprehensive and meaningful partnership—one that meets the needs of the schools, families, and communities—incorporates the following concepts in ways that are unique to the school community: support for communication, school activities, home activities, and lifelong learning; promotion of advocacy and shared governance; and collaboration with community groups. In order to create and *sustain* comprehensive home-school partnership programs, the coalition urges educators to develop written policies that support them, emphasizing that the policies should be developed in collaboration with teachers, administrators, families, students, businesses, community-based organizations, and other key stakeholders. NCPIE notes that policies to promote family and school partnerships are needed at the state and district levels as well as at the level of the local school, and makes the following recommendations.

State/district policies should recognize:

1. The critical role of families in their children's academic achievement and social well-being.
2. The responsibility of every school to create a welcoming environment, conducive to learning and supportive of comprehensive family involvement programs that have been developed jointly with families.
3. The need to accommodate the diverse needs of families by developing, jointly with families, multiple, innovative, and flexible ways for families to be involved.
4. The rights and responsibilities of parents and guardians, particularly the right to have access to the school, their child's records, and their child's classroom.
5. The value of working with community agencies that provide services to children and families.
6. The need for families to remain involved from preschool through high school.

Policies at the local school level should add:

1. Outreach to ensure the participation of all families, including those who lack literacy skills or whose primary language is not English.
2. Recognition of diverse family structures, circumstances, and responsibilities, including differences that might impede family participation. Policies and programs should include participation by all persons interested in the child's educational progress, not just the biological parents.
3. Opportunities for families to participate in the instructional process at school and at home.
4. Opportunities for families to share in making decisions, both about school policy and procedures, and about how family involvement programs are designed, implemented, assessed, and strengthened.
5. Professional development for all school staff to enhance their effectiveness with diverse families.
6. Regular exchange of information with families about the standards

their children are expected to meet at each grade level, the objectives of the educational programs, the assessment procedures, and their children's participation and progress.

7. Links with social service and health agencies, faith-based institutions, and community groups to support key family and community issues. (Guidelines for Good Partnership Policy, para. 1)

FAMILY INVOLVEMENT IN MIDDLE AND HIGH SCHOOL

Most educators agree that getting families involved in their children's education is a challenge more easily met in kindergarten and elementary school than in middle or high schools. Part of the reason is that adolescence is a challenging time for the parent-child relationship. As Billig (2001) points out, "At this stage in a student's life there are overlapping spheres of influence—pushes and pulls from family, school, community, and peers," noting that "research shows that these [school-family] partnerships are not as strong as they could be" (para. 1). Billig reports:

1. The number and strength of school-family partnerships decline with each grade level, beginning with kindergarten, and show the most dramatic decrease at the point of transition into the middle grades. Many parents report that they are no longer able to help their children at this time, either because the children reject their help or because the children feel that their parents lack the expertise to help them.

2. While many parents would like to maintain their involvement during middle and high school years, only a small percent receive guidance from schools on how to help their children. Families lack information on courses, choices, grading procedures, and other facts and issues.

3. Communication between schools and families during middle and high school years tends to be one-way—from the school to the family. Except for parent-teacher conferences, families are seldom asked about their children or about improving school programs. When a family is contacted, it is usually because their child is in trouble.

4. When young adolescents face social, academic, and/or personal problems, there is seldom a coordinated or well-organized effort by families, schools, and communities to address the issues. Lack of coordination often means that mixed messages are received, or that no one provides adequate help.

5. The type of parent involvement desired by adolescents changes. Students now want their parents to be less visible and less active in school settings, often discouraging their parents from volunteering in the school—and, in some cases, even from attending parent-teacher conferences.

Billig points out a number of promising school, family, and community involvement practices. For middle schools, strategies and best practices that can help strengthen school-family partnerships include using the new challenges faced by middle school students as opportunities to build positive interactions and relationships. Schools can provide their staffs with professional development for family involvement. Schools can provide families with information on standards and curriculum that is easy to understand and make special efforts to maintain two-way communication. They can provide parents with examples of how to support their child's academic success. Schools can assess the needs of parents and the community and serve as a catalyst for building relationships. They can actively engage students' families and community members in decisions concerning curriculum and instruction and involve parents in student-mediated conferences about coursework and academic progress.

GETTING STARTED

Three familiar family-involvement programs—parent conferences, home visits, and family resource centers—can become vehicles for launching a comprehensive home-school partnership program.

Parent-Teacher Conferences

Black (2005) notes that schools use several different formats for parent-teacher conferences, but educators agree that no format is perfect. The characteristics of the four most commonly used models are:

1. *Traditional parent-teacher conference.* The focus is on academic progress and behavioral problems, often centering on report cards. These conferences are typically held twice a year. Students do not attend. Parents are scheduled to have 15–20 minutes with the teacher, who sets the agenda. Parents and teachers often feel uncomfortable and tense during the conference.

2. *Arena conference.* Used mostly in middle and high schools, these conferences are usually held in gymnasiums and cafeterias. Parents line up to meet with teachers, who are seated at tables. Parents may be required to attend to receive their child's report card and often spend hours waiting to see their child's teachers. Parents generally are unprepared and may leave out of frustration and dismay at the lack of confidentiality.

3. *Triad conference.* Teacher, parents, and student meet to develop an achievement plan. Teachers run the meetings but students may add information. One teacher meets with the parents. If for scheduling or other reasons, it is not the student's teacher, parents often feel shortchanged.

4. *Student-led conference.* With help from a teacher, students plan and conduct the conference, selecting portfolio and other materials to present and discuss. Teachers spend class time helping students plan and rehearse. Parents are allotted a time slot for the conference, but some parents prefer to talk with teachers without having the student present.

Although schools, especially middle and high schools, are experimenting with alternative parent-teacher formats, the traditional one-on-one conference remains the most commonly used. This conference is one occasion when the expectations of the teacher and the family member should be the same—each speaking and listening to the other, each asking questions—with the two-way communication focused on fostering a student's achievement. These conferences should be a welcomed opportunity for both teachers and families, but frequently the opposite is true. Family members may have only their own school experiences—good or bad—as preparation for the conference. They may be apprehensive, burdened by a perception that the teacher knows it all, the teacher is in control, or the teacher does not really know their child. Teachers may have their own apprehensions based on their own experience—or lack of it—in working with families.

Schools can do much to make the parent-teacher conference successful for both teachers and families. In-service training sessions can be developed, and veteran teachers can give role-playing demonstrations of what to expect and how to react. In scheduling conferences, schools must be sensitive to family demographics and cultural diversity. The child's caregiver and best home contact might be a parent, but it could also be a grandparent, stepparent, foster parent, or even a sibling. Scheduling must be flexible, often including time before school, before or after a family member's job, and on weekends. Translators should be provided if language barriers are expected.

The school can also help families prepare for conferences. Newsletters, parent-teacher association (PTA) meetings, local newspaper features, and television and radio programs can provide tips on how to prepare for a productive meeting, including questions to ask. Some schools recruit volunteers to check on the progress and well-being of students whose parents are either unable or unwilling to come to school.

Ideally, the parent-teacher conference is part of an ongoing parent-teacher partnership, but too often this is not the reality. Teachers can do a number of things that will help make parent-teacher conferences a positive experience for both families and themselves. Shalaway (no date) emphasizes that planning is critical to ensuring an effective conference and recommends the following steps:

1. Prepare a send-home note that invites the parent (or responsible caregiver) to meet with you, states the purpose of the conference, lists potential times, and requests a response to reserve a time slot. It may be appropriate to include the student in the conference.
2. Decide upon the goals of the conference (usually only one or two).
3. Prepare an agenda to share with the parents; include such topics as your general impression of the child, his/her progress in an academic area, standardized test scores, your goals for the child in each content area, and strategies you will use to meet those goals.
4. Plan (and write down) questions to ask, points to make, and suggestions to offer.

5. Ask parents to bring to the conference a list of their child's strengths and weaknesses as they perceive them.
6. List your own perceptions of the strengths and weaknesses of the student and propose actions that might be taken.
7. Collect samples of the student's work to display.
8. Schedule enough time for questions and discussions and be prepared to explain your goals and teaching strategies.

In arranging the setting, a teacher should make the conference area as comfortable as possible, including adult-sized chairs arranged at a table or facing each other, and provide refreshments if possible. Experienced teachers suggest greeting parents at the door, providing pencils and paper for taking notes, and planning a few appropriate activities for younger siblings who may accompany parents. The goal is to put parents at ease.

In conducting the conference, the teacher should first briefly review the prepared agenda, communicate specific information about the student and then listen carefully to parents' responses, answer their questions, explain each point, and ask them if they can confirm the teacher's impressions. Most importantly, the teacher should focus on setting goals together for the child's progress and making plans for keeping parents informed about the progress.

When a teacher must deliver news about an academic or behavioral problem, the conference is stressful for both the teacher and the parents. Shalaway suggests that the teacher focus only on things that can be changed, speaking plainly and avoiding jargon and euphemistic language. It is important to be tactful, but not so tactful that the problem is not adequately communicated. The teacher should limit the number of suggestions for improvements so that parents are not intimidated or overwhelmed and be prepared both to ask questions and to listen to parents' reactions. It is especially important not to overreact to hostility or anger.

Black (2005) reports that Harvard University's study of home-school communication found that the traditional parent-teacher conference consumes a lot of time and energy and seldom by itself improves student achievement. However, she concluded, parent-teacher conferences are an "obvious place to start building better relationships" between teachers and parents. "It's also obvious that home-school communication and relationships—including day-to-day conversations, e-mail, telephone conferences, and, yes, parent-teacher conferences—belong in every school's improvement plan" (Resistance Reluctance, para. 7).

Home Visits

Home visits, another family involvement strategy, have several purposes. They may be used to welcome new families to the school community; survey families for their views on school policies and programs; report on student progress; demonstrate home learning activities; help find solutions to specific problems; etc. They may be conducted by the principal, teachers, community aides, or trained volunteers.

Steele-Carlin (2001) points out that home visits by teachers are not a new idea. The Head Start program has used them for many years, and many kindergartens require home visits by teachers before school starts. According to Steele-Carlin, home visits are being increasingly used as a family involvement and intervention strategy and many school districts have programs that require teachers to visit students' homes at least once a year.

Home visits by teachers can be especially beneficial because they give teachers an opportunity to gain parental support and insights into students' learning styles. This knowledge can help teachers make meaningful connections in instruction and develop activities designed to make use of the knowledge the students bring to school from home. Teacher home visits provide parents with an opportunity to communicate in the security of their own homes, both receiving and giving information about their children. In addition, students may enjoy welcoming teachers into their homes and seeing them in a new, more personal setting.

In researching teacher visits to students' homes, Steele-Carlin found that they take many forms, varying from school to school and from teacher to teacher. The approach chosen may depend on the funding source. In some cases, teachers prefer to travel in pairs when they share the same student, are uncomfortable in some areas of the school community, or need a translator. Other teachers prefer to visit alone, sometimes one-on-one with the parents and sometimes with both the family and the student, depending on the purpose of the visit. Steele-Carlin found that visits lasted from 30 to 90 minutes, depending on the teacher and the type of interaction with the family.

In considering whether to make a home visit, a teacher should keep several principles in mind. The home visit should have a clearly communicated purpose. The teacher must at all times be sensitive to cultural differences and set a tone of mutual respect, realizing that there can be no viable relationship without mutual, demonstrated respect. Preparation for home visits should follow most of the same steps as preparation for a parent-teacher conference, including an advance request to visit and the offer of scheduling options.

A major constraint has historically limited home visits: most teachers have little training in establishing relationships with parents in any setting, although many have developed a degree of competence by working with parents in events held at the school. Because home visits require specific skills, lack of special training may be a formidable barrier.

In practice, a home visit may be refused by a parent or other family member. That person's right to refuse must be respected. Another reality is that some neighborhoods are not safe to visit. In both cases, consideration should be given to holding visits in alternative sites, such as the meeting rooms of a housing project or in a religious or other community facility.

Family Resource Centers

Family resource centers located within a school are often developed based on the growing belief that schools can be the site of a variety of services available to students and their families but located in scattered locations around the community. In these centers, sometimes called parent education centers, schools can offer families a wealth of resources, including written and audiovisual materials in several languages that address a wide range of concerns. Topics may include school issues such as homework, and child development issues such as discipline, communication, self-esteem, and handling stress. Information may also be provided on community resources that families can draw upon. Family resource centers may also provide speakers for community groups on specific topics.

Family resource centers are an effective way for schools to reach out to families. In addition to providing support services, the centers can offer parents helpful information and training on the raising and educating of children. Nicoll (2002) cites research that provides a rationale for schools to provide parent education services because it demonstrates that parenting styles and children's academic achievement are related.

> Across all ethnic groups, education levels, and family structures, the researchers consistently found that of the three parenting styles [authoritarian, permissive, and authoritative], authoritarian parenting was associated with the lowest grades, permissive parenting with the next lowest, and authoritative with the highest grades (mean GPA 3.2). In addition, inconsistent parenting or a frequent switching from an authoritarian to a permissive style was found to be strongly associated with the worst academic outcomes (1.8 GPA). These researchers concluded that parenting style is a more powerful predictor of student achievement than parent education, ethnicity, or family structure. (Conference paper)

Nicoll emphasizes that while the various parenting styles can be found across all income and educational levels, several studies have indicated a tendency for certain parenting styles to appear more frequently in specific socioeconomic populations. He points out that family resource centers can offer parenting information and classes as part of a preventive/intervention program. He contends that formal parent education programs consistent with the authoritative parenting model can be offered to train parents in effective child rearing practices.

Other kinds of family resource centers are not directly connected to a school. Parent Information Resource Centers, an outcome of Goals 2000, are in every state. The Individuals with Disabilities Education Act (IDEA) also provides for parent resource centers, called Parent Training and Information Centers, in every state. The Technical Assistance Alliance for Parent Centers (2005) provides a listing of the regional centers.

TITLE I AS A TOOL FOR PARENT INVOLVEMENT

The Center for Law and Education (no date) recommends using Title I as a tool for building parents' capacity for school involvement. Under Title I, schools are required to provide assistance to parents to help them understand the National Education Goals and the standards and assessment methods that will be used to determine children's progress, and show them how family members may help. Every school district, except the smallest, is required to spend at least 1% of its Title I funds on training and education programs for parents, and parents must be involved in decisions about how this money is spent. Parents must also jointly develop and approve the district's and school's parent involvement policies, which should spell out how this money is spent.

The local education agency's parent involvement policy (Center for Law and Education, no date) must outline how it will:

1. Involve parents in the development of the local Title I plan.
2. Build parents' capacity for involvement in decisions regarding their children's education.
3. Coordinate strategies with parents in other programs, such as Even Start and Head Start.
4. Conduct annual evaluations of the effectiveness of the parent involvement effort.
5. Use the results of the annual evaluations to design strategies for school improvement and revise policy as needed.

Every school that receives Title I funds must have a parent involvement policy as part of its Title I plan. This policy must be developed jointly with, approved by, and distributed to parents, and must include a description of how the school will:

1. Convene an initial annual meeting for parents to explain Title I.
2. Offer flexible meetings for parents. Such meetings should include time to share experiences, brainstorm about creative programs to involve parents, and participate in decisions about the education of their children.
3. Involve parents in planning, review, and improvement of the program.
4. Give parents timely information about the program, including a description of the school curriculum and the assessments used to measure student progress.
5. Implement a school-parent compact.

6. Build capacity to ensure the effective involvement of parents. Schools and school districts are to provide training and materials and must coordinate with other programs, such as literacy training programs, in order to help parents help their children at home. Schools must also help teachers, principals, and other staff work well with parents.

The required school-parent compact must be jointly developed with parents and must outline how the school and parents will work together to help Title I students achieve the high content and performance standards set by the state for all students. The compact must describe the school's responsibility to provide high-quality curriculum and instruction in a supportive and effective environment that will enable students to meet the state standards, and the parents' responsibility for supporting their child's learning. The compact must also address the importance of communication between teachers and parents. The school is required to provide, at a minimum, (1) parent-teacher conferences in elementary schools at least once a year, when parents and teacher will discuss the compact as it relates to an individual child's achievement; (2) frequent reports to parents on the child's progress; and (3) reasonable access to staff and to classrooms to observe activities.

BARRIERS TO FAMILY INVOLVEMENT

One barrier to establishing a school-family partnership may be the community's perception of the school and its staff. A Public Agenda report (no date) analyzed the responses to the question, "How much confidence do you, yourself, have in public schools—a great deal, quite a lot, some, or very little?" over the period 1977 to 2003. The data showed a drop in the percentage of people saying "a great deal" or "quite a lot" of confidence from 54% in 1977 to 40% in 2003. This report and others have been the basis for concluding that public schools are losing public support, but the findings of the 37th Phi Delta Kappa/Gallup Poll (Rose and Gallup, 2005) refute this conclusion.

[An] important conclusion of the poll results is that they should help to destroy one of the myths surrounding the public schools: that the public schools are losing public support. The trend lines in this poll suggest the exact opposite. The grades the public assigns the schools remain as high as ever and are truly impressive when public school parents give their evaluation. The public continues to express a strong preference for change through existing public schools; support for choice shows no sign of increasing and could be said to be lagging; and it is the public schools to which the public turns for closing the achievement gap.

[However,] it seems necessary to comment on the important distinction between the nation's schools and schools in the community. These polls have repeatedly documented that the public has a low opinion of the nation's schools and a high opinion of school in the local community. The media, some education experts, and some government leaders base their comments on the nation's schools and are then surprised when they do not resonate with a public that is concerned primarily with the schools in the community, schools that generally draw approval. As long as those seeking to improve the public schools make their case on the supposed inadequacy of the schools in the community, support for improvement will be hard to build. (para. 2–3)

The obvious conclusion—that the closer people are to the public schools, the higher their regard for them—should make it clear that local educators need to emphasize the importance of family and community involvement in schools. Educators need to be diligent in their efforts to assure that families and the local community have a positive perception of schools and their staffs.

An earlier study by Phi Delta Kappa Foundation (1988) examined the factors with greatest influence on the gain or loss of community confidence in a local school. The top three factors ranked as sources of gain in confidence were, in order: teacher attitudes, administrator attitudes, and student attitudes. The top three factors resulting in loss in confidence were teacher attitudes, the decision-making process, and administrator attitudes. Obviously, teacher and administrator attitudes toward family involvement determine whether there is a welcoming school environment.

Sarason (1991) emphasizes that students have a great deal of influence on the public's confidence in schools. Students are the most important constituency of any school, but they are often left out of decisions. He points out that students are generally treated as products of school, when, in fact, they must want to come to school and be workers in order to learn.

Without student motivation, no kind of school reform, however ambitious, will improve student learning and public education. He adds that is why it is hard to explain why educators do not routinely ask students—especially those in trouble—about how to improve schools.

Finders and Lewis (1994) examine some of the issues that affect how families—particularly minority and low-income families—view schools. They point out that in many schools, the institutional perspective is that children who do not succeed in school have parents who do not get involved in school activities or support school goals at home. The institutional view of nonparticipating parents is based on a deficit model, frequently expressed in terms of "Those who *need* to come, don't come." In many instances, this view ignores the reality of family structures today and employs family involvement efforts based on the model of a two-parent, economically self-sufficient nuclear family.

Parent involvement studies find that most parents want very much to help their children succeed in school. The most commonly cited barriers to parental involvement are lack of time, uncertainty about what to do, cultural differences, and lack of a supportive environment (Decker and Decker, 2001).

The feeling that a parent has nothing to contribute is a common barrier to participation by minority and lower socioeconomic status parents. A similar barrier to involvement is a feeling of powerlessness—the conviction that what one person does or does not do will make no difference. If educators—teachers and administrators—truly want family involvement in school and in the education of children, they will have to find ways to empower families and to share some of their power in making decisions about children's education. Encouragement and support must be offered, and every family must be made to feel wanted and needed.

OVERCOMING BARRIERS

Funkhouser and Gonzales (1997) offer practical suggestions for overcoming common barriers to family involvement in schools.

Overcoming Time and Resource Constraints

Families and school staff need time to get to know each other, learn from one another, and figure out how to work together. Strategies for helping teachers include (1) assigning parent coordinators or home-school liaisons to help teachers make and maintain contact with families through home visits, or by supervising classes so teachers can meet with family members; (2) providing time during the school day for teachers to meet with parents or visit them at their homes; (3) providing stipends or compensatory time off for teachers who meet with families after school hours; and (4) freeing teachers from such routine duties as lunchroom supervision so they can meet with family members. Schools can also provide easier access to telephones and voice mail, provide information hotlines, and use technology in other ways to make communication easier and more efficient.

Schools can demonstrate sensitivity to families' time and safety concerns by scheduling meetings to accommodate families' working schedules, and holding them at places other than the school when advisable. Schools can also help by (1) providing early notices about meetings and activities to allow families time to adjust their schedules, (2) offering the same event more than once, (3) providing information to families who cannot attend a meeting, and (4) establishing homework hotlines and voice-mail systems so families can stay in touch from their homes. Schools can address families' resource constraints by providing transportation and childcare services, holding school-sponsored events in non-school facilities convenient to families' homes, and making home visits.

Dispelling Misconceptions

Training for teachers and other school staff can play a key role in dispelling some of the misconceptions and stereotypes that are barriers to effective partnerships. Schools can provide school staff with information and strategies on how to reach out to families and work effectively with them. Some schools have found that using parent coordinators or parent volunteers to train school staff not only builds parents' leadership skills but also gives staff the opportunity to learn about families from a family member's perspective.

Schools can use a variety of ways to inform and involve parents. Newsletters and school information hotlines can help families stay current with school issues and events. Posting fliers in places where families congregate, developing parent handbooks, and making telephone calls to share positive information can channel information to families. Holding periodic parenting workshops can help families learn about child development. Schools can offer workshops, hands-on training, and home visits to help parents learn how to support children's learning at home. Other programs can help family members capitalize on their skills and expertise and learn how to assist school staff and students as volunteers. Family resource centers can provide a wide variety of information and support services.

Bridging Differences

Language and cultural differences and differences in educational attainment can make communication between families and school staff difficult and may adversely affect family participation in school activities. Some immigrant families have significantly different views of schools and parents' roles in children's education. Schools must be sensitive to the needs of families who may not understand the written communications sent to them or may see themselves as unprepared to help with homework or schoolwork. Family members' memories of their own bad school experiences may also be deterrents to involvement. Overcoming these barriers may require designing new ways for parents who are nonreaders or whose English is limited to work with their children to promote literacy. Schools can give family members opportunities to experience what their children are learning in an environment that is pleasant and nonthreatening, thus helping to allay doubts about the family members' ability to help their children. Schools can provide translation services (written and oral), workshops, and classes in the families' first language. Home-school liaisons can also play an important role in reaching out to parents of different backgrounds, building trust between home and school. Schools can provide training to school staff specifically targeted to bridging cultural differences between home and school.

Tapping External Supports

Schools rarely have funds, staff, or space for all the family involvement activities they want or need to offer. However, they can forge partnerships with local businesses, agencies, colleges, and universities to provide such supports as educational programming and homework hotlines, health and

social services, conferences and workshops, adult education, school refur-
bishing, transportation, and nonschool meeting space. District and state
supports for family involvement initiatives may include funding, training,
and resource centers.

Funkhouser and Gonzales (1997) stress that schools that succeed in
involving large numbers of parents and other family members are investing in solutions, not making excuses. Haugen (2001) suggests that administrators and teachers who are serious about eliminating roadblocks to
parent involvement begin by:

1. Building teacher-parent relations to develop trust.
2. Building and valuing parent strengths, knowledge, and skills.
3. Collaborating to set clear goals and objectives for all involved, as
   well as gathering feedback.
4. Researching and collaborating with colleagues, administrators, and
   community to resolve issues.

Involving Hard-to-Reach Parents

As White-Clark and Decker (1996) point out, the terms *at-risk* and *hard-
to-reach* have become clichés—verbal wastebaskets for a variety of conditions, some of them educational, others personal or societal. The student
population labeled "at-risk" is usually poor and often part of a minority
group, and "hard-to-reach" parents are often assumed to be minorities
with low socioeconomic status, inner-city residence, and little formal education. Another label for such parents is "disadvantaged." Schools often
erect unintentional barriers by adopting a paternalistic or condescending
attitude to those labeled "hard-to-reach."

Educators often perceive Hispanic families as hard-to-reach. Inger
(1992) points out that there is a reason for this misperception.

In Hispanics' countries of origin, the roles of parents and schools were
sharply divided. Many low-income Hispanic parents view the U.S. school
system as "a bureaucracy governed by educated non-Hispanics whom they
have no right to question. . . . Many school administrators and teachers mis-
read the reserve, the non-confrontational manners, and the non-involvement
of Hispanic parents to mean that they are uncaring about the children's edu-

cation—and this misperception has led to a cycle of mutual mistrust and suspicion between poor Hispanic parents and school personnel." (p. 1)

Manning and Baruth (2000) contend that many educators do not understand the important role of the extended family in some cultures—a role that may not extend to involvement in school. At home, children may be nurtured by a number of relatives, but these extended family members may not extend their caregiving role into their children's schools; they may be reluctant to become involved in either their children's education or in school activities.

Inger outlines lessons that have been learned from the efforts of educators and community groups to increase Hispanic parent involvement, lessons that are applicable to working with most populations labeled "hard-to-reach."

1. Programs that increase and retain the involvement of parents follow a simple, basic rule: they make it easy for parents to participate. For example, programs and materials are bilingual, childcare is provided, there are no fees, the times and locations of meetings are arranged for the convenience of the parents, and transportation is provided.
2. Outreach efforts require extra staff. They take considerable time and cannot be handled by a regular staff person with an already full job description. Successful outreach is organized by people who have volunteered, not by people who have been assigned to the job.
3. Parents need to be allowed to become involved with the school community at their own pace. Often before they join existing parent organizations, Hispanic parents want to acquire the skills and the confidence to contribute as equals.
4. The hardest part of building a partnership with low-income parents is getting parents to the first meeting. Impersonal efforts—letters, flyers, announcements at church services or on the local radio or television—are largely ineffective, even when these efforts are in Spanish. The only successful approach is personal: face-to-face conversations with parents in their primary language in their homes. Home visits not only personalize the invitations but help school staff understand and deal with parents' concerns.

5. Since many low-income parents feel uncomfortable in schools, successful projects often hold the first meetings at nonschool sites, preferably at places familiar to the parents. Successful first meetings are primarily social events; unsuccessful ones are formal events held at school, with information aimed at the parents.
6. To retain the involvement of low-income parents, every meeting has to respond to some need or concern of the parents. Programs that consult with parents regarding agendas and meeting formats and begin with the parents' agenda eventually cover issues that the school considers vital; those that stick exclusively to the school's agenda lose the parents.

Educators also often perceive fathers as hard-to-reach. The National Center for Educational Statistics (1997) reports that school programs have traditionally been dominated by mothers, who are more likely than fathers to attend. School programs also tend to focus on mothers because the overwhelming majority of children in single-parent households live with their mother. Nicoll (2002) recommends that schools increase their efforts to involve fathers, citing the observation of the National Center for Educational Statistics (1997) that one plausible conclusion from the existing research is that maternal involvement is beneficial for children's social and emotional adjustment to school, but that paternal involvement may be more important for academic achievement. The 1995 *Kids Count Overview,* "Fathers and Families" (Annie E. Casey Foundation, 1995), documents the negative effect of the absence of fathers in many children's lives, particularly children from minority and low-income families.

Any parent can be "hard-to-reach," of course. Affluent parents who work long hours or parents who lack childcare may be just as hard to reach as parents who fit the common stereotypes of poor and minority. White-Clark and Decker (1996) acknowledge that there are often barriers to overcome in involving parents and families in children's education, and that no one approach will work with all families at all times. They agree that schools should be family-friendly and that every effort should be made to bridge language gaps and cultural differences, but they contend that fewer families would be labeled "hard-to-reach" if educators took a more optimistic approach to them. They recommend that educators:

1. Believe family involvement is important and that educational programs are incomplete without it.
2. Embody an ethic of caring, making a sincere effort to understand the life situations of families who are not involved in the school and, when possible, helping them overcome barriers to involvement.
3. Disregard "hard-to-reach" stereotypes, facing up to their own misperceptions.
4. Develop high expectations for all families, seeking realistic rather than maximum involvement.
5. Conceptualize the roles of parents in their individual situations when designing involvement opportunities.
6. Be willing to address personal concerns, including any of their own experiences that may impede implementation of family involvement activities.
7. Study the framework of family involvement programs in order to develop a clear understanding of their purpose and function.
8. Be willing to work to improve family involvement, including getting out of the school building and into the community when it is beneficial to do so.

PREPARING EDUCATORS FOR FAMILY INVOLVEMENT

The Harvard Family Research Project has been looking into the relative lack of teacher certification requirements in the area of family involvement since 1992. Researchers Shartrand and others (1997) note that the training that is offered is often limited in both content and method. Hiatt-Michael (2001) cites research confirming the inadequacy of efforts to train teachers to work with families continues.

Although the Harvard project's publication *New Skills for New Schools: Preparing Teachers in Family Involvement* (Shartrand and others, 1997) focuses on teacher training, the research findings should interest all educators who seek to involve families in the education of their children. In addition to identifying the skills, knowledge, and attitudes necessary to prepare for family involvement, the research confirms three needs: (1) more direct experience with families and communities, (2) sup-

port in making school conditions conducive to family involvement, and
(3) opportunities to share successful experiences and outcomes with colleagues.

The publication focuses on developing mutual partnerships involving
all families while recognizing a range of types of family involvement. It
places training needs in a framework of content areas:

1. General family involvement
2. General family knowledge
3. Home-school communication
4. Family involvement in learning activities
5. Families supporting schools
6. Schools supporting families
7. Families as change agents

Four approaches are suggested for each of the content areas (see Table
5.2): Functional Approach, based on the work of Epstein; Parent Empowerment, based on the work of Cochran; Cultural Competence, based on
the work of Moll; and Social Capital, based on the work of Coleman
(Shartrand and others, 1997).

TRAINING MATERIALS

The Family Involvement Network for Educators (FINE) (http://www.fi-
nenetwork.org) was launched in November 2000 by the Harvard Family
Research Project to serve as a hub of resources for family engagement in
children's education. Membership in FINE is free. Especially useful is
*Taking a Closer Look: A Guide to Online Resources on Family Involve-
ment* (Weiss and others, 2005); data was collected between January 2004
and March 2005, and periodic updates are planned. The areas covered are
Knowledge Development, Professional Development, Standards, Programs, Tools, Convening, and Special Initiatives. An appendix lists
Resource Guide Organizations.

As part of an ongoing effort to increase family involvement, the Partnership for Family Involvement in Education of the U.S. Department of
Education held a video/teleconference on preparing teachers to work with

Table 5.2. Training Needs by Type of Family Involvement

	General Family Involvement	*General Family Knowledge*	*Home-to-School Communication*	*Family Involvement in Learning*	*Families Supporting Schools*	*Schools Supporting Families*	*Families as Change Agents*
Functional Approach	Attitude that all teachers should learn skills and sensitivity in dealing with parents. Knowledge about the goals and benefits of family involvement and the barriers to it. Skills in involving parents of all backgrounds in school. Knowledge of the role of school administration in promoting or preventing family involvement.	Knowledge of different cultural beliefs, lifestyles, child-rearing practices, family structures, and living environments. Attitude of respect for different backgrounds and lifestyles. Knowledge of the functions of families.	Skills in effective interpersonal communication. Communication skills to deal with defensive behaviors, distrust, hostility, and frustration. Skills in using active listening and effective communication to understand families and to build trust and cooperation.	Skills in involving parents in their children's learning outside of the classroom. Skills in sharing teaching skills with parents.	Skills in involving parents in the school and in the classroom.	Knowledge of how schools can support families' social and educational needs. Knowledge about processes of consultation and communication. Knowledge of the roles of various specialists and interprofessional collaboration. Skills in referral procedures.	Skills in supporting and involving families as decision makers, action researchers, advocates, and parent and teacher trainers. Skills in sharing information to help families make decisions. Skills in sharing leadership and transferring it to parents. Skills in interacting with parents on an equal footing.

Parent Empowerment	Attitude that all parents want what is best for their children and that all parents want to be good parents. Attitude that parents are children's first and most important teachers. Attitude of respect for the family's role in children's nurturance and education. Attitude that the most useful knowledge about rearing children can be found within the community.	Attitude of support toward parents, focused on strengths rather than deficits. Knowledge of power differences among groups in society. Knowledge of the history of disenfranchised groups. Knowledge of the effects of a family's disadvantaged status on its interactions with teachers or other professionals. Knowledge of how families interact with schools and similar institutions.	Skills in effective interpersonal communication. Skills in treating parents as equal partners. Knowledge of the importance of positive communication with parents, even when child is having problems. Attitude that parents should not be controlled, but rather that their views and needs should be understood.	Skills in developing activities that build parents' confidence and facility in conducting home learning activities. Skills in providing constructive feedback.	Skills in making parents feel valued by inviting them to contribute their expertise in the classroom and in the school.	Knowledge of and skills in promoting parent empowerment through adult education and parenting courses. Knowledge of and skills in ameliorating families' basic needs as a first step to helping them help their children academically. Skills in incorporating families' self-identified needs in parent programs and school activities.	Skills in promoting political empowerment for families through: • Advocating shared decision making in schools. • Informing families of governance roles in the school. • Recruiting family members to sit on boards and councils. Preventing families' voices from being overridden in meetings.

Cultural Competence	Knowledge that minority and low socioeconomic status students benefit academically from family involvement. Skills in using culturally appropriate themes in the curriculum.	Knowledge about cultural influences on discipline, learning, and child-rearing practices. Knowledge of personal assumptions, belief systems, and prejudices that can affect relationships with family and community. Skills in understanding and reversing negative stereotypes of parents, families, and community members.	Knowledge of the importance of logistics of obtaining translators for families who do not read or speak English. Knowledge of the styles of communication of different cultural groups.	Skills to incorporate family "funds of knowledge" into homework projects, so that families and communities can contribute to children's learning.	Knowledge of the financial and time constraints of parents. Skills in creating opportunities for parent and other family member involvement in school. Skills in discovering different potential contributions of families.	Knowledge of resources for cultural minorities. Skills in creating opportunities for families with different backgrounds to learn from one another. Sensitive attitude toward different groups' perceptions of school "help" and reciprocity. Skills in incorporating family preferences into parent programs.	Skills in encouraging parents or other family members to run for seats on school councils. Knowledge of importance of providing translators at school council meetings. Knowledge of importance of having teachers from various cultures be present on council to make all families feel welcome.

| Social Capital | Knowledge of the idea of social capital and parental investment in their children's learning. | Knowledge that schools and homes have different norms and values, and that such differences influence partnerships between home and school. Knowledge of common values that span different cultures and institutions. Skills in conflict negotiation and consensus building. | Skills in communicating expectations and values to build a sense of trust among members in the community. Skills in communicating with parents in a way that models how values will be transmitted between other members of society. Skills in being attentive, persistent, dependable, and showing caring over time in relationships with families. | Skills in motivating family involvement in home-learning activities. Skills in home visiting. Skills in fostering community participation in educational activities. | Skills in fostering families' investment in school, by volunteering, attending events, and fundraising. Skills in utilizing resources of other community groups. Skills in building reciprocal exchanges between school and home. | Skills in identifying the expectations and goals of families. Knowledge of how school events can create social capital. Skills in building reciprocal exchanges between school and home. | Attitude that shared decision making is an essential ingredient to establishing and maintaining a common set of core values. Skills in negotiating differences and conflicting opinions. Skills in involving families in the design of curriculum that represents shared values. Skills in codevelopment of mission statement that represents shared values. |

families using the Harvard Family Research Center's *New Skills for New Schools* as a base. A product of that conference, *Partners for Learning: Preparing Teachers to Involve Families* (U.S. Department of Education, Partnership for Family Involvement in Education, 1999) includes a guide to using it for in-service and preservice training.

The federal IDEA emphasizes the importance of family participation in educational decision making. The U.S. Department of Education's Office of Special Education Programs (1999) prepared training materials designed to provide parents and schools with a first tool to ensure that IDEA is consistently and properly implemented throughout the country. Although its focus is on disability programs and policies, the training materials are broadly useful, particularly those related to parent and student participation in decision making. The National Information Center for Children and Youth with Disabilities (http://www.nichcy.org), a national information and referral center, carries the *IDEA 97 Training Package* online.

The National Center for Fathering (NCF), founded in 1990, in response to the dramatic increase in the number of fatherless homes in America, focuses on involving fathers in children's lives and offers resources and training materials for educators and community organizations. NCF conducts research on fathers and fathering and works to develop practical resources (http://www.fathers.com).

REFERENCES

Annie E. Casey Foundation. (1995). *Kids count overview.* Washington, DC: Center for the Study of Social Policy. Retrieved March 22, 2006, from http://www.aecf.org/kidscount/kc1995/overview.htm

Billig, S. (2001). Meeting the challenge of family involvement in the middle grades. *Middle Matters.* NAESP, Winter. Retrieved March 22, 2006, from http://www.naesp.org/ContentLoad.do?contentId = 520

Black, S. (2005). Rethinking parent conferences. *American School Board Journal.* October. Retrieved March 22, 2006, from http://www.asbj.com/2005/10/1005research.html

Center for Law and Education. (no date). Title I as a tool for parent involvement. In *CLE issue/project areas.* Retrieved March 7, 2006, from http://www.cleweb.org/issues/title1/tool.htm

Decker, L. E., and Decker, V. A. (2001). *Engaging families and communities: Pathways to educational success.* Fairfax, VA: National Community Education Association.

Education Week Research Center. (2001). *Parent involvement.* Retrieved March 22, 2006, from http://www.edweek.org/rc/issues/parent-involvement/index.htm

Finders, M., and Lewis, C. (1994, May). Why some parents don't come to school. *Education Leadership, 51,* 9. Retrieved March 7, 2006, from http://www.ascd.org/portal/site/ascd/template.MAXIMIZE/menuitem/

Funkhouser, J. E., and Gonzales, M. R. (1997). *Family involvement in children's education—Successful local approaches: An idea book.* Washington, DC: Government Printing Office. Retrieved May 6, 2006, from http://ed.gov/pdf/docs/97–7022.pdf

Harkavy, I., and Blank, M. (2002). *Community schools.* Retrieved March 22, 2006, from http://www.educationweek.org/ew/articles/2002/04/17/31harkavy.h21.html

Haugen, J. (2001). *Who wants to eliminate road blocks to parent involvement?* Retrieved March 20, 2006, from http://www.ascd.org/portal/site/ascd/templat.MAXIMIZE/menuitem/

Henderson, A. T. (Ed.). (1981). *Parent participation–student achievement: The evidence grows.* Columbia, MD: National Committee for Citizens in Education.

Henderson, A. T. (Ed.). (1987). *The evidence continues to grow: Parent involvement improves student achievement.* Columbia, MD: National Committee for Citizens in Education.

Henderson, A. T., and Berla, N. (1994). *A new generation of evidence: The family is critical to student achievement.* Washington, DC: National Committee for Citizens in Education.

Henderson, A. T., and Mapp, K. L. (2002). *A new wave of evidence: The impact of school, family and community connections on student achievement.* Austin, TX: Southwest Educational Development Laboratory.

Hiatt-Michael, D. (2001). *Preparing teachers to work with parents* (Digest: 2001–02). Retrieved March 22, 2006, from http://web.archive.org/web2002062215158/www.ericsp.org/pages/digests/Teachers-Parents.html

Houston, P. (2001). *AASA poll on public education.* Retrieved September 7, 2001, from http://www.aasa.org/government_relations/08_2001_polling_questions.htm

Inger, M. (1992). Increasing the school involvement of Hispanic parents. *Clearinghouse on Urban Education Digest, 80.* Retrieved March 7, 2006, from http://iume.tc.columbia.edu/eric_archive/digest/80.pdf

Lewis, A. C., and Henderson, A. T. (1997). *Urgent message: Families crucial to school reform.* Washington, DC: Center for Law and Education.

Lynn, L. (1997). Teaching teachers to work with families. *Harvard Education Letter,* September/October. Retrieved March 6, 2006, from http://www.edlet ter.org/past/issues/1997-so/teaching.shtml

Manning, M. L., and Baruth, L. G. (2000). *Multicultural education of children and adolescents.* Boston: Allyn and Bacon.

Moles, O. D., and D'Angelo, D. (Eds.). (1993). *Building school-family partnerships for learning: Workshops for urban educators.* Washington, DC: Office of Educational Research and Development, U.S. Office of Education.

National Center for Education Statistics. (1997). *Fathers' involvement in their children's schools.* Washington, DC: U.S. Department of Education, Office of Educational Research and Improvement.

National Center for Fair and Open Testing. (2002). Will more testing improve schools? *FairTest.* Retrieved March 5, 2006, from http://www.fairtest.org/facts/Will%20More%20Testing%20Improve%20Schools.html

National Coalition for Parent Involvement in Education. (2005). *A framework for family involvement.* Retrieved March 17, 2006, from http://www.ncpie.org/DevelopingPartnerships

National PTA. (2004). *National standards for parent/family involvement programs: An implementation guide for school communities.* Bloomington, IN: National Education Service.

NCLB action briefs: Parent involvement. (2004). Joint Project of Public Education Network and National Coalition for Parent Involvement in Education. Retrieved March 5, 2006, from http://www.publiceducation.org/portals/nclb/Parent_Involvement/PIhome.asp

NCLBGrasssroots.org. (2005). *NCLB left behind: Understanding the growing grassroots rebellion against a controversial law.* Retrieved March 24, 2006, from http://www.nclbgrassroots.org/landscape.php

Nicoll, W. G. (2002). *The case for family involvement programs: A look at the research evidence.* Paper presented at the Academic Achievement and Best Practices Leadership Conference of the Florida Department of Education's Office of Family Involvement. Safety Harbor, FL, April 9, 2002.

Phi Delta Kappa Foundation. (1988). *Handbook for developing public confidence in school.* Bloomington, IN: Phi Delta Kappa.

Policy Institute for Family Impact Seminars. (2005). *Family trends.* Retrieved March 20, 2006, from http://familyimpactseminars.org/trends.htm

Public Agenda. (no date). *Education: People's chief concern.* Issue Guides. Retrieved March 7, 2006, from http://www.publicagenda.org/issues/pcc_de tail.cfm?issue_type = education&list = 2

Rose, L. C., and Gallup, A. M. (2001). The 33rd annual Phi Delta Kappa/Gallup Poll of the public's attitudes toward the public schools. *Phi Delta Kappan, 83*, 1.

Rose, L. C., and Gallup, A. M. (2005). The 37th annual Phi Delta Kappa/Gallup Poll of the public's attitudes toward the public schools. *Phi Delta Kappan, 87*, 1.

Sarason, S. B. (1991). *The predictable failure of educational reform.* San Francisco: Jossey-Bass.

Shalaway, L. (no date). *Planning for parent conferences.* Teachers Scholastic Instructor. Retrieved March 6, 2006, from http://teacher.scholastic.com/prod ucts/instructor/planning_parent_conf.htm

Shartrand, A. M., Weiss, H. B., Kreider, H. M., and Lopez, M. E. (1997). *New skills for new schools: Preparing teachers in family involvement.* Cambridge, MA: Harvard Family Research Project. Retrieved May 6, 2006, from http://www.ed.gov/oubs/Newskills/index.html

Steele-Carlin, S. (2001). Teacher visits hit home. *Education World.* Retrieved March 6, 2006, from http://www.educationworld.com/a_admin/admin/admin 241.shtml

Swap, S. M. (1993). *Developing home-school partnerships: From concepts to practice.* New York: Teachers College Press.

Technical Assistance Alliance for Parent Centers. (2005). *Parent training and information centers and community parent resource centers.* Retrieved March 27, 2006, from http://www.taalliance.org/Centers/index.htm

U.S. Department of Education, Office of Elementary and Secondary Education. (2002). *No child left behind: A desktop reference.* Washington, DC. Retrieved March 5, 2006, from http://www.ed.gov/admins/lead/account/nclbreference/index.html

U.S. Department of Education, Office of Special Education Programs. (1999). *IDEA 97 training package.* Retrieved March 7, 2006, from http://www.nichcy .org/Trainpkg/traintxt/9txt.htm

U.S. Department of Education, Partnership for Family Involvement in Education. (1999). *Partners for learning: Preparing teachers to involve families.* Washington, DC.

Weiss, H. B., Faughnan, K., Caspe, M., Wolos, C., Lopez, M. E., and Kreider, H. (2005). *Taking a closer look: A guide to online resources on family involvement.* Cambridge, MA: Harvard Family Research Project. Retrieved March 27, 2006, from http://www.gse.harvard.edu/~hfrptest/project/fine/resource/guide/ guide.html

Wherry, J. H. (2004). *Selected parent involvement research.* The Parent Institute.

Retrieved March 5, 2006, from http://www.par-inst.com/educator/resources/research/research.php

White-Clark, R., and Decker, L. E. (1996). *The hard-to-reach parent: Old challenges, new insights.* Fairfax, VA: National Community Education Association.

Websites for More Information and Links to Other Relevant Sites

Center for Law and Education, http://www.cleweb.org

Colorado Parent Information and Resource Center, http://www.cpirc.org

Family Involvement Network of Educators, http://www.finenetwork.org

Harvard Family Research Project, http://www.hfrp.org

National Center for Family and Community Connections with Schools, http://www.sedl.org/connections/

National Center for Fathering, http://www.fathers.com

National Center for Parent Involvement in Education, http://www.ncpie.org

National Education Association, http://www.nea.org/parents/index.html

National Information Center for Children and Youth with Disabilities, http://www.nichcy.org

National PTA, http://www.pta.org

Parent Institute, http://www.par-inst.com

Chapter Six

School-Community Collaboration

School consumes a surprisingly small portion of the lives of American children. Young people who have diligently attended school 6 hours a day, 180 days a year, from kindergarten through 12th grade, will, by their 18th birthday, have spent just 9% of their time since birth in school. This fact raises two critical questions: (1) What leverage does the other 91% of children's time have on the goal of achieving academic success? and (2) In what ways can educators build on the positive effects and ameliorate the negative ones from that 91% portion?

These are not new questions. In 1913, American educator Joseph K. Hart pondered basically the same considerations in his examination of the educational resources of villages and rural communities and offered the following thoughts:

> No child can escape his community. He may not like his parents, or the neighbors, or the ways of the world. He may drown under the processes of living, and wish he were dead. But he goes on living, and he goes on living in the community. The life of the community flows about him, foul or pure; he swims in it, drinks it, goes to sleep in it, and wakes to the new day to find it still about him. He belongs to it; it nourishes him, or starves him, or poisons him; it gives him the substance of his life. And in the long run it takes its toll of him, and all he is. (Decker and Decker, 2003, p. 99)

Like children, schools also do not exist independently of their communities. Schools affect and are affected by the health and well-being of the community, and by the attitudes, opinions, and expectations of the community members who surround children during the 91% of time they are not in school. In 1973, 58% of Americans reported "a great deal" or "quite a lot" of confidence in the public schools. Ten years later, this figure had dropped to 39%; by 1999, it had fallen to 36% before, in 2003, increasing slightly to 40% (Smith, 2005). The 2005 Phi Delta Kappa/Gallup Poll of the public's attitudes toward public schools documents a distinct difference in national and local ratings and reveals that, while the public blames the gap in achievement between various groups on factors other than schooling, they hold the schools responsible for closing it.

As Withrow (1999) points out, what the American public expects its schools to do today and in the future is cumulative.

> Schools are still expected to produce ethical, moral, civilized people who can help us sustain our democracy. They are expected to prepare a new wave of immigrants for life in America. And as demands increase, expectations grow, and life accelerates, our schools are expected to produce people who can effectively lead us into a global knowledge/information age. . . . Transformation expected of us is not new. It is simply one of the great benefits and ongoing challenges of living in a free and dynamic society. (p. 94)

The 2005 Phi Delta Kappa/Gallup Poll also documented a strong preference for reforming the existing public schools rather than creating an alternate system—in spite of the fact that "lack of financial support" is identified as the top problem facing schools and has been for the last six years. Given the ambitious goals of high academic achievement and equity for all children, it is not surprising that many observers believe that educational partnerships and collaborative initiatives are the only way schools can fulfill public expectations.

A task force established by the Annenberg Institute for School Reform (School Communities That Work, 2002) concluded:

> Advocating this kind of partnership is hardly new advice. Developing partnerships among city agencies and community-based organizations is rhetorically very popular and many efforts that seek to increase it—integrated services, service co-location, and mayoral councils on child and family issues, to name a few—have been attempted throughout the country. With a few exceptions, these efforts have not lived up to expectations. . . . [Creating educational partnership] is easier said than done. (Introduction, para. 4)

COLLABORATION

In their report, *Building Community Power for Better Schools,* Keleher and Morita (2004) emphasize that collaboration is possible only if the people who make up each organization understand what it means to engage in genuine collaboration. They describe collaboration as:

> A process through which parties who see different aspects of a problem can explore constructively their differences and search for (and implement) solutions that go beyond their own limited vision of what is possible. More specifically, collaborative projects are often viewed by grantmakers and participants as opportunities to address a number of interrelated dynamics, including:
>
> 1. Enhancing the ability of a wide range of organizations to address complex problems by building social infrastructure and realigning organizational relationships;
> 2. Making more efficient use of scarce resources;
> 3. Engaging and empowering disenfranchised community residents;
> 4. Providing a process and structure to address sweeping changes in political context, while affirming group identities and promoting interdependent problem solving. (p. 7)

Keleher and Morita observe that when organizations collaborate they can expand both power and success, but they must achieve an optimal balance between the efficiency and formality of the collaboration. Many trade-offs must be considered. The authors point out, "The reality of some collaborative processes . . . can be time-consuming, frustrating, and often contentious" (p. 42). Table 6.1 Factors of Successful Collaboration illustrates their point.

THE PARTNERSHIP CONTINUUM

In education, partnership encompasses three levels of working relationships that can be viewed as a continuum. *Cooperation* is at one end, implying a simple working together toward a common end. *Coordination* is in the middle range, implying a sharing of resources and joint planning,

Table 6.1   Factors of Successful Collaboration

Factors That Enhance Success	Barriers to Success
Collectively perceived need for collaboration	Costs outweigh actual benefits
Positive attitude toward collaborating among stakeholders	Bureaucracy inhibits communication
	Failure to address power dynamics and internal tensions
Adequate funding and resource allocation	Lack of geographic proximity
Common commitments to a goal	Lack of resources/insufficient funding
Existence of prior relationships	Lack of support for staff work
Environment of honesty and accountability	Sense of competition for resources among participating organizations
Clear and open communication	Differing approaches to leadership and decision making
A complementary diversity exists among staff, leadership, and constituency	
Leadership styles favor collaboration	Organizations fear a loss of program, identity, prestige, or authority
Regular opportunities for exchange among organizations and across constituencies	Inability to address conflict
Respect for diverse organizational structures, capabilities, and needs	Unwillingness to address structural inequities within the collaborative
Support for multiple constituency bases	Different organizational priorities, ideologies, outlooks, or goals
Willingness to invest time, personnel, materials, or facilities	Lack of common "language"
Availability of technical assistance	Historically poor relations between the organizations
Willingness to assess collaboration's internal dynamics and external outcomes	Inability to execute program objectives
	Inappropriate allocation of resources

development, and implementation of programs. *Collaboration* is at the other end, implying a higher degree of sharing and a more intensive, concerted effort, including joint allocation of resources and joint monitoring and evaluation.

There is no single model for an educational partnership. The extent of cooperation or collaboration depends on each partner's willingness to share resources—human, physical, and financial. Table 6.2 suggests what a continuum of school-community partnerships (Decker and Decker, 2003) might include.

The type of involvement and partnership will vary from school to school, depending on local needs and circumstances. The goal is to build a shared ownership for education and the well-being of children. Table 6.3 outlines a partnership continuum of activities and responsibilities representing progressively greater levels of collaboration, shared responsibil-

Table 6.2. The Partnership Continuum

One-on-One (Sponsor → Beneficiary)	Cooperative Agreements (Sponsor ↔ Beneficiary)	Comprehensive Collaboratives (Sponsors ↔ Beneficiaries)
Tutoring	Needs assessment	Needs assessment
Mentoring	Planning	Broad-based multiagency
Field trips	Research and	planning
Guest speakers	development	Research and
Summer jobs	Training in new technology	development
Paid work-study	Teacher/administrator	Long-term institutional
Scholarships	professional	commitment
Incentives and recognition	development	Commonly defined vision
awards	Advocacy policy, laws	Goals/objectives by
Demonstrations	School-based health clinics	consensus
Use of business facilities	Magnet schools	Shared authority/decision
Loaned executives	Funds to support	making
Volunteer services	innovation	New roles/relationships
Minigrants for teachers	Advice on restructuring	Advocacy policy/laws
Teaching assistance	schools	Integration of multiple
Donations of equipment/	Focused programs, e.g.,	cross-institutional
supplies	dropout or teen	programs
Public relations	pregnancy prevention	Comprehensive services
		focused on whole child
		Full-service school

ity, and participation in decision making (Saskatchewan Education, 1999).

"Collaborating with the Community" is the sixth *National Standards for Parent/Family Involvement Programs* (National PTA, 2004). The standard outlined a general framework for educational partnerships and specified quality indicators of successful programs.

Standard VI. Collaborating with the Community

Community resources are used to strengthen schools, families, and student learning. As part of the larger community, schools and other programs fulfill important community goals. In like fashion, communities offer a wide array of resources valuable to schools and the families they serve. The best partnerships are mutually beneficial and structured to connect individuals, not just institutions or groups. This connection enables the power of community partnerships to be unleashed.

Table 6.3. Continuum of Parent and Community Involvement Partnerships

	Meeting Basic Needs	Developing Openness and Two-Way Communication	Supporting Learning in Home and the Community	Participating in Voluntary and Advisory Roles	Building Collaboration and Partnerships	Participating in Governance
Activity and Program Examples	*At home:* safe, caring home environment adequate food, clothing *In school/community:* nutrition programs clothing exchanges "safe rooms" parenting education community kitchens home-school liaison	*At home:* advise teacher of student's likes and dislikes, change to routine, etc. discuss concerns and successes with teacher review information sent home from school attend meetings and school events *In school/community:* welcoming school environment parent, student, teacher conferences school newsletters home visits surveys of parent opinion message board of school events and activities newspaper columns	*At home:* being interested in and encouraging children's learning creating a place to study/work reading to children making learning part of everyday life *In community:* mentoring creating safe, stable communities *In school:* family literacy programs assignments to encourage family involvement learning contracts among parents, teachers, and students summer/holiday learning projects	attending/assisting with school events fund raising volunteering room for volunteers/parents guest speakers tutoring students newsletter coordination leading clubs parent centers providing advice on school issues/programs advising on school policy issues such as code of conduct, discipline, curriculum, program adaptation, schedules, etc.	financial and "in kind" contributions business partnerships and sponsorships integrated services community development youth community service/work in-school daycare early intervention preschool shared facilities adopt-a-school community service work	planning, problem solving making decisions about budget, program adaptations, priorities, criteria for staff and/or staffing training in leadership and decision-making skills program assessment shared management of project, program, or school partnerships with organizations, agencies, and governments
Structure	self-help groups school-community liaison program school-level organization—parent council, school council, home-school association community association	school-community liaison program school-level organizations—parent council, school council, home-school association community association district boards/committees	school-community liaison program school-level organizations—parent council, school council, home-school association community association district boards/committees	volunteer programs school-community liaison program school-level organizations—parent council, school council, home-school association community association district boards/committees	advisory committees interagency committees school-level organizations—parent council, school council, home-school association community association district boards/committees	school councils, parent advisory council, school-community council district boards/committees comanagement board associate schools district board of education

Quality Indicators. Effective programs:

1. Distribute information regarding cultural, recreation..., health, social, and other resources that serve families within the community.
2. Develop partnerships with local business and service groups to advance student learning and assist schools and families.
3. Encourage employers to adopt policies and practices that promote and support adult participation in children's education.
4. Foster student participation in community service.
5. Involve community members in school volunteer programs.
6. Disseminate information to the school community, including those without school-age children, regarding school programs and performance.
7. Collaborate with community agencies to provide family support services and adult learning opportunities, enabling families to more fully participate in activities that support education.
8. Inform staff members of the resources available in the community and strategies for utilizing those resources. (p. 20)

The National Association of Partners in Education (NAPE) (2001) has developed a process to help schools build partnerships with the community. NAPE suggests that it is important to identify all the steps at the beginning of the process and to refer to them repeatedly during development and implementation. Some steps may be more important than others depending on the situation. The steps are informing key populations that a partnership is being considered; gathering and interpreting information in order to formulate goals and objectives; identifying people, materials, equipment, and funding available within a school, school district, business, agency, and community to help meet identified needs; defining the partnership's administrative structure and the rules and regulations under which it will function; engaging people, organizations, and resources in partnership and matching people with the jobs that need to be done; paying attention to training and retention; and, finally, ensuring that monitoring, data collection, and evaluation are completed.

Today's school-community partnerships differ from those of the past in that they reflect a deeper awareness of the devastating effects of noneducational barriers to learning, such as poverty, poor health, or an unstable home life. Collaborative efforts with businesses, universities, medical and social service agencies, foundations, and community-based religious and civic organizations are based on recognition that there is no single solution to school improvement. The challenge in developing partnerships and collaborative efforts is to ensure that all parties are working together to set and reinforce consistent messages and standards for all children.

The Education Policy Studies Laboratory at Arizona State University invited a group of education scholars to review the research on a series of education reform topics, including efforts to better link public schools with their communities; their findings are presented in the publication, *School Reform Proposals: The Research Evidence* (Molnar, 2002). The reviewers found that the challenge in linking schools with their communities is to devise the right mixture of services and programs in organizational situations that are highly idiosyncratic. Their recommendations include:

1. Educational leaders and policymakers should be encouraged to reconceptualize the public school as a vital economic resource that must be nurtured.
2. Schools and other social organizations wishing to provide school-linked services should carefully consider the scope, funding needs, organizational and professional complexities, and types of services to be offered. While perhaps not as compelling or intellectually stimulating, incremental types of school-linked services should be pursued if providers are dedicated to institutionalizing the project.
3. Funding for new community improvement projects should be kept consistent and stable. The bigger and more complex the project, the greater the need for adequate funding. (Executive Summary, section 7, para. 1)

COLLABORATIVE LEADERSHIP

Successful collaboration requires leaders who can broker connections across the community of diverse people and resources, and who can take advantage of emerging opportunities. As Lashway (2003) points out, leading in a collaborative, in which no one has control over all of the people and organizations involved, is different from leading in a traditional organizational setting, where decision making comes from the top. This view of leadership is of a social activity "woven into the threads of the organization which allows leadership to be exercised by different people throughout the organization and the community" (section 4, para. 3). Collaborative leaders must learn to share decision making by distributing leadership inside and outside of the school building and developing leadership capacity in people who do not necessarily see themselves as leaders.

Brubach (2004) emphasizes that sustaining community coalitions is just as important as creating them. She offers seven principles of collaborative leadership that can help coalitions improve their effectiveness and sustainability:

1. *Keep the coalition focused on the goal:* Successful collaborative leaders keep the diverse members attuned to their common goal while keeping an eye on the big picture to help inform group processes.
2. *Locate, persuade, and utilize influential champions and partners within the community:* Strong leaders bring community ties to the table and develop partnerships with organizations and individuals that help sustain the coalition.
3. *Maintain and protect collaborative decision-making, planning, and infrastructure-building processes:* Instead of being the decision makers, collaborative leaders actively seek to continue the group decision-making, planning, and infrastructure-building processes.
4. *Diversify, motivate, and energize the coalition's volunteer base:* In order to increase the coalition's sustainability, leaders should help recruit diverse community members, get them involved in ways that are meaningful to them, and keep them feeling upbeat about their experience as members of the team.
5. *Help resolve member conflicts:* Collaborative leaders can make deliberate efforts to help resolve member conflicts in open, unbiased ways that encourage compromise.
6. *Communicate with the community:* Coalition leaders that bring excellent written and verbal communication skills to the table help

get the coalition message out to the community and potential partners.
7. *Cultivate leadership in coalition members, including youth:* Coalitions gain momentum under the initial inspired involvement of those
   who established the coalition. However, in order for a coalition to
   sustain that momentum, it is crucial that new leadership is both
   allowed and encouraged to develop. (para. 3)

The Role of the Principal

The principal is usually the first-line gatekeeper, the individual who will
determine whether a school reaches out to involve families and the community in the education of children. A principal's willingness and ability
to engage in collaboration are essential to the success of the initiative.
Historically, collaborative skills have not ranked high on the list of leadership abilities needed to be an effective principal, and few principals or
other school personnel receive training in working with parents and families or the community at large.

Recognizing the ever-expanding responsibilities of school principals,
the National Association of Elementary School Principals (NAESP) published *Leading Learning Communities: Standards for What Principals
Should Know and Be Able to Do* (2001a). Introducing the guide, NAESP
president Darrell Rud points out: "Throughout the nation, principals are
redefining their profession and recreating their roles and responsibilities
within it. Regardless of location, racial or socio-economic demographics,
communities demand that principals lead the instructional and academic
performance of their schools" (para. 5). The standards are:

1. Leading schools in a way that puts student and adult learning at the
   center. In addition, principals serve as lead learner and teacher.
2. Promoting the academic success of all students by setting high
   expectations and high standards and organizing the school environment around school achievement.
3. Creating and demanding rigorous content and instruction that ensure
   student progress toward agreed-upon academic standards.
4. Creating a climate of continuous learning for adults that is tied to
   student learning.

5. Using multiple sources of data as a diagnostic tool to assess, identify, and apply instructional improvement.
6. Actively engaging the community to create shared responsibility for student and school success. (para. 7)

In a discussion of school leadership, Lashway (2003) asserts: "In a standards-oriented age, contemporary visions of leadership can be found in the professional standards established by policymakers, practitioners, and university professors. Foremost among these are the guidelines developed by the Interstate School Leaders Licensure Consortium (ISLLC)" (Defining School Leadership, para. 1). He states that the six ISLLC standards have gained rapid acceptance and are now used to guide principal preparation programs in 35 states. The standards "envision these six dimensions as a pathway to one overriding goal—student achievement":

1. Facilitating shared vision.
2. Sustaining a school culture conducive to student and staff learning.
3. Managing the organization for a safe, efficient, and effective environment.
4. Collaborating with families and community members.
5. Acting with integrity, fairness, and in an ethical manner.
6. Influencing the larger political, social, economic, legal, and cultural context. (Defining School Leadership section, para. 1)

Lashway believes that the ISLLC and NAESP standards represent a "best practices" approach based on the judgment of experienced practitioners and knowledgeable observers.

The Role of Municipal Leaders

Building and sustaining educational partnerships requires collaborative leadership on the part of the community as well as the schools. Diverse stakeholders in public education—students, teachers, school administrators, parents, business people, community groups and organizations, and members of the community—must be involved as participants, not merely as audiences, in discussions and actions on behalf of school improvement, increased student achievement, and strengthened families.

Hutchinson and Van Wyngaardt (no date) point out that the 2001 Phi
Delta Kappan/Gallup Poll found that 45% of Americans believe that all
levels of government have a role in closing the academic achievement gap
and that this responsibility is distributed fairly evenly among federal,
state, and local governments—even though municipal leaders typically do
not have direct control or authority over public schools. According to the
authors, "Local elected officials around the country are demonstrating
that local government can make a positive difference in improving
schools—and not necessarily by exerting greater administrative control
over the educational systems" (p. 5). Local elected leaders recognize that
they have an important stake in the success or failure of local schools.
They understand that the health and well-being of communities are
affected by student success—or lack of it—and that successful schools
contribute to economic development and a strong citizenry.

Hutchinson and Van Wyngaardt enumerate ways that municipal leaders, as visible, respected leaders of the community, can use their leadership positions to promote a communitywide approach to improving
schools:

1. Set the public's agenda and articulate the city's vision to reach consensus around specific goals for school improvement.
2. Facilitate ongoing communication with school leaders to build trusting relationships, lay the groundwork for collaboration, and minimize turf issues.
3. Bring community partners together—including business-, community-,
   and faith-based organizations; libraries; museums; and others—to
   assess progress regarding school improvement and to leverage
   resources to support schools.
4. Remove obstacles to achievement by using city resources to help
   children and youth maximize their learning potential, address health
   and social services needs, and enhance student safety.
5. Build public will by engaging parents and community residents,
   using public forums and media outreach to raise critical issues and
   share responsibility for shortcomings and successes. (p. 6)

A report by the U.S. Conference of Mayors (Edelstein, 2006) examines
mayors'—especially mayors of urban cities—growing involvement with

public schools. Mayors are increasingly aware of the impact a good public education system has on the health and wealth of their cities. Public school issues can impact crime rates, health issues, foster care involvement, and a host of other social and economic trends. At the same time, urban residents look to mayors to exercise leadership by using their authority over municipal services and resources to help improve educational outcomes. Edelstein notes that mayors cite a variety of challenges when attempting to improve school systems including unsatisfactory achievement, political conflict, inexperienced teaching staff, and high student mobility. He suggests that mayors can address these challenges by:

1. Working with the school system to develop mentoring and tutoring programs and links to social services.
2. Gathering together the parties involved in school issues.
3. Assisting the school system with employment issues, especially the recruitment and retention of teachers. For example, in some cities mayors have helped provide rental housing and loan subsidies to teachers.
4. Talking with business and education leaders about academic standards and about what students need to know for their future employment options.
5. Offering technical support to help improve the school system including offering to use city administrative functions for school payroll, purchasing, and contract management.

The Forum for Youth Investment (no date) emphasizes that elected officials are often the driving force behind citywide out-of-school efforts, but cautions that a variety of leaders and leadership bodies—city agencies and their directors, community organizations and intermediary leaders, members of the business community and neighborhood leaders—must help in the task of focusing public attention and community resources on out-of-school issues. "There needs to be a balance between top-down and bottom-up leadership, with multiple levels or entry points. Such a balance must protect local diversity and strengths while somehow leveraging citywide leadership" (p. 1).

TYPES OF EDUCATIONAL PARTNERSHIPS

School reform and academic achievement are on the public agenda in almost every community in America, and there is widespread agreement that public schools alone cannot adequately address the many complex issues involved. The idea of using educational partnerships to address problems collaboratively is not new, and a variety of partnership models have been created. The national task force of the Annenberg Institute for School Reform (School Communities That Work, 2002) cautions, however, that effective partnerships must go beyond mere collaboration; the task force recommends that two approaches undergird both the joint work of the partnership and the independent approaches of the individual partners:

1. Assessing and aligning services to promote not only results, but also equity.
2. Considering all current activities and future plans from a youth engagement and development perspective. (p. 2)

Various types of educational partnerships are described below. Some are relatively simple to create, and others are much broader and more complex. Their operation reflects the personalities, agendas, and skills of participants.

Volunteer Programs

Volunteer programs are the oldest and best-known educational partnerships. They take advantage of the American tradition of volunteering. The Bureau of Labor Statistics of the U.S. Department of Labor (2005) reports that about 65.4 million people—almost 30% of the population—volunteered through or for an organization at least once between September 2004 and September 2005. Women volunteered at a higher rate than men, and persons aged 35 to 44 were most likely to volunteer. Teenagers had a high volunteer rate of 30.4%

School volunteer programs recruit and train individuals to work in support of schools and education. Most school volunteers fall into one of four categories. *One-time volunteers* are those who have limited time, usually part or all of one school day. They may volunteer to accompany a field trip, assist with a special event, share a special skill or expertise on a particular topic, or participate in a career education day. *Off-campus volunteers* are those who can work only from home or from another nonschool site. They may have small children, or they may be older or handicapped. These individuals often help develop educational materials or do clerical work such as typing or checking papers, provide a meeting place and leadership for off-campus youth clubs such as Scouts and Brownies, or provide a service such as childcare or transportation to allow others to visit a teacher or work at school. They may help with telephone campaigns or other publicity needs or make telephone contacts to request community agencies' and groups' assistance on special projects. *Short-term volunteers* may offer minicourses or short-term enrichment programs, help with building improvements, assist with assemblies and plays, or provide other in-school services on a short-term project. *Extended volunteers* are those who can work several hours a week over a semester or a year as a tutor, mentor, or classroom or library aide, supervise lunchroom/playground activities, provide classroom or office clerical services, help with a particular subject such as art or music, or assist in coordinating the volunteer program.

Traditionally, parents—primarily mothers—have been the source of school volunteers. However, as family demographics and work schedules have changed, schools have had to reach beyond families to the community and the student body to recruit volunteer assistance. Senior citizens have become a welcome pool of assistance in all kinds of volunteer activities, especially tutoring and mentoring, and as foster grandparents. Students have also been effective as peer tutors and mentors.

Developing a volunteer program is often a school's first step in building partnerships to meet educational needs. Obviously, teachers' and administrators' commitment to using volunteers, knowledge of the role of volunteers, and attitudes and skills in using volunteers are basic to success. Starting a volunteer program requires careful organization and planning. The Points of Light Foundation Tip Sheet (2003) suggests conducting a needs assessment from which volunteer positions can be developed. Time should then be taken to plan for the effective recruitment, supervision, evaluation, and recognition of volunteers. Issues of school safety and security clearances must also be considered.

The retention of volunteers is another vital consideration. Decker and Decker (2003) offer the following advice for retaining volunteer support:

1. Nurture volunteers' feeling of belonging to the educational team. With a sense of pride and ownership, they can become tremendous boosters of public education.
2. Monitor the volunteer/teacher placements. Be sensitive to problems and encourage flexibility when change is indicated.
3. Provide ongoing in-service training when appropriate.
4. Train teachers to work with volunteers. Many problems can be avoided if volunteers and teachers have mutual expectations.
5. Provide feedback about volunteers' performance and suggestions for teaching, discipline, or human relations techniques.
6. Hold informal and formal recognition activities throughout the year.
7. Use suggestions from evaluations when possible. (p. 124)

Mentoring Programs

The term *mentor* is used to describe a one-on-one relationship between an adult and child. Mentors are adult volunteers, usually from the local community, who are willing to make a long-term commitment to act as a role model, teacher, and friend to a child in need of guidance and support. Mentoring programs can be community- or school-based and offer benefits to both mentor and mentee. According to the 1998 Commonwealth Fund Survey of Adults Mentoring Young People (McLearn and others), a majority of mentors report finding the relationship highly satisfying and rewarding and say they would mentor again. Research shows that mentees are likely to have fewer absences from schools, better attitudes toward school and their elders, less abuse of drugs and alcohol, and better relationships with their parents (Herrara, 1999).

School-based mentoring programs differ from traditional community-based models in that they tend to be more focused on school success, are more likely to serve children with academic needs, and tend to require less time from the mentor (Brown, 2004a). School-based mentors require less screening because they work in a supervised setting, and school-based programs may attract volunteers who, because of their jobs, families, age, or other life experiences, may not otherwise be able to volunteer

(Herrara, 1999). Such programs are often cosponsored by local agencies and businesses who allow their employees to take an hour a week of work time to mentor a child.

Mentoring programs offer significant help to the growing number of immigrant children in the United States. Although these children come from a wide range of backgrounds, cultures, and circumstances, they share the stress associated with migration to a new country. Often, their parents have to work long hours, and language and cultural differences may make it difficult for them to understand their children's experiences (Suarez-Orozco and Suarez-Orozco, 2001). According to the National Mentoring Partnership (2005), mentors of immigrant children can help alleviate stress, especially if the mentor is of the same ethnic background as the child; compensate for the void that may have been created by parental absence; bridge the gap between American culture and educational institutions and those of the homeland; and foster identity development by acting as role models in the process of developing a bicultural identity that includes celebration of elements of the ethnic identity while incorporating aspects of the culture of the United States.

The National Mentoring Partnership (2005) cautions that mentoring may not be appropriate for all immigrants, since some cultural and linguistic barriers may be heightened by mentors who are not from the same culture as the mentee. The partnership also warns that the unexpected termination of a mentoring relationship may be particularly harmful to immigrant adolescents who have already suffered separation from or loss of family members and other adults they were close to.

After-School Programs

Donald Kussmaul (2005), former president of the AASA, points out, "In this era of No Child Left Behind, public schools have shifted their focus from providing access to high-quality education to demanding a high level of achievement for all students . . . [a shift that] requires a comprehensive approach to developing the whole child" (para. 1). According to Kussmaul, this comprehensive approach includes three things:

1. Getting children ready for school through comprehensive nutrition and health programs, early childhood education, and ongoing support for families.

2. Getting schools ready for children by redesigning and transforming schools' organization, teaching and learning practices, and leadership strategies to meet the needs of each student.
3. Getting children ready for democracy by preparing young people for active, responsible roles in society.

He acknowledges, "This is a tall order, yet it is partially filled after the regular school day ends—in quality afterschool programs" (para. 2).

The number of after-school programs is increasing rapidly. A survey by the NAESP (2001b) showed that in an era when schools are being asked to do more for children both academically and socially, public schools are stepping in as providers of after-school programming. Two-thirds (67%) of the principals surveyed said that their schools now offer optional programs for children after regular schools hours. Another 15% said they are considering offering an after-school program in the future (NAESP, 2001b, section 1).

The survey's findings in the case of existing programs include:

1. Six in 10 (59%) principals reported that their programs have been operating less than 5 years while 15% said their programs have been operating for more than 5 years, and 25% said their programs are between 6 and 10 years old.
2. Nearly all (95%) after-school programs are located at the schools.
3. Principals believe their extended-day programs are well worth the effort: 91% rated their programs as either successful or very successful and identified improving student academics (34%) and providing a safe haven for students (26%) as their programs' greatest achievements. Almost all (96%) of the principals said their programs offer students help with homework. Most say they provide instruction in literacy and reading (85%) and math enrichment (85%), science (69%), the arts (63%), and computers and technology instruction (62%).
4. More than three-fourths (78%) of principals say their programs offer recreation and sports activities. (section 1)

According to NAESP, attendance in after-school programs can (1) provide youth with supervision during a time when many might be exposed to or engage in antisocial or destructive behaviors, (2) help improve the academic achievement of students who are not accomplishing as much as they need to during regular school hours, and (3) provide enriching experiences that broaden children's perspective and improve their socialization (NAESP, 2001b).

The Children's Aid Society (2002) examined research evidence to determine whether after-school programs did in fact accomplish the goals implied in NAESP's threefold rationale for establishing them. The society's *Fact Sheet on After-School Programs* shows:

1. After-school programs help reduce youth crime and provide a safe environment. About 40% of young people's waking hours are discretionary time that is not committed to other activities such as school, homework, meals, chores, or working for pay. Experts estimate that at least 5 million latchkey children come home to empty houses. Violent juvenile crime triples in the hours of 3 to 8 p.m.; during these same hours children are most at risk of being victims of crime. Recent studies confirm the relationship between availability of after-school programs and reduced rates of juvenile crime.
2. Children who participate in high-quality, constructive after-school programs demonstrate higher school attendance, higher language accumulation rates, and improved performance on standardized tests. In addition, economically disadvantaged children who participate from 20 to 35 hours per week in constructive learning activities during their free time get better grades in school than their peers who do not participate in such activities.
3. In addition to improved academic achievement, children who participate in high-quality after-school programs experience such additional benefits as better work habits, emotional adjustment, and peer relations; improved social skills; and increased ability to maintain self-control, avoid conflict, and make constructive choices in personal behavior.
4. Teenagers, as well as younger children, benefit from participation in high-quality after-school programs.

Chung and Hillsman (2005) recently examined studies evaluating after-school programs and found that:

[A] growing number of studies indicate that after-school programs do make a positive difference in the lives of their participants. Not only do after-school programs provide a safe haven during the nonschool hours, [but] students who consistently participate in quality after-school activities have better grades, greater student engagement in school, increased homework completion, reduced absenteeism and tardiness, greater parent involvement, increased civic engagement, and reduced crime and violence in the non-school hours. . . . [A]fter-school programs [also] provide young people with the opportunity to participate in various activities from which they can learn and grow, including art, dance, music and sports. These activities can contribute to students' overall well-being; improve problem solving, interpersonal, and communication skills; and raise their academic achievement. (para. 6, 9)

In 1998, the Charles Stewart Mott Foundation formed a partnership with the U.S. Department of Education to help fund after-school programs. In the first year, 99 grants were awarded. By 2005, that number had risen to 2,700 grants to provide service to more than a million youth and adult family members in nearly 8,500 local programs. After-school programs come in many different shapes and sizes. In the words of William White, president of the Charles Stewart Mott Foundation:

There is no single formula for a successful school program. That shouldn't come as a surprise because the most effective afterschool programs reflect the needs of the young people they serve, and the resources available within a community to address those needs. By resources I don't mean just money. I'm talking about staff and volunteer commitment, creative approaches to get the job done, and partnerships, whether between schools and other organizations serving youth or between the afterschool providers and the business community. (Charles Stewart Mott Foundation, 2005, p. 6)

Chung and Hillsman (2005) report on an ongoing study to identify the types of after-school programs, or program characteristics, most conducive to positive student outcomes. Early analyses point to programs that offer a wide variety of activities, demonstrate the likelihood of financial sustainability over several years, and indicate high levels of job satisfaction among staff. "[K]ey program characteristics leading to positive student outcomes include physical and psychological safety, appropriate structures, supportive relationships, opportunities to belong, positive social norms, support for efficacy, opportunities for skill building, and integration of family, school and community efforts" (para. 13).

Birmingham and others (2005) examined after-school programs funded by the After-School Corporation that were identified as highly likely to have contributed to improvements in students' academic achievement. The after-school services at each site were delivered by a nonprofit organization that had established a partnership with a public school that served any of the grades K through 12. After-school activities were provided at the school, and all students enrolled in the host school were eligible to participate. Projects provided services free of charge. The researchers found that "[W]hile these high-performing after-school projects were identified through their participants' achievement gains, the projects did not primarily focus on academics" (p. 2). The high-performing after-school projects shared characteristics that include:

1. *A broad array of enrichment opportunities.* For many participants, the after-school project provided their first exposure to new learning opportunities in areas such as dance, music, art, and organized sports. Enrichment activities introduced participants to experiences that could spark interests and expand their goals for their own schooling, careers, and hobbies.
2. *Opportunities for skill building and mastery.* Each after-school project created opportunities to build participants' literacy skills through reading, storytelling, writing activities, and use of formal curricula, such as *Kidzlit* and *Passport to Success.* In addition, they integrated a focus on mastery into arts-based activities by practicing new skills in preparation for an exhibition or performance.
3. *Intentional relationship building.* The process began with each project fostering positive relationships with the host school. Throughout the year, the coordinator worked on relationships with the project's primary stakeholders through ongoing classroom-management training for staff, conflict resolution classes, team-building activities for participants, and regular communication with and the provision of support services to families.
4. *A strong, experienced leader-manager supported by a trained and supervised staff.* The coordinators had experience in youth develop-

ment and a strong connection to the community, the children, and the families they served. There was staff orientation at the beginning of the year, ongoing staff meetings and supervision, and consistent feedback on what worked and what did not work.

5. *Administrative, fiscal, and professional-development support of the sponsoring organization.* In each partnership, the sponsor gave the site coordinator the autonomy and flexibility to manage the after-school project day to day, while providing administrative and fiscal support to the project.

While the value of after-school programs is generally recognized, there is concern that the programs are not equitably distributed. Low-income youth are much less likely than their more affluent peers to have access to them. The Children's Aid Society (2002) reports:

According to the National Education Longitudinal Study, sponsored by the U.S. Department of Education, 40% of low-income eighth graders—compared with only 17% of high-income respondents—do not participate in any organized after-school activities. The likely explanation for this difference is access, not interest, since virtually every survey of American youth suggests that they want to participate in well designed, organized after-school programs. (Fact 4, para. 4)

The Children's Aid Society also notes that there is widespread public support for the expansion of after-school programs. Ninety-four percent of voters say that there should be some type of organized activity or place for children and teens to go after school every day, and 75% of voters (almost a 10% increase since 2000) believe that federal or state tax dollars should be used to expand daily after-school programs to make them accessible to all children.

The NAESP (2001b) survey shows that despite widespread public support and demonstrated success, challenges remain. Principals who do not already have programs identified funding (18%), staffing (32%), and transportation (18%) as the most difficult barriers to starting a program.

Peterson (2005) points out that, increasingly, after-school hours have become the time for new and creative learning opportunities offered in settings where children are supervised by professional educators and community partners. He argues that even though tight local, state, and federal budgets have halted the growth of programs in many districts, "the flat-lining of after-school funding is a very bad mistake" (Multiple Effects, para. 3). Peterson asserts that most school leaders recognize after-school programs as an opportunity to address many vexing challenges, so they are finding ways to leverage existing resources, personnel, and facilities to significantly increase learning time, while recruiting and rallying more allies outside the schools to the cause of expanding learning opportunities.

> Increasingly, school leaders are seeing after-school programs as useful tools to accomplish multiple goals: increasing student performance, expanding learning opportunities in a safe setting, and building greater parent and community support for their community's public schools. With strategic leadership from superintendent and district staff, it is possible to get after-school programs off the ground and keep them afloat even in these days of tightened budgets. Robust and comprehensive after-school programs are one important way to leverage more student success and public support. (District Programs section, para. 4)

Advisory Committees and Task Forces

A task force is usually an ad hoc group formed to focus on a specific issue or assignment. An advisory committee is typically a continuing body that focuses on broad aspects of a school program. These well-known forms of school-community involvement are commonly used to involve the community in educational planning and decision making. They are effective ways to encourage multicultural parent and community collaboration and build new levels of trust through the purposeful inclusion of parents with diverse backgrounds. Although some advisory groups are elected, membership is usually developed through appointment and volunteering. An advisory group may report to the superintendent, the school board, the principal, or the community.

Establishing effective advisory committees and task forces requires a strong commitment and a great deal of work. There are, however, a number of good—even self-interested—reasons for undertaking the serious work of developing and nurturing effective advisory groups. First, and most obviously, community members who become significantly involved with schools develop an understanding of competing interests, are more willing to accept compromise, and tend to support decisions that are made after broad-based consultation. There are other benefits. Special interests tend to balance out. Policy decisions are more likely to be based on complete and accurate information about the community. Importantly, a sense of community cohesion usually begins to develop.

The impact and credibility of an advisory group depend less on the way members are selected than on the degree to which the membership accurately reflects the total community in its ethnic, socioeconomic, and gender dimensions. The group's impact and credibility also depend on the support it gets from school staff, the importance of its assignment, and the clarity of the task to everyone involved.

Decker and Decker (2003) offer the following guidelines for advisory groups:

1. State the goals clearly and precisely.
2. Involve a representative cross section of the community and the school, but keep the group size manageable.
3. Decide on a leadership structure and chain of command.
4. Establish a time schedule with specific intermediary goals, and keep the group on course.
5. Determine if—and precisely—how the group will work with or respond to the news media.
6. Staff the advisory group properly in terms of administrative and other support personnel.
7. Maintain a clear understanding of what will happen to the group's report.
8. Discharge and thank the committee in a meaningful and appropriate manner. (p. 128)

SCHOOL-BUSINESS PARTNERSHIPS

The most publicized school-community partnerships have been those between schools and businesses. Businesses have offered student internships, job counseling, and job-site visits. They have participated in career fairs, assisted administrators in solving management problems, donated money and equipment, funded newsletters and voice-mail systems, served on task forces of various types, provided experts to speak in classrooms and at assemblies, and even used their influence to affect political and financial issues of concern to schools. School and local business partnerships can be especially beneficial to schools that serve poor and minority communities.

Involving the business community in helping to prepare students for the workplace is not a new idea. Vocational students have benefited from participation in cooperative vocation education programs for decades. What is new is the way in which traditional efforts are expanding to reach students from elementary school to college, and the positive way people in the business world are responding to this initiative.

The NAPE (2000) reports that in 2000, 70% of all school districts engaged in some form of business partnership—an increase of 35% since 1990; those partnerships contributed an estimated $2.4 billion and 109 million volunteer hours. According to the Council for Corporate and School Partnerships (2001), small businesses represent the largest share of existing school partnerships—in 2001, 76% of school collaborations with the business community were with small businesses, up from 41% in 1990. Local business and school collaboration programs included English as a Second Language and general equivalency diploma (GED) instruction for parents; math and reading tutors for students; cultural enrichment programs linked to the curriculum; funds for after-school tutoring; and a host of others.

In addition to direct involvement with schools and school programs, the private sector can implement "family friendly" practices that encourage and support family involvement in education. Employers can encourage and recognize employees who volunteer in schools, give employees release time or provide flexible scheduling, or give tangible rewards for volunteering. Employers can also encourage their employees to continue their education, especially those who do not have high school diplomas. Some employers are willing to adjust work schedules or provide scholarship assistance for employees who wish to upgrade their skills or retrain in a new area.

The Council for Corporate and School Partnerships (2001) developed a set of Guiding Principles to illustrate the characteristics of effective partnerships for schools, communities, and businesses interested in developing new partnerships or enhancing existing ones. The council's eight Guiding Principles fall into four thematic categories:

1. *The Foundation:* developing the partnership's core values.
   a. School/business partnerships must be built on shared values and philosophies.
   b. Partnerships should be defined by mutually beneficial goals—short- and long-term—and objectives that are aligned with the educational goals of an individual school and/or district.
2. *Implementation:* translating values into action.
   a. Partnership activities should be integrated into the school and business cultures.
   b. Partnerships should be driven by a clear management process and structure.
   c. Partnerships should define specific, measurable outcomes.
3. *Continuity:* sustaining the partnership over time.
   a. Partnerships should have support at the highest level within the business and school and concurrence at all levels.
   b. Partnerships should include detailed internal and external communications plans that clearly illustrate expectations of all parties.
4. *Evaluation:* determining strengths, weaknesses, and future directions.
   a. Partnerships should be developed with clear definitions of success for all partners.

Although businesses can contribute significantly to the learning experiences of students, there is rising concern that schools have become integral to the marketing plans of some businesses. The seventh annual report on schoolhouse commercialism trends by the Commercialism in Education Research Unit of the Education Policies Studies Laboratory at Arizona State University (2004) describes the basis for this concern:

[C]ommercial interests—through advertising, sponsorship of curriculum and programs, marketing of consumer products, for-profit privatization, and fundraising tied to commercial entities—continue to influence public education. The trend persists despite growing criticism of—and to some degree, attempts to—resist practices that create tighter bonds between public school and private, for-profit corporations. It is driven in large part by continued financial struggles of public school systems to meet the demands of educating children in the face of tighter resources. (Executive Summary, para. 1)

An ERIC Clearinghouse on Educational Management policy report (2001) examined several facets of school-business partnerships, including corporate sponsorships, school-to-career activities, commercialism on the Internet and student privacy, and other legal and ethical issues. The report emphasizes that in the absence of a clear and direct educational benefit to students, the arrangement is not a genuine educational partnership. The report presents eight principles for corporate involvement that have been adopted by the NASBE, National Parent-Teachers Association, AASA, National Council of Social Studies, and National Education Association. The principles are intended to ensure that educational values are not distorted or diluted within the context of a school-business partnership. The report urges educators to adhere to them to help protect the welfare of students and the integrity of the learning environment.

1. Corporate involvement shall not require students to observe, listen to, or read commercial advertising.
2. Selling or providing access to a captive audience in the classroom for commercial purposes is exploitation and a violation of the public trust.
3. Since school property and time are publicly funded, selling or providing free access to advertising on school property outside the classroom involves ethical and legal issues that must be addressed.
4. Corporate involvement must support the goals and objectives of the schools. Curriculum and instruction are within the purview of educators.
5. Programs of corporate involvement must be structured to meet an identified education need, not a commercial motive, and must be evaluated for educational effectiveness by the school or district on an ongoing basis.
6. Schools and educators should hold sponsored and donated materials

to the same standards used for the selection and purchase of curriculum materials.

7. Corporate involvement programs should not limit the discretion of schools and teachers in the use of sponsored materials.

8. Sponsor recognition and corporate logos should be for identification rather than commercial purposes. (para. 9)

Service Learning

Service learning is a growing form of collaboration between schools and community agencies. Summarizing the language of the National and Community Service Act of 1990, the National Youth Leadership Council defines service learning as:

> [S]tudent learning and development through active participation in thoughtfully organized service experiences that meet real community needs and that are coordinated in collaboration with the school and community. The service learning is integrated into the students' academic curriculum and includes structured time to talk, write, and think about what they did and saw during the actual service activity. (Decker and Decker, 2003, p. 134)

This type of collaboration views young people as resources rather than as problems and uses the community as a laboratory for youth development. Service opportunities emphasize the accomplishment of tasks to meet human and community needs and the use of the service experience to accomplish intentional learning goals. Students have opportunities to use newly acquired skills and knowledge in real-life situations in their own communities. The service opportunities enhance what is taught in school by extending student learning beyond the classroom and into the community and help foster the development of civic responsibility and a sense of caring for others.

Service learning can be an important vehicle for bridging the gap that often exists between students and schools, schools and communities, and students and communities. Besides the academic, social, personal, and career benefits to students, service learning activities benefit the school, the community, and the service learning partners. Table 6.4 (Lyday and others, 1998) summarizes these benefits.

Table 6.4.   Benefits of Service Learning

Benefits to School	Benefits to Community	Benefits to Partners
Makes curriculum relevant	Mobilizes youth as a resource of a common community	Provides needed resources
Develops students' responsibility for own learning	Addresses real community needs	Helps achieve partners' goals
Links school to community in positive ways	Builds good, productive citizens	Introduces next-generation leaders to the partners' important work
Develops problem-solving teaming, higher order thinking, time management, and other vital workplace skills	Promotes a "sense of community" for many students who do not have stability in their lives	Bonds agencies with schools and helps build new partnerships
Expands learning environment beyond the classroom	Develops next-generation leaders	Provides opportunities to enhance public image
Motivates reluctant learners	Develops an ethic of service and commitment to the community	Introduces students to career options in partners' area of service
Promotes problem-solving and conflict management skills	Provides shared responsibility for student learning	Gives the partnership a different lens through which to view and assess its work
Helps reduce school problems: behavior, attendance, tardiness	Helps nurture and train the future workforce	Challenges some ingrained ways of doing business
	Makes economic sense	Infuses youthful vitality
	Helps build healthy communities	

Service learning activities can be designed for students of all ages, kindergarten through adults. There are three basic types of activities: direct service, indirect service, and advocacy. The three types are distinguished by the purpose of the activity, the clients to be served, and the method of service delivery.

1. *Direct service* activities require the student to come into direct, personal contact with the recipients of the service. This type of service is often the most rewarding to students, since they are directly involved with the recipient and receive immediate feedback. Direct service also requires the strongest partnerships and greatest amount of planning and preparation, since students must have the knowledge, skills, and attitudes needed to make the experience beneficial for everyone involved. Examples include working with senior citi-

zens, reading to or tutoring another person, and serving meals to the homeless.

2. *Indirect service* activities are easier to manage because students work behind the scenes, and much of the work can be done at school. This type of service might include collecting toys at holiday time, landscaping the schoolyard, cleaning up a vacant lot, or gathering needed items for a homeless family. The required partnerships are more loosely structured than those required for direct service and do not require the same rigor of scheduling, coordination, training, and supervision.

3. *Advocacy* requires that students lend their voices and use their talents to eliminate the causes of a specific problem. Students work to make the community aware of a problem and attempt to get the community involved in seeking a solution. This type of service might include research on a community problem; the development of brochures and pamphlets related to the problem; a series of presentations to other students or community members; a concerted effort to influence political, personal, or community decision making. The partnerships can range from loose coordination with a single agency to a complex array of relationships with multiple community groups. (Decker and Decker, 2003, pp. 135–136)

The service learning project model also affects the nature of the partnership between the school and the agency or organization. In a one-shot model, teachers and students link one service project to their classroom studies, requiring coordination with one agency, one time, on a given date. In an ongoing project, teachers and students link service to their classroom studies on a regular basis throughout the semester or the school year.

Ongoing, direct service projects require continuing communication, interaction, and planning with the agencies and clients involved. In the student placement model, students—individually or in teams—complete internships in a set number of hours in agencies and organizations over the course of the semester or school year, and the agency becomes the students' classroom. The school-agency partnership is more involved, requiring contact, contracts, and written agreements between the school and partnering agencies to ensure meaningful experiences for both the students and the agencies in which they serve.

Many types of service-learning opportunities are possible, but successful programs appear to have common characteristics. *Students in Service to America,* a guidebook from the Corporation for National and Community Service (2002) offers the following hallmarks of effective programs: service activities should be sustained for a minimum of 40 hours over the school year; projects should have specific learning objectives so that students make strong connections between their learning and experience and the curriculum; service learning should be presented as a civic responsibility and there should be adequate time for discussion and reflection; students should be given the opportunity to take leadership and decision-making roles; and mutual goals should be agreed on by all partners.

In 2000, the W. K. Kellogg Foundation, a longtime supporter of service learning, appointed the National Commission on Service-Learning (2002) to study the state of service learning in U.S. schools. Researchers spent a year reviewing research data, visiting schools, and questioning students, teachers, and other advocates in order to determine the prevalence and practice of service learning. The results of this comprehensive study were summarized in the report, *Learning in Deed: The Power of Service-Learning for American Schools.* The commission concluded that service learning is a low-cost, high-impact way of addressing the problems of academic and civic disengagement and recommended: "Every child in American primary and secondary school should participate in quality service-learning every year as an integral and essential part of his or her education experience" (p. 6).

The report notes that, according to the National Center for Education Statistics, nearly one-third of all public schools—and nearly half of all high schools—were organizing service learning as part of their curriculum in 1999. Despite rapid growth, however, the number of schools offering service learning is still limited, and in many of these, only a few teachers participate. The majority of American primary and secondary school students still lack the opportunity to participate in this demonstrably effective means of promoting scholarly achievement and overcoming academic and civic disengagement.

Municipal Partnerships

Municipal leaders in many American cities are beginning to emphasize smart growth policies that encourage in-fill and investment in urban neighborhoods. New self-sustaining neighborhoods are being designed to allow residents to live, shop, work, eat, and educate their children in one location (Brown, 2004a). As a result, municipal involvement in education is growing because city leaders have begun to understand the nexus between economic development, livable neighborhoods, and community schools. In several cities, public schools are becoming an integral part of the neighborhood improvement and revitalization in which cities are investing (Brown, 2004b).

The two largest national municipal organizations, the U.S. Conference of Mayors and the National League of Cities, have made public school improvement part of their agenda. A report from the National League of Cities' Institute for Children and Families (Hutchinson, 2004) suggests that mayors and council members can use their office to:

1. Bring community partners together to monitor school improvement progress and leverage their resources to support schools.
2. Facilitate ongoing communication and trusting relationships among district leaders to lay the groundwork for collaboration and minimize "turf" issues.
3. Advocate for equitable school funding.
4. Create after-school programs to provide safe havens and enrichment opportunities.
5. Turn schools into the center of community life by keeping schools open beyond traditional school hours.

Although it can be challenging for city leaders to plan strategically with other organizations, especially when organizational goals are different and there are at least two bureaucracies to manage, many city leaders are willing to try to surmount these obstacles and work toward a school system that is built on collaboration and actually benefits the whole community (Brown, 2004a).

Public Schools and Community Development Partnerships

Public schools are increasingly becoming partners in community development efforts. The U.S. Department of Education's National Clearinghouse for Educational Facilities, an online research portal, has shown the links between public school facilities and smart growth, sustainable development, and community engagement (Chung, 2005). Public schools are emerging as invaluable partners for community development practitioners on an array of fronts, from enhancing urban revitalization efforts to providing community-oriented spaces.

Chung (2005) points to several trends that have helped accelerate the process.

> In recent years, the nation's school-age population has risen dramatically, and many communities have been challenged to accommodate a growing number of children. At the same time, the nation is facing a school facilities crisis. Many of the country's aging public schools, particularly in low-income urban areas, are in need of capital improvements and modernization. The demand for school facilities is creating intense competition for land and other resources, especially for other community needs, such as affordable housing, parks, and community centers. Out of necessity, some community development practitioners, planners, and public school officials are beginning to combine and coordinate school and community development efforts. Today, whether driven by need or inspired by research, community-based organizations are becoming increasingly involved in the development and support of public schools, generating partnerships that achieve broader community development goals. (p. 3)

According to Chung, the strategies linking schools and community development organizations generally fall into onsite and offsite categories. In onsite strategies, community development organizations directly affect the school—its size, shape, use, location, staff, and student body—in ways that benefit the community. Offsite, or indirect, strategies link nearby community development efforts to a school.

Onsite strategies include:

1. *Public school facility development.* Community developers can use their real estate and development expertise to support a school district's efforts to build more neighborhood-oriented school facilities. They can also use their expertise to assist in the rehabilitation and enhancement of existing school facilities.

2. *Sustainable development.* In-fill strategies can be used to curb "school sprawl"—the trend to build new schools in outlying areas that are disconnected from existing neighborhoods. Community developers can work with local government and school officials to promote smart-growth projects, ranging from building small-sized schools with rooftop playgrounds to the adaptive reuse of buildings and the preservation of historic school facilities.

3. *Joint use.* Community groups can promote the shared use of facilities by schools and other community entities, including the use of public schools as community centers.

4. *Economic development.* Schools are often the largest institutions and employers in a neighborhood, and community developers can tap into their economic influence by linking schools with the local business community and labor force. Some communities are partnering with schools to provide job-training and trade school classes for community members.

5. *Youth development.* Community developers can create neighborhood service-learning opportunities and after-school programs for youth that benefit both schools and communities.

Offsite strategies include:

1. *Affordable housing development.* School quality can have a significant impact on the local housing market, with healthy, stable neighborhoods supported by healthy schools. Developers of affordable housing can enhance the long-term viability of their projects by investing in the quality of nearby schools. Community developers can make neighborhood improvements near a public school to attract families and qualified teachers to a neighborhood, or to increase support for mixed-income housing projects.

2. *Transportation.* Community development organizations can work with schools to alleviate neighborhood traffic concerns and create

safe walks and bike trails for students. They can also advocate for the placement of schools within walking distance of residential areas and transit stops.

3. *Community building.* School reform advocates and community organizing groups can work together to create a unified and comprehensive neighborhood strategy. In cases where there are school closures, school officials and neighborhood groups may organize to advocate keeping the facilities open for other community uses.

Other School-Community Partnerships

Other kinds of school partnerships with community agencies and organizations respond to the recognized need for more school-readiness programs, before-school and after-school enrichment and recreation programs, childcare, and the cooperative delivery of health and social services. An increasing number of initiatives promote the concept of school-community partnerships that turn public schools into full-service community centers that are open all day, all week, year-round, with on-site health and dental clinics, mental health counseling, childcare, extended-day programs, tutoring, adult education, parent education, cultural programs, and summer camp. The daytime academic curriculum is integrated with before-school, after-school, and evening programs, and the schools are open to everyone in the community—children, siblings, teens, parents, and other adults.

Practical examples of successful school-community collaboration can be found throughout the nation. In Chicago, a Community Schools initiative is surging forward with a plan, launched in 2001, to have 100 K–12 community schools in place by 2007. This initiative involves a network of schools, community organizations, businesses, individuals, and other stakeholders who are committed to placing schools at the center of neighborhoods. These new community schools are overseen by a coalition of parents, school personnel, and community partners. Academic success is emphasized, as well as social and health needs. A school resource coordinator ensures that the needs of the community are addressed by the social, health, and educational services provided to the children and their parents. An external evaluation of the schools is currently underway, developed by the Department of Education at the University of Illinois. Early results indicate that 81% of the schools registered improved scores on a statewide test, and, although evaluators are cautioning that it is too early to make substantial claims, there also appear to be reductions in mobility and truancy. This initiative clearly holds great hope for a collaborative system of integrated services that can be replicated in other cities (Chicago Public Schools, 2005).

In California, a not-for-profit agency, New Schools Better Neighborhoods (NSBN), is transforming the planning and service delivery for schools being built in high-need areas to a joint-use and community-centered approach. NSBN serves as a third party intermediary to manage collaborative partnerships between school board officials, community-based organizations, and the business community. A memorandum of understanding drawn up between all partners spells out their agreement to invest staff and resources in a collaborative effort to leverage funds. Key elements of this initiative include smaller, full-service schools, joint-use and multipurpose facilities, an early childhood education component for each school, after-school opportunities, and an emphasis on community engagement. NSBN already has several success stories, the most notable being in Westlake, an impoverished neighborhood near downtown Los Angeles (NSBN, 2005).

In Washington DC, a group of school and community-based groups have come together in a collaboration called BEST (Building Educational Success Together, 2005). The group is led by the 21st Century School Fund and supported by the Ford Foundation. BEST has created a set of model policies to create and support schools as centers of the community, improve facilities management, and secure equitable funding for school facilities. The policies, designed for potential adoption by state legislatures, encourage community partnerships, joint use of facilities, and the locating of new schools within existing communities.

A PRESCRIPTION FOR ACTION

Schools cannot alone address the increasingly complex and diverse needs of families and communities. The need for collaboration is obvious, and developing collaborative relationships should be an important part of a school's comprehensive educational plan. Such collaboration is not developed overnight and must build on the success of other attempts to use community partnerships to meet educational goals.

Planning and organization are essential to success in all types of partnerships and collaborative initiatives. It is crucial not to lose sight of the fact that collaboration takes place among people, not institutions. *People must be the focus of every collaborative effort.*

Don Davies (2002), founder of the Institute for Responsive Education, examined national school reform efforts over the last few years and offers a prescription for action for those educators, parent leaders, and policymakers who are now ready to build the partnerships they have talked about. Davies' plan for action consists of seven recommendations:

1. *Teachers and principals.* Teachers and principals make or break any effort to form partnerships among families, schools, and communities. However, plans for partnerships are often developed with little or no teacher input, and principals are often directed by central office to just do it. Top-down management dooms the partnership effort from the start.

2. *Democratic principles.* Successful partnerships require attention to the essential elements of the democratic process, including recognizing different interests and respecting all participants regardless of color, religion, or educational status. Various methods of conflict resolution—mediation, negotiation, and compromise—are also necessary aspects of the democratic process. Partnerships also mean power sharing. Realistic and workable ways must be found to involve parents and other community representatives in planning, establishing policy, and making decisions regarding educational issues.

3. *Reaching out to parents.* Schools that are friendly and welcoming have an easier time creating good, workable partnership programs. However, making schools attractive and friendly is not enough if educational equity and high standards are the goals. Schools must reach out to those who are thought of as hard to reach. A variety of approaches are necessary and often include recruiting and training parents and other community residents to visit homes to offer information about the schools, academic standards, and how families can support children's learning at home; reaching out by teachers, prin-

cipals, and parent coordinators to family members in community settings rather than waiting for them to come to the school; and offering services to meet family needs through the school's working with health and social service agencies and then communicating with families about education matters.

4. *Grassroots activism.* A revival of parent activism is a key element in rebuilding support for public schools and persuading more schools and districts to make the necessary changes so that all of their students can achieve higher academic standards.

5. *Both choice and voice.* Parent choice is a legitimate and important part of the process of empowering parents and improving schools, as is giving parents an effective voice in decision making. As many reasonable opportunities for choice as possible should be developed, but only within the public school framework, such as magnet and alternative public schools, schools-within-schools, cross-district transfers, and early access to postsecondary education. For parent choice to be genuinely empowering, special steps must be taken to inform families about what they need to know in order to make informed choices.

6. *Increased family responsibility.* With parental power comes increased parental responsibility. In order to close the huge gaps between white and minority children, and between middle-class children and those with lower social status, it is important to spread the responsibility between the home and the community as well as to the school. However, assigning more responsibility to low-income and minority families must be backed up with major efforts to help these families meet their responsibility for rearing and educating their children.

7. *Linking school reform and community development.* Public schools often reflect conditions in their neighborhoods and surrounding communities. Neighborhoods and communities are seldom able to stay healthy and attractive without good schools. Linking schools and community development is important because achieving educational equity requires progress in the areas of access to affordable housing, good health care, jobs, transportation, and safe streets, and in the reduction of alcohol and drug abuse.

Davies emphasizes that his plan is really a plea for changing the culture of schools, so that partnership becomes a way of life that offers benefits to all of the partners and becomes a tradition, not a funded one-time project. He adds two cautions, one for educators and one for partnership advocates.

[*A caution for educators.*] If partnership programs are to be worth the effort, time, and money that they require, they must be able to demonstrate in tangible ways how they contribute to increasing the social and academic development of children in school. This means that programs must be (1) carefully designed, with the participation of all those affected by them; (2) based whenever possible on research evidence; (3) faithfully executed; (4) objectively evaluated; and (5) sustained over time.

[*A caution for partnership advocates.*] Partnerships with families and communities are not the whole answer to school reform that is geared toward equity. They are not a substitute for well-trained, well-paid, and effective teachers and administrators; good books and materials; diverse instructional strategies; commitment to high standards of academic content; good, varied tools for assessing student achievement; ample time for student learning; and safe, orderly, and well-managed schools. Partnership is not the whole answer, but it is one important strategy for school reform. (p. 389)

REFERENCES

Birmingham, J., Pechman, E. M., Russell, C. A., and Mielke, M. (2005). *Shared features of high-performing after-school programs.* Policy Studies Associates. Retrieved April 21, 2006, from http://www.sedl.org/pubs/fam107/fam107.pdf

Brown, P. M. (2004a). The promise of school-based mentoring programs. *Community Education Journal, 17,* 3/4.

Brown, P. M. (2004b). The role of municipal leadership in community education and school improvement. *Community Education Journal, 18,* 1/2.

Brubach, A. (2004). *Sustainability: Principles of collaborative leadership.* Retrieved January 23, 2006, from http://cadca.org/CoalitionsOnline/article.asp?id = 459

Building Educational Success Together. (2005, March). *BEST school facility model policies.* Coalition for Community Schools Conference.

Charles Stewart Mott Foundation. (2005). *Afterschool programs: Giving hope to all our children.* Remarks by William S. White, President. Retrieved January 19, 2006, from http://www.mott.org/21cclc.pdf

Chicago Public Schools website. (2005). *After school and community school programs.* Retrieved January 19, 2006, from http://www.cps.k12.il.us

Children's Aid Society. (2002). *Fact sheet on after-school programs.* Retrieved April 20, 2006, from http://www.childrensaidsociety.org//media/file/Fact sheetafterschool.pdf

Chung, A., and Hillsman, E. (2005, May). Evaluating after-school programs. *The School Administrator.* Retrieved April 21, 2006, from http://www.aasa.org/publications/saarticledetail.cfm?ItemNumber = 2516&snItemNumbe = & tnItemNumber = 951

Chung, C. (2005, Winter). Connecting public schools to community development. *Communities & Banking.* Federal Reserve Bank of Boston. Retrieved April 21, 2006, from http://www.bos.frb.org/commdev/c&b/2005winter/Public.pdf

Commercialism in Education Research Unit. (2004). *Virtually everywhere: Marketing to children in America's schools.* Education Policy Studies Laboratory, Arizona State University. Retrieved September 22, 2005, from http://www.asu.edu/educ/epsl/CERU/CERU_2004_Annual_Report.htm

Corporation for National and Community Service. (2002). *Students in service in America: A guidebook for engaging students in a lifelong habit of service.* Retrieved January 19, 2006, from http://www.studentsinservicetoamerica.org/download/guidebook.pdf

Council for Corporate and School Partnerships. (2001). *Guiding principles for school and business partnerships.* Retrieved January 19, 2006, from http://www.corpschoolpartners.org/pdf/guiding_principles.pdf

Davies, D. (2002). The 10th school revisited: Are school/family/community partnerships on the reform agenda now? *Phi Delta Kappan, 83,* 5.

Decker, L. E., and Decker, V. A. (2003). *Home, school, community partnerships.* Lanham, MD: Scarecrow Press.

Edelstein, F. (2006). *Mayoral leadership in education: An action guide for success.* U.S. Conference of Mayors. Retrieved March 29, 2006, from http://www.usmayors.org/74thwintermeeting/edguide2006.pdf

Education Policy Studies Laboratory. (2004). *Virtually everywhere. Marketing to children in America's schools.* Retrieved April 21, 2006, from http://www.asu.edu/educ/epsl/CERU/Annual%20reports/EPSL-04090103-CERU-exec.pdf

ERIC Clearinghouse on Educational Management. (2001). *Can schools befriend businesses without compromising their mission?* ERIC information: Policy report. Eugene, OR: University of Oregon. Retrieved April 21, 2006, from http://eric.uoregon.edu/publications/newsletter/fal101.html

Forum for Youth Investment. (no date). Leadership and political will. *Moving an out-of-school agenda, task brief #6.* Retrieved April 20, 2006, from http://www.nsba.org./site/pdf.asp?TP=/site/doc//1180/11717.pdf

Hart, J. K. (1913). *Educational resources of villages and rural communities.* New York: Macmillian.

Herrara, C. (1999, September). School based mentoring: What and why. *Public/Private Ventures.* Retrieved January 30, 2006, from http://www.ppv.org/ppv/publications/assets/35_publication.pdf

Hutchinson, A. M. (2004). *Municipal leadership in education yields results.* Retrieved February 19, 2006, from http://www.nic.org/content/Files/IYEF-strongerschoolsreport.pdf

Hutchinson, A. M., and Van Wyngaardt, D. (no date). *Stronger schools, stronger cities.* National League of Cities. Retrieved April 20, 2006, from http://nlc.org/content/Files/IYEF-strongerschoolsreport.pdf

Keleher, T., and Morita, J. (2004). *Building community power for better schools.* Chicago, IL: Applied Research Center.

Kussmaul, D. L. (2005, May). President's corner: Make every minute count. *The School Administrator.* Retrieved October 5, 2005, from http://www.aasa.org/publications/ssarticledetail.cfm?ItemNumber=25280

Lashway, L. (2003, July). *Role of the school leader.* Retrieved January 26, 2006, from http://eric.uoregon.edu/trends_issues/rolelead/index.html#providing

Lyday, W. J., Winecoff, H. L., and Hiott, B. C. (1998). *Connecting communities through service learning.* Columbia, SC: South Carolina Department of Education.

McLearn, K., Calasanto, D., and Schoen, C. (1998). *Mentoring makes a difference—Findings from the Commonwealth Fund.* Retrieved January 23, 2006, from http://www.cmwf.org/publications/publications_show.htm?doc_id=230658

Molnar, A. (Ed.). (2002). *School reform proposals: The research evidence.* Retrieved January 19, 2006, from http://course1.winona.edu/lgray/e1625/SchRef_Proposals/ExecSumm.html

National Association of Elementary School Principals (NAESP). (2001a). *Leading learning communities: Standards for what principals should know and be able to do.* Retrieved January 10, 2006, from http://www.naesp.org/client_files/LLC-Exec-Sum.pdf

National Association of Elementary School Principals (NAESP). (2001b). *Principals and after-school programs: A survey of pre K–8 principals.* Retrieved January 30, 2006, from http://www.naesp.org/ContentLoad.do?contentId=952

National Association of Partners in Education. (2000). *Partnerships 2000: A decade of growth and change.* Alexandria, VA: National Association of Partners in Education.

National Association of Partners in Education. (2001). *Seven stage partnership process: Creating and managing highly collaborative development of community-school partnerships.* Alexandria, VA: National Association of Partners in Education.

National Commission on Service-Learning. (2002). *Learning in deed: The power of service-learning for American schools.* Columbus, OH: Ohio State University.

National Mentoring Partnership. (2005). Mentoring immigrant youth. *Mentor.* Retrieved January 30, 2006, from http://www.mentoring.org/program_staff/index.php?cid=63

National PTA. (2004). *National standards for parent/family involvement programs: An implementation guide for school communities.* Bloomington, IN: National Educational Service.

New Schools Better Neighborhoods. (2005, December/January). New Schools Better Neighborhoods shows that a new model can work in Los Angeles' Westlake neighborhood. *The Planning Report.* Retrieved August 15, 2006, from http://www.planningreport.com/tpr/?module=displaystory&story_id=1051&edition_id=61&fo

Peterson, T. K. (2005, May). Leveraging the after-school value added. *The School Administrator.* Retrieved October 4, 2005, from http://www.aasa.org/publications/saarticledetail.cfm?ItemNumber=2514&snItemNumber=&tnItemNumber951

Phi Delta Kappa/Gallup Poll. (2005). *The public's attitudes toward public schools.* Retrieved January 10, 2006, from http://www.pdkintl.org/kappan/k0509pol.htm

Points of Light Foundation. (2003). *Starting a volunteer program in an organization.* Retrieved January 19, 2006, from http://www.pointsoflight.org/downloads/pdf/VolunteerProgramPlanning.pdf

Saskatchewan Education. (1999). *Parent and community partnerships in education: Policy framework.* Regina: Saskatchewan Education.

School Communities That Work: A National Task Force on the Future of Urban Districts. (2002). *Developing effective partnerships to support local education.* Providence, RI: Annenberg Institute for School Reform. Retrieved April 21, 2006, from http://www.schoolcommunities.org/archive/portfolio/effect_partnerships.htm#intro

Smith, H. (2005). *Report card on America's schools.* Retrieved January 6, 2006, from http://www.pbs.org/makingschoolswork/hyc/report.html

Suarez-Orozco, C., and Suarez-Orozco, M. M. (2001). *Children of immigration.* Boston, MA: Harvard University Press.

U.S. Department of Labor, Bureau of Labor Statistics. (2005). *Volunteering in the United States, 2005.* Retrieved January 10, 2006, from http://www.bls.gov/news.release/volun.nr0.htm

Withrow, F. (with Long, H., and Marx, G.). (1999). *Preparing schools and school systems for the 21st century.* Arlington, VA: American Association of School Administrators.

Websites for More Information and Links to Other Relevant Sites

America's Promise, www.americaspromise.org

Association for Volunteer Administration, www.avaintl.org

Charles Stewart Mott Foundation, www.mott.org

Children's Aid Society, www.childrensaidsociety.org

Coalition for Community Schools, www.communityschools.org

Community Partnerships for Adult Learning, www.c-pal.net

Corporation for National and Community Service, www.nationalservice.gov

Energize Especially for Leaders of Volunteers, http://energizeinc.com

National Association of Elementary School Principals, www.naesp.org

National Association of Partners in Education, http://www.napehg.org

National Dropout Prevention Centers, www.dropoutprevention.org

National Network of Partnership Schools, http://www.csos.jhu.edu/p2000

National PTA, www.pta.org

National Service Learning Clearinghouse, www.servicelearning.org

National Youth Leadership Council, www.nylc.org

U.S. Department of Education, www.ed.gov

U.S. Department of Labor, Employment and Training Administration, www.doleta.govschools/resources.htm

Youth Serve America, www.servenet.org

Chapter Seven

School Public Relations— Bridging the Gap

Public relations (PR) is defined as the art and science of building relationships between an organization and its key audiences—relationships that influence attitudes and bring about desired behaviors. It is a management function focused on presenting the organization in all its complexities to its publics and interpreting the publics' impressions of the organization through a variety of information-gathering and feedback methods.

Chance (2005) explains the relationship-building process in terms of systems theory, in which a system has four basic components: inputs, process, outputs, and feedback loops. *Inputs* encompass information from the external environment, such as laws, policies, community values, and resources. *Process* involves dialogue, teaching, and problem solving that result in some decision or change. *Outputs* are the result of the processes, and *feedback* is provided from the outside environment based upon external perception of the output.

Many people believe that *public relations* and *publicity* are synonyms; they are not (Wikipedia, 2005). Publicity is an important tool in the public relations professional's kit, but it is not the only tool. Wikipedia defines *publicity* as "activities designed to generate favorable coverage of a product, service, candidate, etc., in the print, broadcast, and online media. The most widely known and used techniques are the press release, press conference, interview, and planted article" (Public Relations vs. Publicity section, para. 1).

Wikipedia also notes that PR is often misused as synonymous with unscrupulous efforts to deceive. However, like other disciplines, PR is in itself neither good nor evil.

SCHOOL PR

The National School Public Relations Association (NSPRA) substitutes the word *educational* for *school* in its definition of school PR.

> Educational public relations is a planned, systematic management function, designed to help improve the programs and services of an educational organization. It relies on a comprehensive, two-way communication process involving both internal and external publics with the goal of stimulating better understanding of the role, objectives, accomplishments, and needs of the organization. Educational public relations programs assist in interpreting public attitudes, identify and help shape policies and procedures in the public interest, and carry on involvement and information activities which earn public support and understanding. (NSPRA, 2005, Why Do You Need section, para. 1)

NSPRA also offers a shorter definition: "Educational public relations is management's systematic, continuous, two-way, honest communication between an educational organization and its publics" (Why Do You Need section). Gallagher and others (2005) note that it is NSPRA's contention that sound and constructive relationships between the school and the community are outcomes of a dynamic process that combines:

1. A way of life expressed daily by staff members in their personal relations with colleagues, students, parents, and people in the community.
2. A planned and continuing series of activities for communicating with both internal and external publics about the purposes, needs, programs, and accomplishments of the school.
3. A planned and continuing series of activities for determining what citizens think of the schools, and the aspirations citizens hold for the education of their children.
4. The active involvement of citizens in the decision-making process

of the school and school-initiated community outreach programs so that essential improvements may be made in the educational program and changes made to adjust to social change. (p. 13)

THE NEED FOR SCHOOL PR

Armistead (no date) quotes Tolley, former vice president of public affairs for the Chrysler Corporation as having said, "All institutions live or die by public opinion." Armistead stresses that, while this is obviously true of corporations, it also applies to schools as they "try to deal with pressure groups, governmental mandates, declining budgets, greater demands, and the fallout from societal pressures" (para. 1). He emphasizes that everyone connected with the school engages in public relations— intentionally or unintentionally—and contributes to the school's reputation. Therefore, "while schools don't have the choice of doing PR, they do have the clear choice of whether their total communication program is more positive or negative" (You Don't Have a Choice section).

> A public reputation for [a school] will emerge. It will come about as the result of a carefully-planned and attentively-managed program designed to present the school's positive qualities, or it will come from happenstance, accident and the tremendous influence of the community's grapevine. By not constructing a solid PR program, [school leaders] run the risk of having their school's public reputation created by others who may not have its best interests at heart. The question is not whether a school will have a public reputation, only who will create it. (concluding para.)

A public school's image depends on what its different publics think based on their experiences with the organization and their interpretation of what the school says and does. Because people's perceptions are based partly on objective characteristics and partly on subjective experiences and reactions, not all segments of the community may have the same image of the school. Newsom (2003) points out that "differences of opinion held by various publics produce a fragmented image, and the greater the difference, the more negative the image. When the image is very fragmented, credibility becomes a pivotal issue. People with no direct contact with the school often do not know whom to believe" (p. 41). He explains:

A significant element of the image problem, then, rests on the variety of opinions held by the publics and the sources of information and direct experiences that shape those opinions. Priority publics for schools typically include students, teachers, other employees, parents/guardians, nonparent residents, government officials, equipment suppliers, employers of students and former students, universities that prepare teachers, news media (mass and specialized), and school alumni (even of elementary schools). In many school districts, administrators attempt to communicate with only three of these publics—namely, parents, district employees, and students. (p. 41)

The findings of the Phi Delta Kappa/Gallup polls support the need for educators to engage in school public relations. The 1998 Phi Delta Kappa/ Gallup Poll (Phi Delta Kappa International, 1998) revealed that the schools to which people assign low grades do not exist. Respondents assign low grades to schools in general, or to schools in communities in which the respondents do not live—not to the schools they actually know. The low-rated schools are perceived to exist on the basis of information received from the media. Rose and Gallup (2005) note that the 2005 poll reached the same conclusion. They add, "[I]t seems necessary to comment on the important distinction between the nation's schools and schools in the community. These polls have repeatedly documented that the public has a low opinion of the nation's schools and a high opinion of schools in the local community" (Executive Summary, para. 3). This conclusion may give comfort to educators in terms of their own schools, but the pollsters warn that educators should not ignore people's perceptions that public schools in other communities are bad. Those perceptions may be based on superficial media impressions and misinformation, but they also point to the lack of high-quality, creditable information from school leaders.

The National School Boards Association (NSBA) (Texas Association of School Boards, no date) addressed the issue of inadequate and ineffective school public relations and the potential effect on public education.

There is a pervasive assumption across the United States that the public school system in this country is in crisis and that schools are failing to adequately educate a majority of children. This assumption has, in fact, become conventional wisdom and an unrefuted presumption; when the statement is made that public education and public schools are failing, there are few if any dissents. Even though the perception is often based upon half truths, misconceptions, and factual inaccuracies, the statement goes unchallenged. This perception of failure has led to a serious loss of support for, and belief in, the fundamental role of public education in this country. This loss of support and belief, if not addressed, could lead to the collapse of the American public school system. (para. 1–3)

The association believes that the perception of public education and public schools can be changed through a "concerted effort by educational leaders to [come] to grips with what we—as a county, state, and community—expect of our schools" (para. 7). School PR efforts must focus on prompting a more accurate dialogue among the public and in the media that results in more rational debates about education at the national, state, and local levels. "More honest and straightforward discussions will lead to a better understanding of the role education currently plays in our society. Ultimately, the program is aimed at rebuilding public support for a continually changing education system that is reflective of a continually changing society" (para. 8).

Newsom (2003) points out that unfortunately, too many educational leaders "cling to the idea that sharing selected information with parents, employees, and students constitutes a sufficient communication program. In doing so, these officials may actually be contributing to negative opinions that are more likely to flourish when various publics receive information in less than consistent ways and through a variety of channels" (p. 42). He stresses the need for school officials to understand the broad parameters of the modern practice of PR and the ways in which PR products enhance essential administrative functions. The value of school PR derives from the need for public schools to be open organizations that continuously exchange information with the communities they serve. For this reason, Newsom believes that the modern practice of PR must be infused into the overall administrative structure.

BUILDING SUPPORT FOR PUBLIC SCHOOLS

The NSBA refutes the assumption that the U.S. public education system is in crisis, but it does not deny that changes must be made if schools are to fulfill their mission of educating all children to their highest potential. The association (Texas Association of School Boards, no date) acknowledges:

> While schools are performing better than ever before, the speed at which they are changing to meet new demands has not been able to keep pace with the speed at which the demands themselves are changing. Expectations for schools have increased and diversified over the years. Some of these expectations have been inappropriately placed on schools. Others are appropriate, but we have not equipped [schools to fulfill] them. (para. 6)

According to NSBA, the reality is that if schools are to respond to the swift and substantive changes taking place in society and to the challenges for reform, educators and citizens together must create an environment of support so that public schools _can_ change and improve. "We must shift from bashing public schools to empowering continual public school change" (Texas Association of School Boards, concluding para.).

Research has shown that racial tension and conflict cut across social class boundaries, communities, and neighborhoods. Cooper and Chizhik (2004) argue that effective school reform initiatives will have to include dialogue related to race and racial diversity. They add that race is often a political issue and that, "exacerbated by rapid demographic changes, [it] still serves as a source of division" (p. 205). Cooper and Chizhik pose a series of questions that must be addressed in a dialogue between educators and community members: How do we disrupt the social reproduction of inequality in our schools? How do current policies and programs contribute to racially hostile learning environments? What structures contribute to an environment that fosters feelings of isolation, discrimination, and separation for certain groups of students? How can current curriculum be used to address race, diversity, and pluralism?

Thompson (2003) suggests eight principles that must be embodied in effective community engagement efforts:

1. _Reciprocity._ Those who are engaged and those who do the engaging share mutual commitments, responsibilities, and goals. Community engagement efforts are initiated with the intent to use what is learned in the process in ways that are truly responsive to the per-

spectives and priorities of the internal and external school community.

2. *Proactivity.* Community engagement should begin before a school or school system develops a mission and strategic direction, not just after; the educational mission and strategic direction should be informed by (and, to the greatest extent possible, owned by) educators and the wider community.

3. *Inclusivity.* To fulfill its basic purposes, community engagement must give voice and roles to the diverse constituencies that make up the community and the school system. This requires a demonstrated respect for all participants regardless of race, ethnicity, religion, class, or educational status, and respect for minority viewpoints.

4. *Institutional continuity.* Community engagement involves tapping into the wider community, but it also requires instituting roles for ongoing input (if not leadership) by teachers, parents, and other community members in the educational enterprise.

5. *Centrality.* Engagement of internal and external constituents is not a finite step in a larger process; it is an integral and continuous dimension of creating and sustaining collaborative learning communities.

6. *Coalition building.* Educational endeavors in any community have potential adversaries and potential allies. Influential people and groups who are positively engaged in the planning and implementing of education-related efforts are more likely to become allies.

7. *Ongoing communication.* Messages capturing a district's vision, goals, and priorities—in words that are simple, compelling, and free of jargon—should be in continuous circulation through formal and informal channels of communication, encompassing both internal and external stakeholders.

8. *Balancing listening with leadership.* Authentic leadership involves active listening. What is necessary is to define and defend a nonnegotiable core of values and priorities, while, at the same time, being responsive, inclusive, and collaborative in working out all that is negotiable. The very process of defining the nonnegotiable core is a critical opportunity for engagement through dialogue.

The Learning First Alliance, a permanent partnership of 11 leading national education associations, suggests that educators and others interested in promoting public education in their communities focus the dialogue on how to meet commonly held values. In *A Practical Guide to Promoting America's Public Schools* (2005), the alliance points out: "Educators are accustomed to talking about academics, student achievement, test scores, and other crucial issues that are the core of their work and the basis on which their schools are judged. But research suggests that educators should broaden their message by linking those issues to the vision and values the public holds for public schools" (para. 1).

The alliance suggests seven PR steps educators should use to build supportive partnerships:

1. *Values.* Connect the shared values most important to Americans—hard work, persistence, personal responsibility, and mutual respect—to your public schools. Parents and the public consider test scores one indicator of quality, but they also seek information about the intangibles of schooling that cannot be measured precisely.
2. *School discipline.* Reassure the public that schools take the issue of student discipline seriously. Do not underestimate the importance of Americans' demand for discipline and respectful behavior in schools. Many members of the public are concerned about day-to-day misbehavior that disrupts learning for everyone.
3. *Academics.* Talk about teaching "the basics plus," connecting the curriculum with students' preparation for a successful future. Americans strongly emphasize the need for public schools to teach "the basics," but for them this includes problem-solving skills and preparation for lifelong learning, a productive future, and engagement in the community as responsible citizens.
4. *Benefits of public education.* Describe public schools in terms of the concrete benefits they provide for individual children and for society.
   a. Benefits to children include:
      i. High-quality public schools give every child from every family the chance to learn the skills they need to be successful in life. Public schools are open to all and enable our children to go as far as their talent and hard work can take them.
      ii. Free public schools give every child the opportunity to succeed.

      iii. Most Americans who have worked their way out of poverty have been educated in public schools.

  b. Benefits to the community and the nation include:

      i. Children who get a good education are more likely to become productive members of society.

      ii. Healthy communities need strong public schools.

      iii. A strong national economy requires good public schools to develop new generations of productive employees, good citizens, creative entrepreneurs and innovators, and effective leaders in all fields.

      iv. America needs the best efforts and accomplishments of all our people. That is why we need to come together to support every public school.

      v. Without free public schools, problems like crime and welfare dependency would probably be much worse.

5. *Public information.* Give the public information—and be sure it is the right kind of information. The public wants information that lets them judge overall school performance. Parents also want information about how their own children are doing.

6. *Accountability.* Demonstrate commitment to fiscal accountability and transparency by showing how school funds are spent. Help parents and the public understand where school dollars go by breaking down costs into concrete items. Show how money is spent to support specific activities, materials, staff positions that benefit children, and children's education in the classroom.

7. *Parent involvement.* Acknowledge that parent involvement begins at home and express appreciation for parents who prepare their children to learn and behave respectfully and responsibly in school. Invite parents to be partners with the school to ensure that children succeed; offer ideas on what they can do.

Carlsmith and Railsback (2001) emphasize that school leaders must recognize that the public has changed from earlier generations:

The difference is that people today want to be a part of any changes that are planned at their local schools. . . . This means that to create a satisfying partnership with the community, one that will reap the reward of community support, educators must seek outsiders' input in areas that used to be the sole province of administrators: designing new assessments, approving new graduation requirements, setting standards, providing input on new constructions, hiring key staff, [etc.]. . . . And that is the public relations challenge: to sincerely accept and welcome public input, and to lose the insular tendency to deny outsiders' opinions, while still maintaining the integrity of an administrator's ability to be the final arbiter in any decision. It is a fine line, one that educators years ago did not have to walk. (pp. 9–10)

Simply put, school PR is not about letting everyone make decisions. It is about letting families and community members know that their input is valued and taken seriously, and that they are welcome and needed. How well a school leader is able to meet the school PR challenge will depend in large part on his or her ability to communicate—communicate to inform and develop high morale among staff members, communicate to build a team with families focused on the education of their children, and communicate to develop public support within the community and among elected leaders.

COMMUNICATION

The scope of successful school public relations has expanded from the mostly written communication of the past to a greatly increased need for face-to-face communication with a variety of publics. The process of communicating with others is not simple. George Bernard Shaw memorably observed, "The greatest problem of communication is in the illusion that it has been accomplished." From the perspective of a communicator, Freeman Teague, Jr., said, "Nothing is so simple that it cannot be misunderstood." Goethe put it this way: "No one would talk much in society if they knew how often they misunderstood others."

All types of communication, oral and written, have five basic components (Decker and Decker, 2003):

1. *Source:* the person with an idea to communicate.
2. *Message* (structure and content): what the person wants to communicate, expressed in words, gestures, and symbols.

3. *Channel:* how the idea is expressed: sight, sound, touch, smell, taste, or a combination; selecting the right channel is important if the idea is to reach the intended receiver.
4. *Receiver:* the person(s) to whom the message is directed. Considering the receiver's characteristics is crucial as the source develops the idea into a message and chooses a channel to express it.
5. *Effect:* an indication of whether or not the receiver understood the message. (p. 152)

Oral communication is also affected by nonverbal behaviors (Clark, 1997). Eye contact helps to regulate the flow of communication. It signals interest in others and increases the speaker's credibility. Facial expressions convey emotions. Smiling is a cue that transmits happiness, friendliness, warmth, and liking, and often makes people more comfortable and more willing to listen. Gestures capture the listener's attention, make the conversation more interesting, and facilitate understanding. Posture and body orientation affect how a message is interpreted. Standing erect and leaning slightly forward communicates to listeners that the speaker is approachable, receptive, and friendly, whereas speaking with one's back turned or looking at the floor or ceiling conveys discomfort or lack of interest. Cultural norms dictate a comfortable distance for interaction with others. Variations in tone, pitch, rhythm, timbre, loudness, and inflections help keep listeners' attention.

Successful oral communication involves the listener as well as the speaker. Listening is not the same as hearing. Hearing is involuntary and refers simply to the reception of aural stimuli. Listening is a selective activity that involves both reception and interpretation of aural stimuli; it involves decoding sound into meaning. Listening may be passive or active. Passive listening is little more than hearing. Active listening involves listening with a purpose; it requires the listener to attend to the words and feelings of the sender.

It has been suggested that an active listener listens first to what someone is *saying,* then tries to listen to what a person is *not saying* and to what a person *wants to say but does not know how.* What the listener perceives as being said is as important as what is actually being said. The listener's perceptions can affect both the meaning assigned to the words and the meaning of the complete message.

Effective communication occurs only if the receiver accurately understands the information or idea that the sender intends to transmit. Several kinds of barriers can keep the message from being understood in the way the sender intends. These barriers may be internal or external (Decker and Decker, 2003):

1. *Filters:* senders and receivers may have different opinions, concerns, or value systems.
2. *Jargon:* specialized terms, acronyms, or unfamiliar expressions.
3. *Semantics:* words that mean or imply different things to different people.
4. *Information overload:* too much information and/or not enough time to comprehend.
5. *Nonverbal behavior:* body language, facial expressions, gestures, proximity, vocal elements.
6. *Emotional climate:* fear, anger, hostility, or distrust. (p. 153)

The most effective communication channel is oral and face-to-face, especially one-on-one. The more people involved, the greater the chance that the message will not be received or will be misunderstood. Written communication, however carefully thought out and precisely worded, is more likely to encounter barriers—filters, semantics, and information overload. Thus, when the intent of the communication is to advocate or persuade, person-to-person exchanges, telephone calls, dialogues, or workshops are preferable. When the intent is to inform, mass media sources—media memos, newsletters, brochures, news releases, radio and television spots, videotapes, websites—may be viable options.

There is no single formula or style of communicating that works every time. The best approach depends on a number of factors including the type of communication and the characteristics of the targeted stakeholders. Cultural background, work schedules, and other individual differences influence the extent to which individuals are receptive and responsive to different types of communications. The Mid-Continent Research for Education and Learning (MCREL) (2003) suggests five guiding questions in the selection of communication methods:

1. Is information being delivered, or is dialogue needed?
2. What kind of information is being delivered?

3. Is the information sensitive or potentially confusing?
4. Is feedback needed?
5. What methods are most appropriate and effective for communication with stakeholders? (p. 1)

MCREL makes recommendations on three aspects of communication—the appropriateness of the method, the desirability of dialogue, and the clarity and accessibility of the message.

1. *Appropriate communication methods.* All communications are considered in terms of the tool or strategy that is most appropriate given the type of communication and the audience.
2. *Dialogue.* Many opportunities for dialogue with and among all stakeholders are available. School leaders and staff members reach out to stakeholders and create opportunities to exchange ideas, information, and perspectives.
3. *Clarity and accessibility.* Communications by all educators are consistently clear and free of jargon. There is an expectation that communications will be clear and accessible to stakeholders. School leaders model communicating in clear and accessible ways.

The National Academy for Superintendents presented a panel of active superintendents who were asked to address how their position and responsibilities have evolved over the past decade and what specific skills had changed the most. Panelist Ralph Johnson (2005) said that the function of communication had made the most profound shift and singled out three developments that contributed to that perspective. Johnson's arguments reflect MCREL's strategies for effective communication:

[First] communication became more effective when it flowed from the perspective of "we." In other words, messages, information, reporting, and discussion were all done acknowledging a broader community context. Messages were not just about "the schools"; messages were about the schools as part of the broader community, touching on the social, economic, religious, and governmental fabric of the whole civic tapestry. Educating the community on education's impact permeated every message.

Second, the type and frequency of communication . . . have drastically shifted because of the quality and number of competing messages from the media and the business world. Schools now compete in a sophisticated marketplace of ideas and media. Ideas and messages are subject to a process of natural selection whereby the strength of resonance sorts key ideas into a hierarchy of importance, sometimes crowding out schools. Schools and their messages can be left behind, or worse—their mission and function are being defined by others. Schools under-invest in communication.

Finally, the role of the staff as key "communicators" for the organization, and how each member manifests communication, emerged as an essential element. . . . This human factor brings a subjective quality to the definition of school communication. Teachers, administrators and even classified employees help to strengthen or weaken the school's "brand." Effective schools have their employees as ambassadors in a focused "on-message" way that promotes the mission and values of the schools. Acknowledging and developing those skill sets became a rapidly growing organizational priority. (pp. 7–8)

The Internal Public

Gallagher and others (2005) agree that in order to be effective a school PR plan needs a solid internal communications program. They point out that administrators must recognize that they alone cannot gain continued public support for education; they must enlist the help of those directly connected to the school and doing so requires a structured internal communications program. They emphasize that a good internal communication program must be a priority because a good external communication program cannot survive without it.

The school's internal public includes all those directly connected to and affected by the school and its operation: the professional and support staff, students, and families. These are also the people who affect the internal climate of a school. Their importance cannot be overstated. Their actions and personal relationships not only affect student achievement and staff morale, they create the public image of a school and the type and level of community support a school enjoys.

Woodland (2001) believes that without a core emphasis on staff communication, a school's image is doomed. He stresses that public confidence in a school is highly influenced—positively or negatively—by the school's faculty and support staff. He asserts that the conclusion of the 1988 Phi Delta Kappa Commission on Developing Public Confidence in

Schools—that the employees of a school rank first as the general public's information sources and are the most powerful determinants of a school's image—is even truer today than it was in 1988. To many people, the staff *is* the school.

Every school staff member—from administrator and teacher to nurse, custodian, bus driver, and contract worker—needs to know his or her importance as a member of the school PR team and needs to believe that responsibility for creating good PR is within their job description. A school PR plan needs to contain provisions for (1) orientation of staff to their respective roles in PR, (2) ongoing staff development on how to enhance public confidence in schools, and (3) ongoing sharing of information about programs, program changes, new directions, etc., to keep all staff up to date and informed.

Obviously, the school PR plan should also include provisions for keeping students and families informed. They, too, have a vested interest in high-quality PR because of the importance of good community-school relations in carrying out the mission of the school: the academic success of all children.

The External Public

To say that everyone who is not part of a school's internal public is part of its external public sounds simplistic, but it is true. Some people—alumni, volunteers, and others who have some kind of a collaborative relationship with the school—may perceive themselves as having an indirect or secondary connection to a school. Others may think that they have little or no connection to public schools and therefore have no reason to support them.

A comprehensive PR program must include strategies directed at all segments of the external public to build and maintain the conviction that everyone in the community benefits from the academic success of all children. Whether or not community members believe that a school is able to carry out its mission of educating all children—or is at least making progress toward carrying out that goal—depends on how well the school's PR program has informed its external public, appropriately involved them, sought their opinions or invited them to participate in decision making, and provided them with opportunities to be of service to the school.

Image Matters

Marketing consultants often advise clients that image is more important than reality, because image—the sum of perceptions, attitudes, beliefs, ideas, and feelings about something—makes people act in certain ways and shapes their attitudes toward a product, service, or organization. Whether perceptions or beliefs about a school or school system are deserved or undeserved, positive or negative, they in large measure determine the strength or weakness of public support for education.

Image matters. But as Woodland stresses, "[G]ood public relations is not about making everyone think you are wonderful" (Open and Accountable, para. 2). The one overriding, paramount reason to do school public relations is to encourage "involvement in the education process and support for student achievement" (Open and Accountable, para. 2).

Because image does matter, one of the first steps in developing a school's PR program is finding out what the community's image of the public school actually is. As PR consultant William Harms (Newquist, 2004) points out, good PR begins with the cost-free investment of thoughtful evaluation of all interactions and communications with the public by everyone connected to the school. Good PR should be something everyone involved with a school is practicing every day.

Harms stresses that careful attention should be paid to assessing communications. He notes that the tricky part is knowing what the various stakeholders want to know and what they will perceive as propaganda. A school can begin improving its PR by evaluating everyday communications. Newquist (2004) warns: "The biggest public relations budget in the world won't matter if your school projects a poor image in its most basic communications" (Return Those Phone Calls section, para. 1) and suggests the following self-examination:

1. How are people treated when they call the school? Is the person answering the phone courteous, friendly, and helpful?
2. If there is a voice-mail system, how well does it work? Do callers get led through a frustrating phone maze? Most important of all, if a caller leaves a message, does the call get returned and if so, how promptly?
3. How often are meetings held? Are they accessible? Are families and

community members notified well in advance? Most important, is time allowed for audience discussion?

4. Is the community notified of school events? Are families given enough notice so they can arrange schedules to attend?
5. How well do teachers and administrators communicate with families? Does the communication take into consideration any language and cultural issues, as well as the other barriers to family involvement? Is the communication meaningful, clear, and engaging?

Assessing a school's image benefits the school staff in several ways. It requires a school to look at both its internal and external publics and systematically identify community perceptions so that planning can be based on fact, not speculation. It helps to build better PR by letting community members know that their opinions are important. It provides school staff with baseline data to measure long-term increases in support, monitor changes in image over time, and keep in touch with the opinions of key community groups.

The techniques for assessing a school's image are similar to those used for conducting a needs assessment. The objectives should be clearly defined, written, and formally agreed upon. The research design should be realistic and achievable, involving decisions on whether data will be collected just from targeted groups or from a sampling of the entire community. The design should ensure that the desired information is gathered in the most judicious, expedient, cost-effective, and reliable manner possible. This may involve a blending of qualitative and quantitative methods.

Carroll and Carroll (2001) stress that public schools need to practice *outside-inside* marketing so that strategies and resulting actions are based on information and data coming from the community to the school, not on decisions often made in isolation in a faculty meeting. Decision making should not be "an insular process, occasionally interrupted by poorly attended public hearings" (para. 2). Educators need to systematically assess the needs, wants, perceptions, preferences, and satisfaction of the total community using such techniques as surveys, focus groups, and in-depth interviews. Carroll and Carroll point out that "using such strategies builds long-lasting, meaningful relationships with the community and fosters a loyalty to the public school. Relationship building is the key to getting and keeping community support, and to do this, public schools must start 'outside' with their communities" (para. 3).

Based on data collected in an image assessment, a school can develop a plan to enhance the impact of positive factors and decrease that of negative ones. The planned actions and supporting data must be communicated to the targeted groups.

MARKETING COMMUNICATIONS

A school's PR strategies should include marketing communications—that is, communications directed at persuading the external public of the value of supporting public education in general and a specific school in particular. Marketing communications are tools used to persuade; their major purpose is to provide information to, and develop a relationship with, community groups.

There are three basic types of marketing communications: advertising, publicity, and personal contact. Advertising includes traditional methods—purchased time or space and outreach materials, such as fact sheets, brochures, newsletters, and videotapes. Publicity includes newspaper and magazine articles, press releases, radio and television coverage, discussion panels, guest appearances, and other special efforts. Personal contact involves one-on-one discussions, public speaking, special events, and tables or booths at community gatherings.

SOCIAL MARKETING

According to Weinreich (2003), social marketing began as a discipline in the 1970s, when Kotler and Zaltman realized that the same marketing principles that were being used to sell products to consumers could be used to sell ideas, attitudes, and behaviors. Social marketing employs general marketing strategies to deal with social issues and to affect behavioral change. It differs "from other areas of marketing only with respect to the objectives of the marketer and his or her organization. Social marketing seeks to influence social behaviors not to benefit the marketer, but to benefit the target audience and the general society" (para. 2).

Weinreich explains that in social marketing, as in commercial marketing, the primary focus is on the consumer—learning what people want and need—and the message speaks to the consumer, and is not about the product. The planning process takes this consumer focus into account by addressing the four elements of the *marketing mix: product, price, place* (distribution), and *promotion*—often called the Four P's of marketing. Social marketing adds a few more P's: *publics, partnership, policy, politics,* and *purse strings.*

The following is a discussion of the social marketing mix in the context of a campaign to generate support for educational partnerships.

Product. A continuum of products exists, ranging from tangible, physical products, to services, practices, and less tangible ideas. The product or program must have benefits that are recognizable by those who are participating. In order for a product to be viable, people must first perceive that they have a genuine problem or need, and that the product offered is a good solution. It takes research to discover consumers' perception of the problem or need and the product, and to determine how important they feel it is to take action toward achieving a solution.

Price. There is always a *cost* involved in efforts to increase participation in a program. This cost may be monetary or may require the consumer to give something intangible, such as time or effort, or risk disapproval. If the cost outweighs the benefit for an individual, it is unlikely the product will be adopted. The cost-benefit ratio may not be clear-cut. If a product is priced too low or is free, it may be viewed as low in quality. If the price is too high, some people may not be able to afford it. It should be remembered that language may be a cost on the part of the marketer as well as the consumer when it is a barrier to communication.

Place. Place describes the way the product reaches the consumer. For a tangible product, it is the distribution system. For an intangible product, place refers to decisions about the channels through which consumers are reached. An element of place is determining how to ensure accessibility. Messages need to be in places where the target audience will see or hear them. Research may be needed into audience demographics in order to match a target group's characteristics with the most effective media. Holding meetings at convenient times in comfortable locations and creating a friendly and positive atmosphere promote open communication and meaningful sharing. A variety of approaches should be tried. When a simple, clear message is repeated in many places and formats throughout the community, it is more likely to be seen and remembered.

Promotion. Because of its visibility, promotion is sometimes mistakenly perceived as comprising the whole of social marketing, but it is only one element. The focus is on creating and sustaining a demand for the product. Research is needed to determine the most effective and efficient methods to reach the target audience and increase demand. Promotion may be conducted through one-on-one contact, advertising, PR, promotional samples, media advocacy, public service announcements, or any other *selling* vehicle. Social marketers need to be aware of any competing messages that are being directed at the target audience. Environmental factors may affect people's reaction, political changes may require a new approach, news events may change the context in which people hear the message, and efforts of other agencies or organizations may affect how the message is received. All products, promotional material, and services should be test marketed with a target audience to gauge their potential effectiveness. Forums and surveys are common methods of assessment.

Publics. Social marketers usually have to address a variety of different audiences, or publics, if the program is to be successful. *Publics* refers to both the external and internal groups involved in the program. There is no such thing as selling to the general public. Target audiences must be segmented into groups that are as homogenous as possible, and messages must be created for each segment. Some target audiences may be reached more successfully when the message comes through a secondary group.

Partnership. Education, social, and health issues are so complex that no one agency can offer a total solution. Teamwork in the form of agency cooperation and collaboration is needed to be effective. Research is needed to determine which agencies and organizations have similar goals and to identify ways in which they can work together in partnership toward the solution of a problem or the fulfillment of a need. By pooling resources with other agencies and organizations working to achieve a goal, social marketing programs can increase their impact as well as gain access to new audiences.

Policy. Social marketing programs can motivate individuals, but support may be difficult to sustain unless the environment in which the product is offered is supportive for the long run. Often policy changes are needed.

Politics. The issues addressed by social marketing programs are often complex and frequently controversial. Some political diplomacy may be needed to gain community support, get access to a target audience, or deal with potential adversaries.

Purse strings. Most organizations that develop social marketing programs operate through funds provided by such sources as foundations, government grants, or donations. A strategy concerning where to get money to create and maintain the program must be in place.

Evaluation must occur throughout the social marketing process. As a program is developed, messages and products must be tested with members of the target audience and refined as needed. When the program is implemented, activities must be monitored and assessed to determine whether they are functioning as planned. Periodically, the program must be evaluated to see whether it is having its desired effect. The actual impact of a social marketing program may be difficult to assess accurately, especially in the short run. However, at whatever level the evaluation is performed, the information gained should be used to improve the program in the future.

WORKING WITH THE NEWS MEDIA

Schools deal with two things very dear to most people: their children and their tax dollars. People want to know how well schools are teaching students, and they want to know how their tax dollars are being spent. Studies consistently show that the prime sources of information about the school are students and newspapers. As the number of households with children in school continues to decrease, the power of the press to influence public opinion about schools continues to increase. Newsom (2003) points out that in some school districts, fewer than 20% of households have children in school and thus any direct source of information. The other 80% probably rely heavily on the news media for information about the schools.

The result of the 37th Phi Delta Kappa/Gallup Poll (Rose and Gallup, 2005) documented the power of the media to influence the public's perception of public education and public confidence in schools. The poll and other studies underscore the need for educators to work with the media to ensure that attitudes toward schools are not based on misinformation or misunderstanding. Working with the news media is only one part of a school's overall public relations plan, but it is such an important part that expending time and effort to do it well can pay big dividends. Doing it poorly can have disastrous effects. Public confidence takes a long time to build but only a short time to destroy.

According to Gallagher and others (2005), "[T]he astute administrator will not underestimate the power of the press. Appreciating the power of the press, the administrator then must understand the role of the press in its dealing with the public schools" (p. 196). The reality is that the press believes it has a responsibility to report on all public institutions, including public schools. Accountability requires educators to show where the money is going and taxpayers want answers on how schools are being run, so it is imperative that school leaders work with reporters to ensure that they are knowledgeable about school activities, achievements, and problems.

> School officials should know the state law on the public's right to know. School administrators who are aware of the reporter's right to information can save themselves and their schools severe embarrassment. Too frequently school officials refuse reporters information that is eventually made public when a court intervenes. More damaging than the harm done to the relationship with the reporter is the mistrust generated by hiding the facts. (pp. 196–197)

One of the facts that school leaders—both new and experienced—know is that, like it or not, they will have contact with the news media on a fairly regular basis. Working with the media involves a variety of encounters, from a full-scale news conference to a brief telephone call. Unfortunately, most educators have little or no communication and PR training. Carlsmith and Railsback (2001) state that "[m]any are uncomfortable in 'selling' themselves and their services" (p. 6). However, the fact is that schools must promote themselves, because an absence of facts makes it possible for rumors and misinformation to circulate as fact. The authors point out that a trained communication, marketing, or public relations professional is the best way to ensure effective PR. If a trained professional is not available, the job must be delegated to a person who has the resources and ingenuity to undertake the PR function, form PR goals and objectives, plan strategies, and be accountable to school leadership.

Gallagher and others (2005) also stress that each school and school system should identify one person who will be the media liaison with full responsibility for media relations. The media relations director for a school system should work directly with the superintendent, hold a position in the school system's cabinet, and be involved in and informed about the details of all programs and important decisions. The designated person should have the authority to speak for the school system on any issue that might arise and to call on others for their knowledge and expertise as needed.

Harms (Newquist, 2004) reminds school leaders that, whether a school hires someone to manage PR or decides staff members can handle it, it is important to give PR the attention it deserves. He points out what should be obvious: if there is to be good, consistent press coverage, the person handling PR responsibilities must take the time to know reporters, develop a trust relationship and a reputation for honesty, and demonstrate a willingness to help reporters do their job.

In an orientation guide for new school spokespersons, Mullen (1999) recommends that, in addition to taking time to get to know media personnel, the spokesperson define three positive points—facts, issues, or messages—that he or she wants everyone to know about the school. In deciding which messages to promote, the spokesperson should think of how various issues of the day affect community members, identify school strengths and vulnerabilities, brainstorm with others, and keep saying *why?, so what?,* and *prove it!* until three positive points are identified. Next, the spokesperson should anticipate reporters' questions by making a list of questions that have been asked in the past or could be asked, including questions he or she hopes not to get. Then the spokesperson should practice answering them, making sure to find a way back to the three positive points. Finally, the spokesperson should personalize responses as much as possible, using the words *we* and *you,* and keeping in mind the 10 C's that describe a good source: concise, candid, conversational, clear, correct, calm, compassionate, compelling, complete, and credible.

Gallagher and others (2005) offer practical tips for working with print or broadcast media:

1. Compile a directory of key news contacts. Know each reporter's audience and what kind of stories are most likely to interest a particular reporter.
2. Know what is news. Talk to reporters to improve your understanding of what constitutes news. Answering the question, "How many readers will this item interest?" will help determine whether it is newsworthy.
3. Be available when negative news occurs. Be prepared to tell the facts of the situation and how the school intends to respond.
4. Answer questions honestly. Be sure that what you say is true. Avoid educational jargon. Stick to the facts and do not speculate. Don't be afraid to say "I do not know the answer, but I will call you back." Be sure to respond as promptly as possible.
5. Be accurate, although it may sometimes be unnecessary to be precise. When all the figures and details are not available, an approximation may suffice.
6. Remember that "no comment" is a comment. The words imply that the speaker has something to hide or is condescending. If you cannot answer a question, tell the reporter and explain why.
7. Remember talking to a reporter "off the record" means that you are offering information for their knowledge but that it is not for publication. Talking off the record can be risky unless the trust relationship is very strong.
8. Be fair to all media. Distribute even the most routine news releases at the same time to all media outlets and do not inadvertently time the releases to give one news organization an advantage over others.
9. Be sensitive to reporters' deadlines.
10. Don't blame reporters for things they cannot control. A reporter

generally has little or no control over whether a story will actually be used; how a story is positioned and presented in relation to other stories; the length of a story, either in print space or air time; deletions that are made because of time or space constraints; and the headline and presentation.

11. Remember that reporters, like educators, occasionally make mistakes. If an error occurs in a story, it may mean a reporter misunderstood something you said. Keep in mind that good reporters base their livelihoods on their credibility.

In working with the news media, it is helpful to keep in mind that anyone who expects fair, balanced, accurate, interesting coverage by the media must be fair, balanced, accurate, and interesting with the media. Both schools and the news media need to understand that occasional conflict is a fact of life. Mutually productive relationships should be sound enough to weather the storms of controversy.

KEY COMMUNICATOR NETWORK

Many schools' PR plans include a strategy for using another group of people besides news media personnel to bridge the gap between the school and the community. Often called "key communicators," these are supportive people—internal and external—who are kept well informed about the school. Their job is twofold: (1) to spread accurate and supportive information quickly to other members of the community, and (2) to serve as listening posts in the school and community, alerting school administration to rumors and concerns. They should represent a cross section of the community. A key communicator can be almost anyone who is respected and listened to in his or her circle of contacts, regardless of the size of the circle. They may be business people, regular volunteers, bus drivers, crossing guards, substitutes, parents of students and former students, former students themselves, interested citizens, etc. Within the school, they are often secretaries and custodians. Students may also be key communicators.

Holliday (2003) explains that key communicators are the people in the community that friends, relatives, and neighbors listen to and trust, especially in times of change or crisis. He stresses that school leaders should identify the people who are key information sources for the community and get to know them well. Key communicators can keep school leaders updated on the perspectives of various segments of the community. When a change is planned or a problem arises, they are the people who must be given the facts immediately so they can pass along accurate information.

All communities have opinion leaders. As school communities become increasingly diverse, the use of key communicators is a relatively easy and inexpensive way to reach out to all of the school's publics. Carlsmith and Railsback (2001) point out that key communicators are especially effective when a school or district is trying to reach a non-English-speaking community. Bilingual community members can pass information back and forth in ways that benefit both the school and the community.

The Oregon School Boards Association (OSBA) (2005) emphasizes that no matter how sophisticated and well planned a school's or school district's communications programs may be, the community grapevine is the way a large portion of school news gets around. OSBA observes that as a communication system, the grapevine is frequently unreliable and goes only one way; setting up a key communicator network is a simple way to mitigate the grapevine problem, according to OSBA. A key communicator system can actually harness the power of the grapevine because people tend to believe friends and neighbors more than they believe the media or publications. (Research shows that mass communication generally does not change minds but only reinforces existing positions, thus activating opposition as well as support. In addition, the media usually report the ideas of others.) OSBA explains why key communicators, or opinion leaders, are critical:

> A well-organized, one-on-one campaign targeting opinion leaders anticipates issues and discourages attacks by going straight to the people who bring issues to the media. . . . [O]pinion leaders are critical for a simple, but seldom expressed reason. Publics, or groups, don't act *en masse*. They follow leaders who are pacesetters. These persons jump-start behavior within the group. Left to their own devices, publics may choose to be led in any direction. The choice is whether or not to influence this direction. (Why section)

OSBA suggests five beneficial effects of formalizing a key communicator network:

1. A person-to-person program enables school officials to establish two-way communication and thus to be able to get a quick pulse of the community.
2. The program helps to bridge the distance between school officials and the community—community members get to know school officials as individuals, not as figureheads in a central office or boardroom.
3. Regular communication to key opinion leaders increases opportunities to convey positive accomplishments of the schools.
4. The program provides a mechanism for rumor control and grapevine correction, because the facts about volatile issues or confrontations can be quickly communicated to opinion leaders.
5. Communicating negative news or problems to key communicators conveys candor and openness and ultimately establishes credibility.

The Principal's Partnership (no date) says that the principal must be the face of the school even though the operational duties of the key communicator network may be assigned to another staff member. The partnership recommends these steps in establishing a network:

1. Bring together a small group of trusted people who are knowledgeable about all segments of the community to brainstorm a list of opinion leaders—those who have people power, not position power. That list will be the foundation for the network.
2. Create a realistic list from all the names gathered, making sure that all segments of the community are represented and the number is small enough to be manageable.
3. Send a letter with a response form to the potential members inviting them to a meeting to discuss the concept. Explain the goal of creating a communications group to help the community understand the challenges, successes, and activities of the school. Stress that the key communicator network will not take an inordinate amount of anyone's time.
4. Make follow-up phone calls to those who do not return the response form, especially those who will be important to have in the network.
5. Start the first meeting by explaining that those in the audience have been invited because they are respected community members who

are known to care about the education students are receiving. Describe the school's objectives in organizing the key communicator network—(a) to provide network members with honest, objective information about the school; (b) to encourage network members to deliver this information to others in the community when they have an opportunity; and (c) to listen to questions or concerns community members might have about the school and report them to the person in charge of the network so they can be dealt with.

6. Establish a newsletter specifically for the key communicators. The newsletter should include new information and when appropriate, respond to rumors by providing the facts.

7. After the first year, send out a short evaluation form or schedule a meeting to discuss how the network is working and how it might be improved. Emphasize the importance of the perceptions of the network.

USING TECHNOLOGY

While technology cannot replace face-to-face communication, word processing, e-mail, voice mail, faxing, videoconferencing, paging, chatting, web surfing, and CDs and DVDs have become common tools for communicating ideas and accessing information. Electronic communication provides 24-hour public access to school information and allows the school to communicate the same message in different languages. Homework hotlines and e-mail to and from teachers enable two-way communication not constrained by geography or time.

For PR personnel, the Internet can be a powerful tool. A school's website can deliver messages incorporating text, audio, graphics, still pictures, animation, and full-motion video. It can deliver virtual-reality environments in which services or products can be demonstrated and educational facilities toured. The Internet can deliver, in real time, interactive and customized messages to any type of public.

Studies show that people are increasingly turning first to the Internet for information. Paine (2002) points out:

The biggest difference between the web and traditional media is its interactive nature. Thus, it becomes a perfect medium for building relationships with your publics. In chat rooms and on websites, around the world or in your neighborhood, dialogue is occurring daily, even hourly, with constituencies, customers, and prospects, as well as enemies. The goals of all those dialogues are the most basic public relations objectives: to educate, convince, win over, make aware, and persuade. (Relationship Building section)

Paine also notes that the web can be used effectively in reactive crisis management. Schools can develop "crisis communications" websites to turn on when necessary. The sites should contain contact information and background data, as well as current information.

Machine translation is a technology that automatically translates text from one language to another. An IBM report (Booth, 2002) on emerging technologies underscores the fact that machine translation is continuously being improved. As of 2002, nine language pairs were supported: English to/from French; English to/from Italian; English to/from German; English to/from Spanish; English to/from Simplified Chinese; English to/from Traditional Chinese; English to/from Japanese; English to Korean; and English to Brazilian Portuguese. The report emphasizes that:

> The source and/or the target language medium might be text or speech, but most [machine translation] systems work with text. If speech source or speech target is of interest, then speech recognition or speech synthesis modules could convert speech to or from text, and the machine translation could work with the text form. . . . Machine translation is particularly useful for translating web pages, email, and chat. It not only translates the text, but it also carefully preserves links and pictures and renders fonts nicely in the target text. (Machine Translation section)

Slowinski (2000) points out that a number of web- and computer-based technologies are breaking the barrier to multilingual communication. He notes that, although online translation is not always accurate, it is a useful tool for language learners and provides effective support for learning and communication.

Technology can contribute to academic achievement for all students, but, as Valdez and Svedkaustkaite (2002) point out, "[T]he benefits of technology are even greater for students with limited English proficiency. Not only can they gain . . . new knowledge but they also increase their

English language use at the same time" (The Power of Language section). Valdez and Svedkaustkaite list several free online translation services:

1. Babelfish translation, babelfish.altavista.com
2. Mezzofanti translations, www.mezzofanti.org/translation/index .html
3. SYSTRAN, www.systranlinks.com/systran/cgi (The Power of Language section)

Valdez and Svedkaustkaite also note the availability of collaborative and cross-cultural "email pals." They mention two sites: International Education and Resource Network (www.iearn.org) and ePALS Classroom Exchange (epals.com).

Slowinski (2000) also points out two multilingual search engines: AltaVista Digital can search for websites in 25 languages, and Euroseek can find resources in 29 languages. He notes that many other search engines support language resources on the web and urges school administrators and teachers to identify the languages used by their students at home and look for search engines in these languages.

The growth in local cable television has given rise to a variety of local community-produced programs and provides yet another means of communicating with local audiences. Local cable television can be used to attract new attention and promote dialogue about school issues. Local cable shows enable school leaders to communicate regularly with various audiences at relatively low cost.

Technology is also being used to create "virtual schools." In one project, part of a National Science Foundation initiative, the College of Human Relations and Education and the Computer Science Department at Virginia Tech University in Blacksburg, Virginia, are working with county schools to develop a network-based virtual school. In another venture, Blacksburg residents are being linked into what is called an "electronic village." The idea is to link community members to each other, to information sources, and to worldwide networks. The Blacksburg Electronic Village (BEV) (no date) is a collaborative project involving the town government, Virginia Tech University, and the regional telephone company. BEV services provided to the community include electronic mail, technical support for users, dial-up modem access to the Internet, direct connections in local offices and apartments, online polls and referendums, classes, and training about how to use the Internet.

GETTING A PR PROGRAM STARTED

The role of school PR is to maintain mutually beneficial relationships between the school and the many publics it serves. The NSPRA (2005) emphasizes that each school and school district has "its own unique way of carrying out this role, but there is one common element in all successful public relations programs: they are planned." According to NSPRA, exemplary PR programs follow a four-step process:

1. *Research:* up-front analysis of where the school or district stands in regard to all the publics it wishes to reach.
2. *Plan:* developing an action plan related to the public relations goals, objectives, and strategies that go hand-in-hand with the school's or the district's overall mission and goals.
3. *Communicate:* performing the tasks necessary to meet the goals and objectives.
4. *Evaluate:* judging the effectiveness of actions taken and determining what changes are needed in the future. (School Public Relations Plans, para. 3)

The process for developing a comprehensive school PR program is similar to the process used in the development of any strategic plan. It should:

1. Be strategic in that it contributes to the school's and school district's mission and overall objectives.
2. Market the school and the district and their educational values, as well as their programs, facilities, and services.
3. Focus on both internal and external publics, especially targeting those stakeholders with whom public relations need to be improved.
4. Be part of a schoolwide and a districtwide effort that supports and is supported by other organizational functions (i.e., operation, programming, home-school-community outreach efforts).

5. Recognize that the success of public relations and ultimately the entire home-school-community partnership initiative depends on the quality and strength of the relationship with all of the community's educational stakeholders, with an emphasis on long-term satisfaction.

6. Be viewed, budgeted, and evaluated as an investment, not as an expense. (Decker and Decker, 2003, p. 173)

A detailed PR plan should have eight integrated components: (1) the organization's mission, goals, and objectives; (2) a needs/situation assessment; (3) PR objectives; (4) internal and external populations, including segmentation, targeting, and positioning; (5) the mix of strategies; (6) budget; (7) implementation plan; and (8) evaluation. The NSPRA and the NSBA can supply reference materials and written examples. Most large school systems are willing to share their plans and offer assistance to smaller districts. A school or school district may also use an advisory committee that represents educators, students, families, businesses, and community members in all their diversity.

In spite of compelling evidence of the importance and effectiveness of PR, many school boards have not yet adopted a school PR policy or employed a full- or part-time PR person. Budget constraints may be blamed, but the real reason may be that, despite the evidence, PR is not viewed as a priority. When PR is deemed a priority, creative resource allocation and staffing can usually be formulated. In larger districts, it is not difficult to justify the hiring of at least a part-time PR coordinator with an adequate operations budget. In smaller districts or at the local school level, the superintendent or principal may have to personally perform many of the PR tasks, especially those needed on a regular basis. However, even in those cases it is usually possible to designate several people—from staff or the community—to be responsible for specific aspects of the plan. For example, a staff member could be given time to write a newsletter and news releases. Trained volunteers could be used to conduct surveys and publicize student and staff achievements. Students could be trained to research community opinions and attitudes, providing valid data to a public relations coordinator.

STEPPING FORWARD

Bob Chase, former president of the National Education Association, has quoted a bumper sticker that says, "Change is good. You go first." Increasingly, schools and school districts are daring to go first with new ideas and initiatives to revitalize public schools. Many are reaching out to families, social service agencies, businesses, and the public in general to build broader support for their mission. Central to their public relations efforts is the concept of keeping the "public" in public education and involving the community in raising the child.

Jean Johnson, executive vice president of Public Agenda (2005), notes the strong differences in public opinion about what public schools should be doing to help children achieve their potential and warns that addressing these deeply human differences requires genuine give-and-take among people inside and outside of education. Only by "engage[ing] broader swaths of the public—and doing it in more human, tangible ways—will [schools] engender positive results," (para. 7) she believes. She recommends Public Agenda's program, Education Insights, which works with schools and communities to build open, consensus-seeking environments.

A variety of PR efforts are starting to bridge the gap that separates schools and communities. One technique—initiating conversations with the public—is gaining popularity. Schools are using town meetings and community forums as a means to take the public's pulse on education issues. Some local forums are patterned on forums sponsored by Phi Delta Kappa (2004) in cooperation with the Center for Education Policy and the National PTA. These forums are structured around three fundamental questions: (1) What are the purposes of the public schools? (2) How effective are the public schools in achieving those purposes? (3) What changes are necessary to make the public schools as effective as we want them to be?

Education leaders should raise these questions in their communities at every opportunity, recognizing that effective educational reform requires inclusive visioning and planning. However, as Kowalski (2005) cautions, democratic processes require citizen involvement and activities that inevitably reveal or accentuate philosophical differences that may lead to conflict. He stresses that successful public involvement requires "both effective leader communication and a comprehensive public relations program producing credibility, confidence, reciprocity, goodwill, continuous two-way communication and social harmony" (p. 226).

REFERENCES

Armistead, L. (no date). Public relations and the high school principal. *The Principal's Partnership.* Retrieved April 11, 2005, from http://www.principals partnership.com/feature1003.html

Blacksburg Electronic Village. (no date). *Blacksburg electronic village: Digital library.* Retrieved April 10, 2006, from http://www.bev.net/about/research/digital_library/planning.php

Booth, A. (2002). *Extending the reach of enterprise application with transcoding and machine translation.* Retrieved April 6, 2006, from http://www.128.ibm.com/developerworks/websphere/library/techarticles/0206_booth/booth.html

Carlsmith, L., and Railsback, J. (2001). *The power of public relations in schools.* Portland, OR: Northwest Regional Educational Laboratory.

Carroll, S. R., and Carroll, D. (2001). Outside-inside marketing. *School Administrator* web edition. Retrieved April 10, 2006, from http://www.aasa.org/publications/saarticledetail.cfm?ItemNumber = 3504

Chance, P. L. (2005, Spring). Engaging communities through vision development: A systems approach to public relations. *Journal of School Public Relations, 26,* 2.

Clark, D. (1997). *Big dog's communication and leadership.* Retrieved April 10, 2006, from http://www.nwlink.com/~donclark/leader/leadcom.html

Cooper, R., and Chizhik, E. W. (2004, Spring). Talking about race in schools post-Brown: A public relations challenge. *Journal of School Public Relations, 25,* 2.

Decker, L. E., and Decker, V. A. (2003). *Home, school, community partnerships.* Lanham, MD: Scarecrow Press.

Gallagher, D. R., Bagin, D., and Moore, E. H. (2005). *The school and community relations.* New York: Pearson Education, Inc.

Holliday, A. E. (2003). Communicating on a peanuts budget. *The School Administrator.* Retrieved April 10, 2006, from http://aasa.org/publications/saarticle detail.cfm?ItemNumber = 1774

Johnson, J. (2005, November 8). It's time to address the human factor in education reform. *School Board News.* Retrieved November 18, 2005, from http://publicagenda.org/aboutpa/aboutpa_articles_detail.cfm?list = 25

Johnson, R. (2005, Winter). Observation from the National Academy for Super-intendents: Three shifts in thinking toward better school communications. *Journal of School Public Relations, 26,* 1.

Kowalski, T. J. (2005, Summer). Broadening research on communication and school public relations. *Journal of School Public Relations, 26,* 3.

Learning First Alliance. (2005). *A practical guide to promoting America's public schools.* Retrieved April 10, 2006, from http://www.learningfirst.org/publications/pubschools

Mid-Continent Research for Education and Learning. (2003). *Communication.* Retrieved February 1, 2006, from http://www.mcrel.org/pdf/LeadershipOrganizationDevelopment/5031TG_commfolio.pdf

Mullen, M. (1999). How to work with media reporters. *Journal of Educational Relations, 20,* 3.

National School Public Relations Association. (2005). *Public relations.* Retrieved April 10, 2006, from http://www.nspra.org/main_schoolpr/

Newquist, C. (2004). Public relations 101: How-to tips for school administrators. *Education World.* Retrieved April 5, 2006, from http://www.educationworld.com/a_admin/admin/admin123/.shtml

Newsom, D. (2003, Winter). When "community relations" won't cut it: PR for public schools. *Journal of School Public Relations, 24,* 1.

Oregon School Boards Association. (2005). *Key communicator network.* Retrieved April 6, 2006, from http://www.osba.org/commsvcs/kcnetwrk.htm

Paine, K. D. (2002). *Measures of success for cyberspace.* Retrieved April 6, 2006, from http://www.instituteforpr.org/pdf/2002_onlinemeasurement.pdf

Phi Delta Kappa International. (1998). *The 30th annual Phi Delta Kappa/Gallup poll of the public's attitudes toward the public schools.* Retrieved November 17, 2005, from http://www.pdkintl.org/kappan/kp9809-a.htm

Phi Delta Kappa International. (2004). *Forums on the public schools.* Retrieved April 10, 2006, from http://pdkintl.org/advocacy/forums.htm

Principal's Partnership. (no date). *Key communicator network.* Retrieved April 6, 2006, from http://www.principalpartnership.com/keycommunicator.doc

Rose, L. C., and Gallup, A. M. (2005). The 37th annual Phi Delta Kappa/Gallup poll of the public's attitude toward the public schools. *Phi Delta Kappan, 87,* 7.

Slowinski, J. (2000). Breaking the language barrier. *Electronic School.* Retrieved February 3, 2006, from http://www.electronic-school.com/2000/01/0100f3.html

Texas Association of School Boards. (no date). *Supporting schools: Building support for public education.* Retrieved April 10, 2006, from http://www.tasb.org/schools/building

Thompson, S. (2003, Fall). Community engagement: Moving from words to action. *Journal of School Public Relations, 24,* 4.

Valdez, G., and Svedkaustkaite, A. (2002). Tecnología para todos: Using technology to break through language barriers in schools. *Learning Point.* Retrieved February 3, 2006, from http://www.ncrel.org/info/nlp/lpf02/todos.htm

Weinreich, N. K. (2003). *What is social marketing?* Retrieved April 10, 2006, from http://www.social-marketing.com/Whatis.html

Wikipedia, The Free Encyclopedia. (2005). *Public relations.* Retrieved November 11, 2005, from http://en.wikipedia.org/wiki/Public_relations

Woodland, B. (2001, August). Beyond image: Learning-based communications. *School Administrator* web edition. Retrieved April 10, 2006, from http://www.aasa.org/publications/sarticledetail.cfm?ItemNumber = 3498

Websites for More Information and Links to Other Relevant Sites

IASB: Community Relations, www.ia-sb.org/communityrelations

Institute for Public Relations, www.instituteforpr.org

National School Public Relations Association, www.nspra.org

Public Relations Society of America, www.prsa.org

Chapter Eight

Community Relations in a Political Context

Public schools were once universally recognized as a vital part of the community, educators were viewed with respect, and the general public believed in the power of public education to uplift and improve the society. Today, the power of public education is questioned and, in many communities, public schools are struggling for public support. Social changes and pressures and the complexities of modern life are undoubtedly responsible for some of the decline in the prestige of public education, but the AASA (2005) suggests that politics has also played a large role.

> Over the course of the past twenty years public education has been served up as "failing" by those eager to see its downfall. . . . Why has public education gone from a positive issue, around which members of both major political parties have coalesced for years, into a target for Washington domination of this most local of institutions? Much of the credit can be taken by those who have manipulated public opinion through speeches, newspaper and television interviews and editorial opinion, and an endless barrage of expensive print and electronic media advertisements. (para. 2, 4, 5)

AASA points to the passage of the No Child Left Behind Act as evidence of the success of these efforts. "With the passage of the No Child Left Behind Act—a law that uses a negative concept as its reason [for being]—those who seek the downfall of public education now have a tool that virtually guarantees a system that will lead to the 'failing' label for nearly every school system in the nation" (para. 3).

Sugarman (1997) believes that one reason anti-public education efforts have succeeded is that child welfare and education organizations have failed to give cohesive political support to congressional representatives who are committed to children's issues. "Advocates continued to believe that reliance on data, reason, and virtue in advocacy [is] sufficient to win support as distinct from hard political infighting. Similarly, there has been a continuing failure to rally child advocacy organizations to common causes" (para. 2). Sugarman says that local school leaders have not been—but could be—important catalysts in developing consensus among those interested in children's issues.

POLITICAL REALITIES IN EDUCATION

Today, no one seriously disputes the proposition that politics plays a significant role in decisions about schools and educational practices. Many people in the community have a stake in education—even if they see it only as an expenditure of their tax dollars—so it is not surprising that they want a voice in the ongoing debate about schools. Even in communities that are committed to equal opportunity for all children, meeting that commitment almost inevitably involves money—public money—and therefore controversy. Such things as early childhood education, smaller classes, expanded technology, more comprehensive social services, etc., are all expensive, and it is a reality that *any* decision about the expenditure of public money involves politics and the community power structure.

Schools and educators are expected to remediate society's social and economic ills, but if their attempted reforms fail to produce quick fixes, critics may make scapegoats of them, as evidenced by the fact that the average tenure of big-city school superintendents is less than three years. Keedy and Björk (2001) state that the superintendency, now more than ever, is a political position.

Still, the proposition that educators should stay out of politics is strongly rooted in the profession and continues to be espoused by some school leaders.

Overtly political efforts to move an agenda forward, build coalitions of support and, when needed, force concessions which encourage broad-based community involvement are more and more the standard [rather] than the exception. Still, political engagement remains, in many administrators' thinking, an intrusion in the business of schooling. Much remains to be done to move these educational leaders away from thinking that the nobility of their mission guarantees public support. . . . Recognition that confidence in the schools comes as much from influential individuals and political support as it does from student outcomes is a concept many educators only grudgingly accept, if at all. (Berg and Hall, 1999, p. 8)

Berg and Hall warn that if educators do not become political players, they will be at the mercy of the political system.

Educators need to understand political power—where it comes from and how it can be used to improve schools. Not only must educational leaders engage in politics, they must be active in efforts to create widespread community engagement in politics. "Acting alone, professional educators have neither the leverage nor the political capacity to conceptualize or implement the changes needed, to build the necessary broadbased coalitions, or to attract the substantial human and financial resources required" (Hale and Moorman, 2003, p. 2).

POLITICS

In his definitive publication, *Reweaving the Fabric* (1993), Cortes examines the strategy for using power and politics in rebuilding the quality of life in primarily poor and moderate-income communities that have seriously deteriorated. He explains that politics is about collective action initiated by people, it is "about relationships enabling people to disagree, argue, interrupt one another, clarify, confront, and negotiate, and through this process of debate and conversation to form a compromise and a consensus that enables them to act" (Importance of Political Renewal section, para. 2). It is this process that enables people to change the nature of schools—or any other institution—recreating and reorganizing the way in which people, networks, and institutions operate.

If the process of debate and conversation is to lead to consensus, people must be given the opportunity to develop practical wisdom and the kind of judgment that includes understanding and responsibility. Cortes argues, "In politics, it is not enough to be right, that is, it is not enough to have a position that is logically worked out; one also has to be reasonable, that is, one has to be willing to make concessions and exercise judgment in forging a deal" (Importance of Political Renewal section, para. 2). Understood in this sense, decisions made by voting are "not to discover what people want, but to ratify decisions and actions the political community has reached through argumentative deliberations" (Importance of Political Renewal section, para. 2).

Keedy and Björk (2001) believe that the political process is an institutional centerpiece within a democratic society and essential to the viability of local schools. They point out that educators, especially superintendents, encounter three types of politics, which they label participatory, partisan, and patronage. *Participatory* politics occurs when group membership is fluid and alliances are ad hoc and reflect the complex and changing interactions among interested groups and individuals. *Partisan* politics encompasses circumstances in which distinct political groups or parties compete over educational issues. *Patronage* politics occurs in a context in which programs, jobs, or funds are allocated or withheld on the basis of personal affiliations.

Citizen Politics

Politics in the American democracy is the give-and-take, messy, everyday work of citizens themselves. Politics is the way citizens deal with public problems—the issues of their common existence—in many settings, not simply through government. It is the way people *become* citizens—accountable players and contributors. Contained in the broad meaning of citizenship is the "concept of citizen as a creative, intelligent, and above all 'political' agent in the deepest meaning of the word *political*—someone able to negotiate diverse views and interest for the sake of accomplishing some public task" (Boyte, 2002, para. 11).

Mathews (2002) suggests that three gateway questions be answered before Americans take the first step toward becoming political citizens. Each question is generated by an immediate problem or by a growing awareness of a threat to everyday life. The gateway questions are:

1. *Is this a problem that affects me?* People have to find a connection between the problem they hear about and their own sense of what is

valuable—"valuable" going well beyond financial—before they will get involved.

2. *Can I do anything?* When citizens find a handle—something they can do personally—they usually become convinced that they might make a difference, and this sense of possibility engenders political energy.

3. *Who will join me?* At the same time that people are trying to find out whether they can make a difference, they test to find out whether others will join them. Instinctively, they know that they are relatively powerless alone but powerful when they band with others. (p. 19)

Boyte (2002) emphasizes that citizen politics is different from the civic acts of volunteering and community service. There are differences in six aspects:

1. *Goal.* Service is to fix problems (or people); citizen politics is to build democratic power, a democratic way of life.

2. *Definition of citizenship.* Service is viewed in terms of voluntarism; citizen politics is to work toward the public good.

3. *Motive.* Service is more altruistic; citizen politics, dynamically understood, is more self-interested.

4. *Method.* Service is in programs; citizen politics is public leadership development.

5. *Site.* Service tends to be in programs; citizen politics is usually in public spaces.

6. *Outcomes.* Service results in projects and reports; citizen politics results in cultural and human change.

Community Politics

The practice of deliberation is the cornerstone of community politics. Mathews (2002) explains that community politics harnesses the power of an engaged public—the power of "a diverse body of people joined together in ever-changing alliances to make choices about how to advance their common well-being. . . . Members of an engaged public have decided among themselves on a course of action and are political actors directly involved in making changes; an engaged public owns its problems and its institutions" (p. i). In this context, *politics* is used to describe "the things citizens do both with other citizens and with governments to change their communities" (p. iii). Ultimately, it is about developing ways to allow a deeper, more deliberative form of public engagement to take root in the habits, traditions, and culture of a community on an *ongoing* basis.

The National Civic League (NCL) was founded in 1894 at a time in American history of great distrust between American citizens and their government. Its focus was on community politics, advocating a concept of self-government in which citizens play a key role in making communities work. Gates (2000), NCL president, observes, "Ironically, 105 years after the founding of the [NCL], we find ourselves in the situation where, once again, America's democracy is in need of repair" (p. 1). He points to four of the most prominent obstacles to effective community politics and an engaged public:

1. *Frustrated and angry citizens.* NCL asserts that reports of widespread public apathy are inaccurate. Citizens-at-large are not so much apathetic as they are frustrated and angry with politics and politicians. Most feel that public life is beyond their control, that they are unheard, and that their own values and interests are not reflected in the policies that shape the larger society.

2. *Presumption of bad intent.* People assume that individuals must have ulterior motives or a hidden agenda when making policy proposals. Suspicion of government officials severely limits the community's ability to address the challenges it faces.

3. *Negative media.* The media plays a powerful role in creating the community psyche. The inclination toward the negative perpetuates the public's cynicism, suspicion, and anger.

4. *Dysfunctional politics.* People used to believe that politics mattered and social change could occur through political activity. Today, for many community members, politics has become a target of jokes, sarcasm, and cynicism. Like other dynamics, dysfunctional politics provides the public with a number of excuses for *not* becoming more involved in their communities.

The Kettering Foundation's contention (Mathews, 2002) is that changing political practices, particularly the way in which issues are framed, choices made, and action taken, will result in greater public engagement and "put the public back into the public's business" (p. 20). The foundation recommends these changes:

1. *Naming and framing issues for deliberation.* The way a problem is named determines who will get involved and the response that may emerge. For a broad array of citizens to become engaged with an issue, it must be named in a way that connects with or reflects what is valuable to them. In order to make sound decisions regarding what should be done about a problem, people must consider a range of approaches to solving it. Most importantly, issues must be presented in a way that reveals the inevitable conflicts among and within each approach. Framing an issue in a way that reveals the conflicts among several approaches makes deliberation possible.

2. *Making choices through deliberation.* Deliberation is a natural kind of talking and reasoning people use when a difficult decision has to be made, and it involves weighing the costs and consequences of various approaches to a problem against what people consider most valuable. The goal of deliberation is not a clear agreement or a compromise, but rather a general sense of direction and purpose bound by limits. Deliberation produces a reading on how the public thinks about an issue, after people have had the chance to engage each other in discussion. It creates public knowledge about whether there is a shared sense of direction or purpose, even when citizens cannot agree fully and are unwilling to compromise. Informed and shared public judgment is the foundation for wise policymaking.

3. *Acting publicly.* Deliberation can stimulate citizens and organizations to take action on particular issues by triggering a sense of possibility. It contributes to public action, not by developing consensus, but by discovering a sense of purpose or direction. Out of this sense of direction, people—individually or jointly with other citizens or organizations—can start acting in mutually reinforcing ways around an issue, although they may still disagree on certain aspects of the problem.

4. *Connecting citizens and officeholders.* Community politics arises

out of a vision of politics in which the public takes on a central role with greater control over, and greater responsibility for, issues important to them. Its goal is to supplement and reinforce, not replace, the activity of officials. There are no prescribed models or answers to demonstrate how citizens and officeholders can interact most constructively. However, whatever the approach, all are working to find innovative and workable ways for citizens and officeholders to become partners—coproducers—of sound, sustainable policy.

5. *Judging progress.* Judging progress refers to the process of taking stock—a form of evaluation in which people involved in the common work of community politics ask themselves: "How are we doing?" The judging process is about creating opportunities for citizens to come together to assess the value of what they have done and what they have learned from it. It is key to sustaining momentum for community politics.

COMMUNITY ORGANIZING FOR SCHOOL REFORM

Meier (2003) believes that one of the troubling things about 20th-century school reform was the vigorous efforts by administrative and classroom progressives to insulate schools from the community, deeming their own judgment superior to that of ordinary citizens. The distancing of schools from the community is one of the base causes of erosion of confidence that public schools are serving the best interests of families, especially in low- and moderate-income communities. Johnson (2003) suggests that the increasing emphasis on accountability is a product of distrust and notes that in some cases there may be a "manufactured culture of distrust for public schools by external detractors" (para. 2).

Gold and Simon (2002) argue that community organizing for school reform, sometimes called *educational organizing*, is a new paradigm for school reform, "one in which the connection of schools and communities is central to school change. In this paradigm, the strengths and knowledge of parents and community members are essential to transforming schools to serve the best interests of families in low- to moderate-income communities" (Reframing the Paradigm section, para. 1).

Lopez (2003) points out important differences between educational organizing and standard parent involvement. The goals of educational organizing are focused on system change and school accountability; the work is directed toward changing the system for all children. The primary issues addressed are accountability, parent engagement, school environment, equity, standards and performance, special programs, and quality of instruction. Educational organizing encourages families to exercise their responsibilities as citizens to make needed changes in schools and focuses on raising parents' consciousness and their increasing awareness of their collective power to effect change. Educational organizing focuses on relational power. Organizers work to bring people into relationships with one another so that they can identify and act on school issues.

Lopez stresses that the emphasis on building relational power makes educational organizing different from the other types of parent involvement. Standard parent involvement avoids issues of power. School-based shared decision making gives families some influence, but educators remain in control. Community organizing "intentionally builds parent power—it equips parents with the skills to leverage a more even playing field when it comes to tackling educational issues and shaping solutions" (p. 1).

Lopez acknowledges that community organizing for school reform is only one of several approaches to rebuild the connection between schools and communities. She states that:

> What community organizing shares with these other approaches is the social capital that works toward the best interests of students. What makes it different is turning social capital into political capital. Community organizing focuses not only on school reform, but also on empowerment. . . . Because school reform is a political issue, organizing builds the political will to ensure that poor schools gain access to resources they need to improve the quality of education. (p. 8)

POWER

Understanding politics requires an understanding of power, because both power and politics are involved in the allocation of resources for the public good.

Two kinds of power—unilateral and relational—exist in communities (Cortes, 1993). Unilateral power treats the opposition as an object to be instructed and directed; it tends to be coercive and domineering. Relational power involves a personal relationship, subject to subject. This kind of power involves, not just the capacity to act, but the capacity to allow oneself to be acted upon. A kind of empathy permits a meaningful understanding of other people's subjects and allows them to understand one's own.

Understanding politics also requires an understanding of the relationship between leadership and power. The Center for Leadership Studies (1999) points out that power is the resource that enables a leader to influence followers. Because of the integral relationship between leadership and power, leaders must not only assess their leadership behavior in order to understand how they actually influence other people; they also must examine their possession and use of power. The center warns that inappropriate use of power or inappropriate use of certain power bases will ultimately undermine a leader's credibility.

The Center for Leadership Studies' Power Perception Profile (1999) uses the seven bases of power identified by Hersey and Natemeyer (1979):

1. *Legitimate power* is based on the position of the leader. The higher the position, the higher the legitimate power tends to be. A leader high in legitimate power influences others because they believe that he or she has the right, by virtue of position, to expect suggestions to be followed.

2. *Information power* is based on the leader's access to information that is perceived as valuable to others. This power base influences others because they need the information or want to be in on things.

3. *Expert power* is based on the leader's possession of expertise, skill, and knowledge, which gains the respect of others. A leader high in expert power is seen as possessing the expertise to facilitate the work of others, and respect for this expertise leads to compliance.

4. *Reward power* is based on the leader's ability to provide rewards for other people, who believe that their compliance will lead to being rewarded with positive incentives, such as increased pay, promotion, or recognition.

5. *Referent power* is based on the leader's personal traits. A leader is

generally liked and admired by others because of personality. A liking for, admiration of, and identification with the leader influences others.

6. *Connection power* is based on the leader's connections with influential or important persons inside or outside the organization. A leader high in connection power induces compliance from others because they aim at gaining the favor or avoiding the disfavor of the powerful connection.

7. *Coercive power* is based on fear. It induces compliance because failure to comply is seen as leading to punishment, such as undesirable assignments, reprimands, or even dismissal.

The power structure of a community consists of the formal and informal networks that make things happen. Power is structured differently in different communities, and power structures change over time. Relational power comes into play when two or more people, groups, organizations, or agencies come together, debate their concerns, develop a plan, and take some sort of action. In citizen politics, community politics, and educational organizing, the challenge is for people to acquire enough power to do the things they think are important. Gaining enough power usually involves building coalitions with other people and learning the rules of politics and power. One lesson is clear: effective political leaders learn from, and are influenced by, a community of collaborators and supporters. Effective leadership is both informed and collegial, and power and politics are intertwined.

POLICYMAKING

In a generic sense, a policy is a broad guideline describing a course of action approved by a governing entity in a given situation. Policymaking is the process by which a course of action is determined, worded, executed, and interpreted. It functions as a sorting-out process for the aspirations, needs, and concerns of the individuals and groups involved. Policy is an outcome of the sorting-out process.

Policymaking is a special type of decision making that takes place in a political context. The focus is on the policymakers and on the processes they establish to control access to the development of policies. Education policymakers are influenced by the representational and distributive nature of educational policy, and the ongoing nature of the decision-making process. The participants and their orientations are basic factors in the policymaking process. As interests and values change, policy priorities also change.

Policymaking serves both problem-solving and power-balancing goals. In problem solving, policies are adopted to help the organization pursue its goals more efficiently through technical processes. The resulting policies describe the extent to which the governing body intends to solve the problem, how it intends to solve it, the activities required to solve it, and the resources to be allocated. In power balancing, policymakers engage in a set of interactions they hope will shape the authoritative allocation of values. The policies developed represent an equilibrium: the balance of power among the various bodies, individuals, and groups with responsibility for governing education, or with an interest in the decisions. In its power-balancing aspects, policymaking is a political process designed to allocate money, jobs, prestige or status, and primary responsibility.

Policies tend to follow from political interaction and a complex set of forces that together produce effects. To understand who or what makes policy, one must understand the characteristics of the participants, what roles they play, what authority they hold, and how they deal with and control each other. Lindblom and Woodhouse (1993) make an important distinction between policymaking and problem solving. Policies tend to follow from political interaction rather than from rational analysis, while conventionally conceived problem solving is an intellectual process.

In the United States, policies regarding the allocation and use of resources result primarily from political interaction that blends the values and definitions of the *public good* of political subcultures. These subcultures may exist side by side, or they may even overlap; differences in their cultural values significantly affect local and state education systems. Patterson (2000) argues that even though there has been a nationalization of American politics, distinctive subcultures remain:

1. *Individualistic.* This subculture is located primarily in the middle part of the United States, from Massachusetts to Maryland and westward through Illinois and Missouri to southwestern states such as

Arizona. Government is viewed simply as a utilitarian institution created to handle those functions that cannot be managed by individuals. Government need not have any direct concern with the question of the good society or the general welfare. The democratic order is viewed as a marketplace. Emphasis is on private concerns, and a high value is placed on limiting community intervention into private activities. Government exists only to give the public what it wants, and public officials are normally unwilling to initiate new programs or to open new areas of governmental activity. Political conflict is rough and tumble, political power is closely guarded, and public policy is often narrowly applied.

2. *Moralistic.* States in the northern tier of the nation have been characterized by an emphasis on good government (public interest), clean government (honesty), and civic government (public participation). This subculture emphasizes that politics is part of the people's search for the good society, and that the good life can be achieved only through the good society. Individualism in this view is tempered by a general commitment to use communal power to intervene in public activities when it is necessary to do so for the public good. Participation in community affairs is seen as a civic duty for every citizen, and public officials are viewed as having a moral obligation to promote the general welfare even at the expense of individual loyalties and political friendships.

3. *Traditionalistic.* This subculture typifies the states of the old Confederacy and a few states bordering on it. The main role of government is viewed as the maintenance of the existing social order. It accepts government as a positive factor in the affairs of the community—but only to the extent that government maintains and encourages the traditional values and patterns of life. Social and family ties are paramount, and real political power is confined to a relatively small and self-perpetuating group drawn from an established elite of *good old families.* (Framework of Analysis section)

In addition to its political subcultures, every community has interest groups. The most common political tactics of interest groups are public relations to create a favorable climate, electioneering to elect sympathetic individuals, and lobbying to influence decisions.

Four kinds of interest groups account for most of the attempts to exert influence on state and local governments:

1. *Economically motivated groups.* Government policies will either cost or save members money. Business and labor groups are the most obvious examples.
2. *Professionally motivated groups.* Government policies may affect their members' professional activities. Medical and teacher associations are examples.
3. *Public agency groups.* These groups provide opportunities for public officials to exchange ideas, lobby collectively, and get up-to-date information on developments and concepts that affect their agencies. Examples are the U.S. Conference of Mayors and the National Association of Counties.
4. *Ideological groups.* Most of these groups claim to represent a public interest. Many are not permanent but arise in response to a specific issue. Environmental and religious groups are examples. (Decker and Decker, 2003, p. 192)

Other groups, often not readily identifiable, may also affect the political interaction of a community. Some may not be well informed about what is happening in local schools, may not understand the theory and practices behind educational jargon, or may feel excluded from serious discussion about school matters. Individuals in these groups are often targeted by opponents of various school initiatives, who may give them biased information in order to enlist their support in opposition.

FRAMEWORK OF AN EDUCATIONAL PARTNERSHIP POLICY

Decision making in the development of an educational partnership policy must be done within the political context of a community. There is no question that democratic decision making requires a lot of processes to work through competing and conflicting interests. The process of developing a comprehensive policy involves documenting existing conditions, defining goals and objectives, generating and evaluating alternatives developed by key interest groups, and making decisions.

The National Coalition for Parent Involvement in Education (no date) advocates that state and district school leaders acknowledge the following concepts in the development of partnership policies:

1. The critical role of families in children's academic achievement and social well-being.
2. The responsibility of every school to create a welcoming environment conducive to learning and supportive of comprehensive family involvement programs that have been developed jointly with families.
3. The need to accommodate the diverse needs of families by developing, jointly with families, multiple, innovative, and flexible ways for families to be involved.
4. The rights and responsibilities of parents and guardians, particularly their right to have access to the school, their children's records, and the children's classrooms.
5. The value of working with community agencies to provide services to children and families.
6. The need for families to be involved from preschool through high school. (Guidelines section, para. 1)

The coalition emphasizes that school-level policies should include:

1. Outreach to ensure participation of all families, including those who lack literacy skills or for whom English is not the primary language.
2. Recognition of diverse family structures, circumstances, and responsibilities, including differences that might impede participation. (Policies should include participation by all persons interested in a child's educational progress, not just the biological parents.)
3. Opportunities for families to participate in the instructional process at school and at home.
4. Opportunities for families to share in making decisions, both about school policy and procedures and about how family involvement programs are designed, implemented, assessed, and strengthened.

5. Professional development for all school staff to enhance their effectiveness in working with diverse families.
6. Regular exchange of information with families about the standards their children are expected to meet at each grade level, the objectives of educational programs, the assessment procedures, and their children's participation and progress.
7. Linkages with social service and health agencies, businesses, faith-based institutions, and community organizations and groups to support key family and community issues. (Good School Policies section, para. 1)

Including these considerations will result in a policy that contains the broad outlines of a course of action. How that course of action is chosen, phrased, approved, executed, and interpreted will be determined by sorting out the diverse aspirations, needs, and concerns of individuals and groups in a particular community. The result of this sorting-out process should be a policy uniquely tailored to that community.

DISCOVERING THE COMMUNITY POWER STRUCTURE

An important first step for anyone who wants to make changes in schools or educational programs is to identify the leaders in the community's power structure. It is only then that appropriate communication linkages can be built, involvement strategies designed, and alternative plans developed. There are four basic ways to identify the power actors in a community (Hiemstra, 2000):

1. *Positional method:* identifying the individuals who occupy key authority positions, usually formal roles, in the community's major organizations, groups, and strata. An important basic assumption is that power and decision-making ability reside in those who hold important positions in a community's formal organizations.
2. *Reputational method:* identifying knowledgeable citizens who can provide the names of top community power actors according to their reputations for social power. The basic premise is that a reputation

for having the potential to affect community decisions is an accurate index of influence, and that such reputations are slow to change.

3. *Decision-making method:* tracing the history of decision making in a particular issue area. Influential people are those who can be identified as the main participants in any such activity. A basic assumption is that the social power to influence decisions within a community can be measured by a person's actual participation in various problem-solving or decision-making activities.

4. *Social participation method:* making lists of the formal leaders of a variety of voluntary associations. The assumption is that social participation, active membership, and holding a leadership role are important prerequisites to the accumulation and use of community influence.

Hiemstra explains why it may be necessary to use more than one method to arrive at an accurate picture of a community's leadership:

In reality, each method may identify different power actors and leaders within a community. At times, the overlap of individuals determined by the various methods will be fairly small. The positional method yields institutional leaders, office holders, and highly visible leaders; the reputational technique identifies reputed leaders, generalized leaders, and frequently, non-visible leaders; the decision-making method can delineate both generalized and specialized activists; and the social participation method often identifies primarily "doers," those in the public eye, and voluntary association leaders. Thus it may be necessary for the educational change agent to employ more than one technique to obtain a comprehensive understanding of the community's leadership. . . . [Moreover,] actors will change over time. Consequently, any one method may need to be repeated periodically so that such changes can be determined. (Chapter 6, Power Structure Analysis section)

POTENTIAL FOR CONFLICT

Bolman and Deal (2002) propose conceptualizing school organizations through a political frame of reference—a setting in which different interest groups compete for power and scarce resources. In their view, schools are "alive and screaming political arenas that house a complex variety of individual and group interests" (Political Frame section, para. 3). The potential for conflict is everywhere. Five propositions summarize this perspective:

1. Organizations are coalitions composed of varied individuals and interest groups (for example, hierarchical levels, departments, professional groups, gender and ethnic subgroups).
2. There are enduring differences among individuals and groups in their values, preferences, beliefs, and perceptions of reality. Such differences change slowly, if at all.
3. Most of the important decisions in an organization involve the allocation of scarce resources; they are decisions about who gets what.
4. Because of enduring differences and scarce resources, conflict is central to organizational dynamics, and power is the most important resource.
5. Organizational goals and decisions emerge from bargaining, negotiation, and jockeying for position among members of different coalitions. (Political Frame section, para. 3)

Jehl and others (2001) point out that educators and community builders frequently differ on their perception of conflict and its importance, both within and outside of collaborative partnerships.

> For educators, conflict is a sign of something going wrong, while for community builders it is seen as a valuable tool for change. Community building organizations work in neighborhoods and with individuals who have little institutional or financial clout. Their power comes from a willingness to resist a "consensus" position that is balanced against them and to clearly voice their own interests. Many community builders see conflict and confrontation as a healthy part of collaboration—essential tools for equalizing power relationships and creating positive change. School leaders operating in a hierarchical bureaucracy with an inside strategy for decision-making are more likely to see conflict as a sign of breakdown. They may find it easier to suppress debate than to allow strong disagreement. (p. 10)

Bolman and Deal see bargaining, negotiation, and compromise—and sometimes coercion—as part of everyday organizational life. They suggest that the following political skills are essential for school leaders:

1. *Agenda setting:* the ability to establish a purpose for the organization and a coherent strategy for achieving that purpose.
2. *Networking and coalition building:* the ability to build personal relationships with members of the school community who can help neutralize potential opposition to the agenda and become allies in striving to achieve it.
3. *Negotiating and bargaining:* the ability to manage the constant clash of different interests in the organization. (Educational Leaders Must Be Effective Political Leaders section)

SOURCES OF CONFLICT

Keedy and Björk (2001) also emphasize that conflict is not a bad thing. They view politics as a process where individuals and groups openly express needs and interests and reconcile differences. They point out that educators face conflicts over values and interests, heightened levels of political activism within communities, changing power structures, and challenges to traditional purposes and goals of public education. Understood as an essential part of the democratic process, conflict can lead to personal growth and better outcomes.

Ascher and others (1996) list some of the current sources of disaffection and conflict facing today's educators.

1. Business has been worried about the United States' loss of international competitiveness since the early 1980s and has been putting pressure on public education to raise its standards.
2. Liberals and families of color have become discouraged by the failure of public education to realize the promise of the Supreme Court's desegregation decision in *Brown v. Board of Education* and there is growing anger among minority and lower socioeconomic groups at the failure to improve opportunities and outcomes for their children.
3. At the same time, protracted efforts to achieve equal educational opportunity, particularly student busing, have caused a backlash among some white families.
4. Persistent problems result from the United States' property-based

method of school financing, exacerbating the disparity in resources available for public schools.

5. Public schools, particularly in troubled cities, are being asked to respond to a widening range of student needs, many of them generated by worsening economic conditions in some urban areas.

6. Public education is bearing the brunt of anti-union and anti-government sentiments that have mushroomed in the United States in recent decades.

7. A long-term decline in civic consciousness and public engagement and increasing privatization in many areas have contributed to negative attitudes toward public education.

8. Some conservative and religious groups blamed public schools for a perceived decline in Christian and other traditional values, branding public schools as part of "big government" and crusading to replace public education with free market institutions.

Keedy and Björk (2001) emphasize the weakening of common ground—the shared values and beliefs that undergird responsibility and the meaning of citizenship. They assert that the positions of education professionals, especially administrators, are highly politicized when viewed within the context of how public education will be defined. They contend that the very existence of community interest groups requires educators to mediate and negotiate among competing groups to gain a consensus about how public schools might serve their communities.

FINDING COMMON GROUND

Most educators and community members believe that there are advantages to working together. Effective school-community partnerships combine insider expertise with outside resources and support. However, as Jehl and others (2001) report in *Education and Community Building: Connecting Two Worlds,* building insider/outside relationships is not always easy. On one hand, not all educators accept the role of families and community members as active players in the effort to reform schools. On the other hand, many families and community members do not understand the education system they are trying to change. Jehl and others outline several "sticking points" in the process of building bridges and finding common ground:

1. Differences in organizational size, structure, and staffing can easily lead to communication problems. School personnel may find it hard to communicate with people whose communication style and values reflect the community rather than a specific educational discipline or profession. Community members and organizations may find "working through the channels" arduous and exasperating while their lack of knowledge about "how things are done" can waste time and irritate school personnel.

2. Differences in the role and expectations of leaders may lead to friction when partners fail to recognize the legitimacy of both kinds of leadership—one based on credentials and training, and the other on relationships. Misunderstandings in school-community relationships are most likely to occur when partners are unwilling to take the time to build relationships, trust, and appreciation for one another; when school personnel misjudge the abilities of people whose formal education may be limited; or when community members underestimate the range of challenges, responsibilities, and occupational obligations school leaders face.

3. As education reform focuses more exclusively on academic achievement, differences in views about the role of schools and schooling create considerable distance between school personnel and community members. Educators sometimes feel that community members do not understand the magnitude and complexity of the challenge to improve student achievement. Community members worry that an exclusive focus on academics ignores other important areas in which young people can develop skills and abilities.

4. School personnel, who see their jobs, as well as their students' futures, on the line, are sometimes unwilling to share power and resources with partners who seem to have less to lose. As long as there is only one measure of accountability—test scores—partnerships between schools and communities may experience imbalance and tension.

5. Both institutional and people power are necessary to improve student learning and build communities, but connecting them is often

difficult. The propensity of school administrators is to look for partners with demonstrable "clout" and overlook the potential power of organized groups of residents and family members.

6. All parents, regardless of background, can benefit from ongoing, school-sponsored parent involvement programs. However, not all educators can visualize an active role for parents and community residents in helping to design and implement school reform. In addition, many parents, especially those who have little formal education or who have had negative experiences with schools, may be reluctant to participate in school-organized activities—especially when they are cast in the role of students who must be taught, rather than adults who have a great deal to teach.

7. Community builders and many educators believe that actions taken to benefit communities ultimately benefit schools. Nevertheless, tough issues inevitably arise when community members ask for support from schools: negotiating shared use of school facilities and equipment, responding to parent challenges to school policies, and dealing with community concerns about school performance. The "two-way street," with give and take on both sides, is often difficult to establish.

The process for seeking common ground relies on many of the same techniques used to build communities and allocate social capital. In this case, a school's *social capital* is the attention and resources it gets from responsible adults in the community. Cortes (1993) notes that thinking about relationships as *capital* helps put decisions about the allocation of resources into a helpful perspective.

To create capital, individuals must invest labor, energy, and effort in the here-and-now to create something for later use. . . . Investment requires the ability and the discipline to defer gratification, to invest energy not only in the needs or pleasures of the present, but also in the potential demands of the future. Capital also requires maintenance and renewal. . . . Knowledge and skills must be updated and refined. Similarly, the partners in a venture must renew the means of trusting one another. (Social Capital section, para. 4–5)

Almost all educational advocates acknowledge the difficulty in finding common ground. Although most Americans want decisive action to improve schools, they disagree about both the problems and the solutions. Public support is up for grabs, and advocates of none of the contending perspectives can confidently count the public on their side.

BUILDING INSIDER/OUTSIDER RELATIONSHIPS

Hale and Moorman (2003) suggest that schools of the 21st century require a new kind of school leader, one who effectively fulfills three roles:

1. *Instructional leader:* one who is focused on strengthening teaching and learning, professional development, data-driven decision making, and accountability.
2. *Community leader:* one who is imbued with a big-picture awareness of the school's role in society; shared leadership among educators, community partners, and residents; close relations with parents and others; and advocacy for school capacity building and resources.
3. *Visionary leader:* one who has demonstrated commitment to the conviction that all children will learn at high levels and is able to inspire others inside and outside the school building with this vision. (p. 7)

The success of the school leader in fulfilling all three roles depends to a great extent on effective communication skills and processes. When the goal is to revitalize citizenship at the local level by bringing collaborative problem-solving and conflict-resolution techniques to diverse groups of community stakeholders, school leaders must be able to communicate the rationale for bringing people into the process and a clear understanding of the problems to be addressed. They need to promote diversity as an advantage and create a sense of wholeness that incorporates diversity.

Finding common ground may require changes in policies and practices and almost certainly requires efforts by a variety of people and groups. For this reason, no single approach is likely to accomplish all the goals and objectives. Hiemstra (2000) describes four basic strategies for achieving change and notes that unless the desired change is simple—and already has wide acceptance—a combination of strategies will be needed.

Strategy 1. Learn who the primary community leaders are. Understand how they control or affect the decision-making process, and establish an acquaintanceship or friendship with them. Those who propose or plan change need to involve or consult such influential persons at various stages of the planning process. If such involvement is not facilitated, the planner risks program blockage or failure.

Strategy 2. Identify with and use existing groups and organizations that will support the desired change. This approach involves the coordination of two or more groups. A professional planner or other expert is frequently needed to promote this cooperation.

Strategy 3. Affiliate with an organization whose function can include directing or guiding the change. Because such organizations often perform a change-agent role, their employees are knowledgeable about the means used to achieve various changes and have skills in human relations, problem diagnosis, and use of resources to achieve specific goals.

Strategy 4. Form committees or groups around particular content areas or particular needs. This involves getting agencies or organizations with certain physical and organizational resources to cooperate with groups that have special skills or access to particular clients. This strategy is especially useful in addressing unique minority-group needs.

A publication of the Southwest Educational Development Laboratory (Ashby and others, 2003) focuses on the topic of public deliberation as a tool for connecting school reform and diversity. Its authors point out that public deliberation is a structured process of face-to-face exchange for making decisions that lead to actions. Deliberation is dialogue based on the premise that many people have pieces of the answer and that together they forge new approaches and solutions. It asks people to put aside their own interests and hear what others feel and think.

The settings for public deliberation are varied. Sometimes the groups are small and informal. At other times, they are formal and involve large numbers of people. The authors emphasize that what is common about the varied groups is their decision to take responsibility for common problems.

Three types of formats are commonly used for public deliberation:

1. *Forums and study circles.* A forum tends to gather from about 30 to 200 people and typically meets once to discuss a single issue. Study circles are typically made up of 10 to 15 people who meet weekly for two hours over four weeks. The purpose of both a forum and a study circle is to engage participants in making—or at least working toward—a decision about how they will act on a problem or policy they think is important to their community or country. The dialogue sessions last about two hours and are led by a moderator whose role is to focus the discussion, engage participants, and enforce mutually agreed upon ground rules. Moderators clarify by asking questions and help the group consider a variety of views.

2. *Focus groups.* Focus groups are designed to gauge how different groups view an issue. Different types of groups, made up of 10 to 15 representative members, provide distinct points of view. A focus group is a structured conversation organized around a set of questions and typically lasting about two hours. The information gathered from several focus groups discussing a single topic can be used to design questions for a survey or town meeting and to craft community forums, public policy, or written materials. If the goal is also to partly educate the larger community on a complex topic, a series of many separate focus groups over an extended period can help to inform the community. Typically, focus groups are held over two days on one topic.

3. *Citizens jury.* The citizens jury brings together citizens representative of the community to examine an issue and make a judgment. The jury arrives at a solution after hearing and discussing expert testimony and listening to recommendations. A jury is made up of 12 to 24 jurors who have been selected to constitute a microcosm of the community. Jurors are briefed in detail on all the background and current thinking about a specific issue and asked to deliberate and make recommendations to the larger community. Hearings are led by a moderator, last four to five days, and involve briefings by expert witnesses. The witnesses are the sole source of information.

Whether in a large body or in smaller groups, jurors study the information, cross-examine witnesses, and discuss various aspects of the issue. The jury's conclusions are presented to the body that commissioned them. The verdict need not be unanimous nor its recommendations binding. However, the body that commissioned the jury must inform the general public of the jury's findings and undertake to carry out the recommendations or give reasons why it chooses not to.

Sokoloff (2003) suggests that a

fruitful place to start [in building inside/outside relationships] would be with a conversation about what people value in their community—why they live there, what . . . [characteristics of] the community they want to protect and expand, and how the schools support those values. My experience is that starting with what the community itself values almost always brings people in and helps them understand anew their stake in schools their own children no longer attend. (Conversations with the Community, para. 6)

POLITICS AND ACADEMIC SUCCESS

Politics are a fact of life in public schools because many people in the community have a stake in public education. Educators must understand and use politics and the community power structure to help them achieve their mission of academic success for all children. They must both master basic political skills and adopt an attitude that values politics as an honorable means of achieving educational goals. They have an obligation to engage and inform the public and to protect schools from manipulation by special-interest groups who seek to misinform the public in order to advance their own agendas. Even some who advocate sharing power with families and communities may, at times, be motivated by their own educational and social objectives.

Educators must accept the fact that issues related to home-school-community relations have entered the arena of political policy and action. Whether overt opposition exists or not, educators must develop ways to communicate, through a democratic process, with a wide variety of people in the community. Without public understanding, support, and participation, initiatives to achieve academic success for all children will be difficult, if not impossible, to sustain. The reality is that the greatest benefit of the involvement process may be that members of the community will learn to work together to improve learning for all children.

REFERENCES

American Association of School Administrators. (2005). *Backers of the bashers.* Retrieved April 10, 2006, from http://www.aasa.org/policy/content.cfm/Item Number = 4680

Ascher, C., Fruchter, N., and Berne, R. (1996). *Hard lessons: Public schools and privatization.* New York: The Century Foundation. Retrieved September 9, 2002, from http://www.tcf.org/Publications/Education/Hard_Lessons/ Chapter1

Ashby, S., Garza, C., and Rivas, M. (2003). *Public deliberation: A tool for connecting school reform and diversity.* Southwest Educational Development Laboratory. Retrieved January 24, 2006, from http://www.sedl.org/pubs/1c06/ together.html

Berg, J. H., and Hall, G. E. (1999). The intersection of political leadership and educational excellence: A neglected leadership domain. *AASA Professor, 22,* 4.

Bolman, L. G., and Deal, T. E. (2002). *Reframing the path to school leadership: A guide for teachers and principals.* Thousand Oaks, CA: Sage Publications. Retrieved December 21, 2005, from http://www.sagepub.book.aspx?pid = 8899

Boyte, H. C. (2002). *A different kind of politics: John Dewey and the meaning of citizenship in the 21st century.* Retrieved April 11, 2006, from http://www.cpn .org/crm/contemporary/different.html

Center for Leadership Studies. (1999). *Power perception profile.* Retrieved December 19, 2005, from http://www.situational.com/leadership/accessories

Cortes, E., Jr. (1993). Reweaving the fabric: The iron rule and the IAF strategy for power and politics. In H. G. Cisneros (Ed.), *Interwoven destinies: Cities and the nation.* New York: W. W. Norton and Company. Retrieved April 11, 2006, from http://www.cpn.org/sections/topics/community/index

Gates, C. T. (2000). Introduction: Creating a healthy democracy. *The community visioning and strategic planning handbook.* Denver, CO: National Civic League Press.

Gold, E., and Simon, E., in partnership with Brown, C. (2002). *Successful community organizing for school reform: A report in the indicators project of educational organizing series: Strong neighborhoods, strong schools.* Retrieved January 23, 2006, from http://comm-org.wisc.edu/papers2003/goldsimon/goldsimon.htm

Hale, E. L., and Moorman, H. N. (2003). *Preparing school principals: A national perspective on policy and program innovations.* Institute for Educational Leadership, Washington, DC and Illinois Education Research Council, Edwardsville, IL. Retrieved February 17, 2006, from http://www.iel.org/pubs/preparingprincipals.pdf

Hersey, P., and Natemeyer, W. E. (1979). *Power perception profile.* Escondido, CA: Center for Leadership Studies.

Hiemstra, R. (2000). *The educative community: Linking the community, education, and family.* Baldwin, NY: HiTree Press. Retrieved April 11, 2006, from http://www-distance.syr.edu/commindx.html

Jehl, J., Blank, M., and McCloud, B. (2001). *Education and community building: Connecting two worlds.* Washington, DC: Institute for Educational Leadership.

Johnson, F. (2003, September). "Community" must be everyone. In Conversations along the road. *American School Board Journal, 190,* 9. Retrieved January 11, 2006, from http://www.asbj.com/2003/09/0903coverstory2.html

Keedy, J. L., and Björk, L. G. (2001). The superintendent, local boards, and the political arena. *AASA Professor, 24,* 4.

Lindblom, C. D., and Woodhouse, D. J. (1993). *The Policy-making process.* Englewood Cliffs, NJ: Prentice-Hall.

Lopez, M. E. (2003). *Transforming schools through community organizing: A research review.* Cambridge, MA: Family Involvement Network of Educators and Harvard Family Research Project.

Mathews, D. (2002). *For communities to work.* Dayton, OH: Kettering Foundation Press.

Meier, D. (2003, September). The road to trust. *American School Board Journal, 190,* 9. Retrieved January 11, 2006, from http://www.asbj.com/2003/09/0903coverstory.html

National Coalition for Parent Involvement in Education. (no date). *Developing family and school partnerships: Guidelines for schools and school districts.* Fairfax, VA: National Coalition for Parent Involvement in Education. Retrieved April 11, 2006, from http://www.ncpie.ore/DevelopingPartnerships/Policy Guidelines.html

Patterson, T. E. (2000). *The American democracy* (5th ed.). Retrieved December 20, 2005, from http://www.mhhe.com.com/socscience/polisci/americangov/stateandlocal.html

Sokoloff, H. (2003). Conversations with the community. In Conversations along the road. *American School Board Journal, 190,* 9. Retrieved January 11, 2006, from http://www.asbj.com/2003/09/0903coverstory2.html

Sugarman, J. (1997, May). Advocacy groups must find common cause. *The School Administrator.* Retrieved January 23, 2006, from http://www.aasa.org/publications/saarticledetail.cfm?ItemNumber = 4766

Websites for More Information and Links to Other Relevant Sites

National League of Cities Institute for Youth, Education, and Families, http://www.nlc.org/IYEF

Principals.org—Legislation and Advocacy, http://www.principals.org/s-nassp/sec.asp?CID = 14&DID.14

Chapter Nine

School Safety and Crisis Management

The term *school violence* was not widely used in the United States until 1992 (Furlong and Morrison, 2000). The meaning of *violence* has evolved over the last decade and is "now conceptualized as multifaceted acts of aggression in schools, which inhibit development and learning, [and] . . . harm the school's climate" (p. 1). Various definitions range from limited—for example, related to guns—to very broad, to include all youthful misconduct. *In the Spotlight: School Safety,* a report of the National Criminal Justice Reference Service (2002), uses the definition of the Center for the Study and Prevention of Violence: "[A]ny behavior that violates a school's educational mission or climate of respect or jeopardizes the intent of the school to be free of aggression against persons or property, drugs, weapons, disruptions, and disorder" (p. 1). Pamela Riley, former executive director of the Center for the Prevention of School Violence (National Governors Association Center for Best Practices, 1999), emphasizes that school violence is not a special genre of violence; instead, it is "youth violence that happens at school" (p. 2) and goes far beyond what occurs between 8:00 a.m. and 3:00 p.m.

The fact is that most schools are safe. "The victimization rate for students aged 12–18 generally declined . . . at school between 1992 and 2002" (DeVoe and others, 2004, p. 5), but school leaders now recognize that every school has the potential for violence, making school safety an issue of concern for all educators.

ISSUES MANAGEMENT

Issues may be categorized as critical, ongoing, or emerging. Critical issues require immediate attention. A school crisis falls into this category if it requires quick action to prevent harm, ward off additional damage, or provide emotional support. Ongoing issues are those that have to be dealt with regularly. Emerging issues are just beginning to appear and may not even be recognized as issues because they are in an early stage.

The term *issues management* is somewhat misleading. The issue may be a trend or a condition that, either in the school or in the broader society, does or will or may affect the school's mission of educating all children. What the educator hopes to *manage* is not the issue itself—which may well be beyond any individual's ability to control—but the school's response to it. Although schools have no control over some natural and man-made hazards that may affect them, they can take actions to minimize or mitigate the impact. Ronald Stephens (2005), executive director of the National School Safety Center, points out, "[T]here are two types of school administrators: those who have faced a crisis and those who are about to. One of the keys to success is preparedness: knowing which issues are already out there, and which are lurking around the next corner, and having a general plan for responding to them" (para. 1). "In reality . . . current data on youth crime and violence in this country provide reasons for both optimism and concern. . . . School safety must be approached from both an immediate and a long-term perspective and incorporate prevention as well as intervention strategies" (Lumsden, 2001, Striving for Solutions section, para. 1).

SCHOOL SAFETY

The issue of school safety is important not only for the obvious reason that students must be kept safe from harm, but also because of the effect of violence on academic achievement and overall school climate. As DeVoe and others (2004) point out, "For youth to fulfill their potential in school, schools should be safe and secure places for all students, teachers, and staff members. Without a safe learning environment, teachers may have difficulty teaching and students may have difficulty learning" (Executive Summary, para. 1). Simply put, school violence in whatever form and at whatever level hinders a child's ability to learn.

In 1999, the U.S. Departments of Education and Justice presented one of the first all-inclusive portraits of the state of violence and crime in schools nationwide over the period 1992–1999. Summarizing the findings of the jointly issued report, then U.S. Secretary of Education Richard Riley said: "This comprehensive report proves that the vast majority of America's schools are still among the safest places for young people to be" (p. 1). Specifically, the report found:

1. *Schools are basically safe places.* Forty-three percent of schools reported no incidents of crime; 90% reported no incidents of serious violent crime (defined as physical attack or fight with a weapon, rape, robbery, murder, or suicide); 47% reported at least one crime that was less serious or nonviolent; and 10% reported one or more incidents of serious violent crime. From a general perspective, our schools have been successful in keeping most of their students and employees safe from injury. Overall, school crime has decreased since 1992.

2. *Despite recent well-publicized occurrences, schools should not be singled out as especially dangerous places in a community.* Most school crime is theft, not serious violent crime. In 1996, theft accounted for 62% of all crime against students at school.

3. *Teachers' unease about their own security is justified.* From 1994 through 1998, there were, on average, 133,700 violent crimes against teachers at school, plus 217,400 thefts, as reported by both public and private schools for an annual rate of 31 violent crimes and 51 thefts for every 1,000 teachers. In urban schools, 40 out of 1,000 teachers were likely to be the victims of violent crime; the comparable number in suburban or rural schools was 24 out of every 1,000 teachers.

4. *Far fewer students are bringing weapons to school and engaging in physical altercations at school.* Between 1993 and 1999, there was a marked decline—from 12% to 7%—in the rate of students in grades 9 through 12 who reported carrying a weapon to school on one or more days during the previous month. During the 1998–1999 school year, states and territories expelled approximately 3,523 stu-

dents for bringing firearms to school, a decrease from the previous school year (1997–1998), in which 3,658 students were expelled for the same reason. Student fighting declined during the same period, from 16% to 14% of students reporting that they had been involved in a physical conflict on school property during the previous year.

5. *A decreasing school crime rate results in a decline in students' fear.* Crimes against students and teachers contribute to an environment of fear. Since 1995, there has been a notable decline in students' fear of attack at school, as well as in their reporting of a gang presence at school. Students reported fearing an attack less often in 1999 than in 1995. In 1995, 29% of students reported that street gangs were present in their schools; this number fell to 17% in 1999.

6. *A majority of schools nationwide are implementing security measures on campuses.* In the 1996–1997 school year, more than 95% of public schools reported having some kind of security measures at their school. Measures ranged from zero tolerance policies for firearms, alcohol, and drugs, to monitored and controlled access to school buildings and grounds, to requiring visitors to sign in before entering school facilities. (Key Findings section)

Indicators of School Crime and Safety has continued to be updated. In a press release on the 2004 update, the U.S. Department of Education (2004) stated, "The rate of violent crimes in school settings against students ages 12 to 18 dropped by half between 1992 and 2002" (para. 1). Other key findings of the 2004 report were:

1. Between 1993 and 2003, the percentage of students in grades 9–12 who reported being in a fight on school property declined from 16% to 13%.

2. In 2003, 7% of students ages 12–18 reported that they had been bullied at school. The comparable percentage had increased from 5% in 1999 to 8% in 2001; no difference was detected between 2001 and 2003.

3. In 2003, 12% of students ages 12–18 reported that someone at school had used hate-related words against them (i.e., derogatory words related to race, religion, ethnicity, disability, gender, or sex-

ual orientation). During the same period, about 36% of students ages 12–18 saw hate-related graffiti at school.

4. Twenty-one percent of students ages 12–18 reported that street gangs were present at their schools in 2003. Students in urban schools were the most likely to report the presence of street gangs at their school (31%), followed by suburban students and rural students (18% and 12%, respectively).

5. Every year, from 1998 to 2002, teachers were the victims of approximately 234,000 nonfatal crimes at school, including 144,000 thefts and 90,000 violent crimes. The figures translate into an average annual rate of 32 thefts, 20 violent crimes, and 2 serious violent crimes per 1,000 teachers. (para. 4)

Despite the fact that school shootings make up a very small percentage of incidents of school violence, they have had a tremendous effect on the nation's perception of the potential for horrific acts. The Safe Schools Initiative, a collaborative effort of the U.S. Secret Service and the U.S. Department of Education (National Threat Assessment Center, no date), focused on this component of school violence, labeling it "targeted violence." The term was developed by the Secret Service to refer to "any incident of violence where a known (or knowable) attacker selects a particular target prior to their violent attack" (p. 13). The study examined school shootings in the United States from 1974 to 2000, analyzing a total of 37 incidents involving 41 student attackers. The goal was to identify information about a school shooting that may be identifiable or noticeable before the shooting occurs, to help prevent any future attacks. The study found:

School shootings are rarely impulsive acts. Rather, they are typically thought out and planned out in advance. In addition, prior to most shootings, other kids knew the shooting was to occur—but did not alert an adult. The study findings also revealed that there is no "profile" of a school shooter; instead, the students who carried out the attacks differed from one another in numerous ways. However, almost every attacker had engaged in behavior before the shooting that seriously concerned at least one adult—and for many had concerned three or more adults. (para. 2)

While most researchers acknowledge that indicators show a decrease in school-based crime, some question the accuracy of the figures. Ronald Stephens, executive director of the National School Safety Center (Hurst, 2005), emphasizes that some conclusions are based on three- to four-year-old data that may not provide an accurate picture of the most current trends. Other experts (Hurst, 2005) say that the federal No Child Left Behind Act, "which requires states to identify schools with high amounts of criminal or violent activity as persistently dangerous, has only exacerbated the problem of underreporting. Schools faced with the possibility of being labeled 'persistently dangerous' have no incentive to accurately report episodes of violence" (para. 18).

School safety concerns are much broader than weapons possession or shootings. The vast majority of criminal and victimization incidents that occur in schools do not involve physical violence. Hurst believes that the public needs a broader understanding of all the kinds of incidents that are related to the issue of school safety.

A broad range of student misconduct is labeled as school violence. The Safe and Responsive Schools Project (2000) reported that behaviors one group of teachers and administrators "perceived as escalating most dramatically were not the types of deadly violence that appear to concern us most—drugs, gang involvement, or weapons-carrying—but behaviors that indicate incivility, including rumors, verbal intimidation and threats, pushing and shoving, and sexual harassment" (para. 5).

PREVENTION AND INTERVENTION

Evidence has long supported the proposition that prevention and early intervention will lead to a reduction in violence and other inappropriate student behavior. The National Governors Association Center for Best Practices (1999) pointed out that early identification is probably the best strategy for preventing school violence. In its report, *Making Schools Safe,* the center emphasized that delinquency and violence are closely related and recommended that early identification efforts should focus on the risk factors for delinquency and violence, early warning signs of violence, and imminent warning signs of violence.

The report cited a multiyear, longitudinal study of recidivism rates among juvenile offenders in Oregon that found that youth with a combination of any three of six risk factors had an 80% chance of offending again, and that race and type of arrest were not related to the probability of future detainment. The six risk factors were (1) arrest of father, (2) arrest of mother, (3) documented involvement with child protective services, (4) major family transition (one parent either left home or returned since birth), (5) special education services received by child, and (6) early history of delinquent/criminal activity (child arrested before the age of 14).

Safeguarding Our Children: An Action Guide (Dwyer and Osher, 2000) highlights 16 early warning signs, but cautions that care must be made to interpret the signs in the larger context of each student's situation to avoid the risk of stigmatizing the student. The signs are:

1. Social withdrawal.
2. Excessive feelings of isolation and being alone.
3. Excessive feelings of rejection.
4. Being a victim of violence.
5. Feelings of being picked on and persecuted.
6. Low interest in schoolwork and poor academic performance.
7. Expression of violence in writing and drawings.
8. Uncontrolled anger.
9. Patterns of impulsive and chronic hitting, intimidating, and bullying behaviors.
10. History of discipline problems.
11. Past history of violent and aggressive behavior.
12. Intolerance for differences and prejudicial attitudes.
13. Drug and alcohol use.
14. Affiliation with gangs.
15. Inappropriate access to, possession of, and use of firearms.
16. Serious threats of violence. (pp. 17–18)

Imminent warning signs are very clear indicators that a youth is in distress and needs immediate attention. Violent youth will typically exhibit one or more of the early warning signs with increasing frequency and increasing severity. The signs include:

1. Serious physical fighting with peers or family members.
2. Severe destruction of property.
3. Severe rage for seemingly minor reasons.
4. Detailed threats of lethal violence.
5. Possession and/or use of a firearm or weapon.
6. Self-injurious behaviors or threats of suicide. (p. 18)

The Center for the Study and Prevention of Violence (CSPV) at the University of Colorado at Boulder initiated a project to identify juvenile violence prevention programs that could provide the nucleus for a national violence prevention initiative. The CSPV identified 10 prevention and intervention programs that proved effective in reducing adolescent violent crime, aggression, and substance abuse (Muller and Mihalic, 1999). The 10 model programs are the basis of the Blueprints program of the U.S. Department of Justice, Office of Juvenile Justice and Delinquency Prevention. *Blueprints: A Violence Prevention Initiative* (Muller and Mihalic, 1999) is based on the belief that many antisocial behaviors can be avoided by providing early intervention programs for youth. The Blueprint programs are:

1. *Prenatal and Infancy Nurse-Home Visitation.* This program sends nurses into the homes of at-risk women pregnant with their first child to ensure the health of the mother and child. Home visits promote the physical, cognitive, and emotional development of the children and provide overall support and parenting skills to the parents from the prenatal period to two years after the birth of the child.

2. *Bullying Prevention Program.* This school-based initiative is designed to reduce victim/bully incidents among primary and secondary school children. It identifies and addresses episodes from teasing and taunting to intimidation and physical violence and attempts to restructure the school environment to reduce opportunities and rewards for bullying behavior.

3. *Promotion of Alternative Thinking Strategies.* This multiyear, school-based prevention model for elementary school youth is designed to promote emotional and social competence, including the expression, comprehension, and regulation of emotions.

4. *Big Brothers/Big Sisters of America.* This mentoring program primarily serves 6–18-year-old disadvantaged children from single-parent households. The goal is to provide a consistent and stable mentoring relationship. Typically, a mentor will meet with his/her assigned youth at least three times a month for three to five hours.

5. *Quantum Opportunities.* This educational incentives program focuses on disadvantaged teens. It provides educational, developmental, and service activities combined with a sustained relationship with a peer group and a caring adult during the high school years. The goal is to help high-risk children from poor families and neighborhoods graduate from high school and attend college by improving their basic academic abilities.

6. *Multisystemic Therapy (MST).* This program targets specific factors in a young person's ecology (i.e., family, peers, school, neighborhood, and support network) that contribute to antisocial behavior. MST is a short-term, intensive program by credentialed therapists that has been proven to be effective in decreasing antisocial behavior of violent and chronic juvenile offenders.

7. *Functional Family Therapy (FFT).* This family treatment model is designed to engage and motivate youth and families to change their communications, interaction, and problem-solving patterns. FFT has been applied successfully to a variety of youth with problems ranging from conduct disorder to serious criminal offenses such as theft or aggravated assault.

8. *The Midwestern Prevention Project.* This comprehensive, community-based program is designed to prevent the use of cigarettes, alcohol, and marijuana among junior high and middle school students. The program introduces five intervention strategies in sequence over a five-year period; the strategies involve mass media, school, parents, community organizations, and changes in health policy to combat drug use in the community.

9. *Life Skills Training.* This three-year primary prevention program targets the use of cigarettes, alcohol, and marijuana (the initial year includes 15 lessons; booster sessions are provided in the second and third years). The program teaches general life skills and social pressure resistance skills to junior high and middle school students to increase their knowledge and improve attitudes toward drug use.

10. *Multidimensional Treatment Foster Care.* This program targets teenagers who have problems with chronic delinquency and antisocial behavior. Youth are placed in well-supervised foster families for six to nine months and undergo weekly individual therapy. Foster families receive weekly group supervision and daily telephone monitoring. Biological parents learn management techniques to ensure that gains made in the foster settings are maintained after the children return home.

Dwyer and Osher (2000) emphasize that understanding the causes of violence and familiarity with evidence-based practices can help schools identify and address warning signs so children can get help before it is too late. Lumsden (2001) adds a caution: "Although some strategies aimed at reducing school violence are nearly universally applauded and supported, others are more controversial" (Some Areas of Controversy section, para. 1), raising moral, ethical, and legal questions. For example:

1. *Engaging in student "profiling" and other techniques.* The primary concern is that certain students may be stigmatized or classified inappropriately because they seem to fit a profile.
2. *Increasing building security.* The concern is that the gains achieved as a result of installation of metal detectors and other security-related hardware may be offset by detrimental effects on school climate and culture.
3. *Imposing stiffer sentences for juvenile offenders.* The concern is that the focus on punishment turns attention away from prevention and treatment.

CHARACTERISTICS OF A SAFE SCHOOL ENVIRONMENT

The National School Safety Center (Stephens, 2005) defines a safe school as one in which "students can learn and teachers can teach in a welcoming environment, free of intimidation and fear. It is a setting where the educational climate fosters a spirit of acceptance and caring for all students; where behavioral expectations are clearly communicated, consistently enforced, and fairly applied. A safe school is also one that is prepared to respond to the unthinkable crisis" (Message from Director section).

A U.S. Department of Education publication, *Safeguarding Our Children: An Action Guide* (Dwyer and Osher, 2000) delineates characteristics of a safe school by highlighting such key components as prevention, intervention, and responsive strategies, all properly functioning within a school community. These strategies work best in school communities that:

1. *Focus on academic achievement.* Effective schools express the belief that all children can learn and achieve academically and behave appropriately, while simultaneously appreciating children's individual differences. Students who receive the support they require are less likely to behave in antisocial ways.

2. *Involve families in meaningful ways.* School communities make parents feel welcome in school, address barriers to their participation, and keep families positively engaged in their children's education. Students whose families are involved in their growth both in and outside of school are more likely to experience success at school and less likely to become involved in antisocial activities.

3. *Emphasize positive relationships among students and school staff.* Research demonstrates that positive relationships with an adult who is able to provide needed support are crucial in preventing school violence. Effective schools both ensure opportunities for adults to spend quality personal time with students and promote positive student interpersonal relationships, encouraging students to assist each other and to feel comfortable helping others get help when necessary.

4. *Develop links to the community.* Everyone must be committed to improving schools. Schools that have close ties to families, support services, community police, faith-based communities, and the community in general benefit from the numerous resources all of these groups are prepared to provide.

5. *Design ways for students to share their concerns.* Research shows that peers often know in advance about potential school violence. Successful schools promote and support positive relationships between students and adults in order for students to feel safe about

providing information to responsible adults about antisocial behavior and potentially dangerous situations.

6. *Discuss safety issues openly.* Students arrive at school harboring numerous and varying perceptions and misperceptions about death, violence, and weapons use. Effective schools are able to reduce the risks of violence by teaching students the dangers of weapons and appropriate ways to address feelings, express anger, and resolve conflict. Schools teach students that actions have consequences for which they will be held responsible.

7. *Treat students with equal respect.* A major source of conflict in many schools is the perceived or real problem of bias and inequitable treatment of students and staff because of ethnicity, gender, race, social class, religion, disability, nationality, sexual orientation, physical appearance, or some other trait. Effective schools communicate to students and the community at large that all children and staff are valued and respected. There is a deliberate and systemic effort to establish an atmosphere that demonstrates care, concern, and a sense of community.

8. *Help students feel safe expressing their feelings.* It is vital that students feel safe when expressing their needs, fears, and anxieties to the staff of the school.

9. *Establish a system for appropriate referral of students who are suspected of being abused or neglected.* The referral system must reflect federal and state guidelines.

10. *Offer extended day programs for children.* School-based before- and after-school programs that are well supervised and provide a range of support services and activity options (including counseling, tutoring, mentoring, homework help, and community service) can be effective in reducing violence.

11. *Promote good citizenship and character.* Effective schools reinforce and promote the shared values of their communities, including honesty, kindness, responsibility, and respect for others, while recognizing that parents are the primary moral educators of their own children.

12. *Identify problems and assess progress toward viable solutions.* Schools must openly and objectively examine conditions that are potentially dangerous for students and school staff. Effective

schools share this information with their students, families, and the community in general.

13. *Support students in making the transition to adult life and the workplace.* Young people require assistance in planning their future and developing skills that will result in success. In cooperative relationships with the community, effective schools provide students with community service opportunities, work-study programs, and apprenticeships that help them connect with caring adults in the community. As an outcome of these opportunities, relationships develop and, when established early enough, foster in children a sense of confidence in the future.

PLANNING FOR SAFETY

The National Center for Education Statistics (2002) says that two priorities have emerged for public schools. One is to demonstrate that all children are meeting high academic standards as measured by state assessment. The other is to create an environment that is safe and orderly. The center emphasizes that these are not separate missions: children need a safe and orderly school in which to learn.

In the National School Safety Center's safe school planning guide, Stephens (2005) states that "placing school safety on the educational agenda is a mandatory first step toward safer and better schools" (para. 2). He recommends that school safety be incorporated into the educational mission statement to reflect the context in which the school community wants academic learning to take place. For example, the statement, "To learn in a safe, secure, and peaceful environment, free of violence, drugs, and fear" supports the school's legal position to create and enforce policies promoting a disciplined school climate and adds to the validity and credibility of the efforts to create and preserve a safe environment.

The CSPV (no date) emphasizes that creating a safe school plan is not a static process. The plan should be perceived as a framework for action that may be used as a guide for current and future planning. In an effort to provide some guidelines for school and community leaders to follow when devising a safety plan for their own schools, CSPV designed a research-based model for those involved in school safety preparation.

Entitled *A Blueprint for Safe Schools,* the guide outlines the five recommended components:

1. *Convene a safe school planning team.* The planning team is the driving force behind the planning process and should be composed of representatives of the entire school community, including school personnel, students (if age appropriate), parents, religious leaders, law enforcement officials, and government representatives.

2. *Conduct a school site assessment.* An annual school site assessment must be conducted and used as both an evaluation and planning tool to determine the extent of any school safety problems or school climate issues.

3. *Develop strategies and implement violence prevention programs.* In an effort to meet the needs identified in the annual school site assessment, some strategies to consider are:

   a. Establish a clear Code of Behavior that includes the rights and responsibilities of both adults and students within the school community.

   b. Include all young people in positive, rewarding activities and relationships at school to foster a healthy learning environment.

   c. Review federal, state, and local statutes and relevant school and district policies related to student management and school order with the school district attorney.

   d. Control campus access and implement a uniform visitor screening process.

   e. Maintain accurate and detailed records of all school crime incidents.

   f. Promote an ongoing positive relationship with local law enforcement, local businesses, and other community organizations.

   g. Establish a school/district hotline that may be accessed anonymously to report threats or pending violent incidents.

   h. Identify effective violence prevention programs that meet the needs of the school community. Include both in-school and community-based programs such as bullying-prevention programs, life skills training, preventive intervention, and family strengthening programs.

i. Establish guidelines and procedures for identifying students at risk of violence, either as victims or perpetrators.

4. *Establish a social support team.* The focus is to help improve the school climate. Members should include teachers, parents, counselors, mental health workers, and law enforcement officers who are able to help identify students who are at risk and provide the most appropriate support for them.

5. *Develop a crisis response plan.* A crisis response plan outlines specific procedures to follow during an emergency. Having such a plan in place can save an enormous amount of time and energy and maintain the commitment to safety when unforeseen problems arise.

The CSPV stresses that no two school communities are the same. Each must identify its own needs and the strategies to meet them in an ongoing planning, assessment, implementation, and evaluation process.

Paine and Sprague (2000) suggest that planners assess their particular schools' needs in six areas and devise strategies to meet those needs. The areas are (1) community collaboration, (2) antiviolence curriculum, (3) preventative student-discipline policies and procedures, (4) safe physical environment, (5) staff and student training and support, and (6) crisis response.

The director of the Center for the Study and Prevention of School Violence (Riley, 2000) suggests that the strategies in the plan address the *Three P's*—place, people, and purpose. *Place* refers to the physical environment of the school, *people* to the relationships between and among those who are a part of the school community, and *purpose* to a steady focus on the educational purpose of the school, so that the emphasis on safety and security does not have the effect of making a school take on the characteristics of a prison. These Three P's relate to the conditions of being safe, orderly, and caring, as well as to the reason schools exist—education. Table 9.1 defines *safe, orderly,* and *caring* and presents an analytical process to determine if a school *is* safe, orderly, and caring.

COMPREHENSIVE SCHOOL SAFETY PLAN

Violence in neighborhoods and communities often finds its way into schools. School violence frequently reflects a broader problem that can be

Table 9.1. How to Determine If Your School Is . . .

	A Safe School	An Orderly School	A Caring School
Definition	A *safe school* is one whose physical features, layout, policies, and procedures are designed to minimize the impact of disruptions and intrusions that might prevent the school from fulfilling its educational mission. It is characterized by a climate that is free of fear. The perceptions, feelings, and behaviors of members of the school community reveal that the school is a place where people are able to go about their business without concern for their safety.	An *orderly school* is one characterized by a climate of mutual respect and responsibility. Students relate to each other and to teachers and school staff in acceptable ways. Expectations about what is acceptable behavior are clearly stated, and consequences for unacceptable behavior are known and applied when appropriate. Students and staff feel responsible for the successful operation of the school.	A *caring school* is one that is inviting and supportive of students and staff. Students and staff are provided with opportunities to relate to each other in appropriate ways. The perceptions, feelings, and behaviors of members of the school community reveal that the school is a place where people are comfortable, feel welcome, and are able to be successful.
Indicators	The existence and implementation of a plan, policies, and procedures that address the "safety" of the school. Measures: • number of trespassers • number of guns and other weapons • number of break-ins • incidents of vandalism • rates of/reasons for absenteeism • survey results • school-specific indicators	The existence and implementation of a plan, policies, and procedures that address the "orderliness" of the school. Measures: • referrals to the office • reasons for referrals • number of in-school suspensions • number of out-of-school suspensions • survey results • school-specific indicators	The existence of a plan, policies, and procedures that enable the school to provide a "caring" environment. Measures: • rates of/reasons for absenteeism • number of/reasons for transfers • staff turnover • levels of involvement/participation • survey results • school-specific indicators
Evaluation	To evaluate the safety of a school, assessments of the safety concerns of members of the school community (through surveys, for example) need to occur. Information from surveys and other safety measures should be used to create the safe school plan so that safety concerns can be addressed. Continuous measurement of safety concerns needs to take place so that actions can be adjusted to address safety concerns.	To evaluate the orderliness of a school, assessments of the reasons for disorder need to occur. From these assessments, a code of conduct reflecting behavioral expectations can be established as part of the safe school plan. Review of the reasons for disorder should help establish the code of conduct. Adjustments to the code should be made based upon continuous review of the school's orderliness.	To evaluate how caring a school is, assessments of the perceptions, feelings, and behaviors of members of the school community need to occur. Such assessments will reveal how much these members feel *cared for* and will provide direction to school efforts that are intended to create a *caring* environment.

addressed only when everyone—school, home, and community—works together. Unfortunately, even when schools, families, and communities work together, schools are not insulated from the negative conditions in the surrounding communities. Thus, schools everywhere—in the most densely to the most sparsely populated communities—must recognize the need to plan and prepare for a variety of situations, including incidents of violence.

A U.S. Department of Education publication, *Safeguarding Our Children: An Action Guide* (Dwyer and Osher, 2000), is a companion piece to the department's *Early Warning, Timely Response: A Guide to Safe Schools* (Dwyer and others, 1998). Highlighting evidence-based practices, the *Action Guide* is geared to developing strategic, coordinated, and comprehensive plans that involve schoolwide prevention, early intervention, and intensive services for students with significant emotional or behavioral needs, including needs manifested by disruptive, destructive, or violent behaviors. The authors emphasize that "the most promising prevention and intervention strategies extend beyond the schoolhouse door; they include administrators, teachers, families, students, support staff, and community agency staff. Everyone's support is important to safeguard our children" (p. 7).

A comprehensive school safety plan must be tailored to meet the specific needs of the school and its surrounding community in providing a safe and orderly environment for learning and must address the areas of discipline, promotion of tolerance, conflict resolution, and crisis response. Gallagher and others (2005) caution schools and school districts not to simply adopt the plan of another school or district. They stress that the process of developing a plan not only ensures that the plan will fit the needs of a specific setting, but will also lead to ownership and understanding by school personnel, students, families, and the community at large—in other words, by all those affected by the plan.

Discipline

Discipline has been a recurring problem in public schools for many years. A new study, *Teaching Interrupted* (Public Agenda, 2004), suggests that "educators have made only limited progress addressing it. The issue continues to bedevil teachers, concern parents, and derail learning in schools across the country" (p. 2). According to a random national survey of teachers and parents of middle and high school students, there is strong agreement among teachers (97%) and parents (78%) that a school needs good discipline and behavior in order for students to succeed academically. There is also strong agreement among teachers (93%) and parents (88%) that, in addition to teaching the three R's, the school's mission is to teach youth to follow rules so they can become productive citizens.

These findings suggest that today's school discipline policies may not be working very well, but teachers and parents agree that "the discipline problem" is not insurmountable. Proposals that garnered support in the survey fell into the following categories:

1. *Dealing with "persistent trouble makers."* Teachers (93%) and parents (89%) supported the establishment of zero-tolerance policies. In addition, teachers (84%) and parents (70%) supported giving principals more authority to handle discipline issues as they see fit.
2. *Putting more responsibility on parents.* Teachers (94%) supported finding ways to hold parents more accountable for students' behavior.
3. *Limiting lawsuits on discipline.* Teachers (82%) and parents (78%) supported limiting lawsuits to serious situations like expulsion, and teachers (82%) and parents (69%) supported removing the possibility of monetary awards for parents who sue over discipline issues.
4. *Consistently enforcing the little rules.* Teachers (91%) and parents (88%) supported strictly enforcing the little rules so the right tone is created and bigger problems are avoided. (pp. 4–5)

In the safe schools guide, *Early Warning, Timely Response,* Dwyer and others (1998) state that "a growing number of schools are discovering that the most effective way to reduce suspensions, expulsions, office referrals, and other similar actions . . . is to emphasize a proactive approach to discipline" (p. 21). Effective schools implement schoolwide campaigns that establish high expectations and provide support for socially appropriate behavior. They develop and consistently enforce schoolwide rules that are clear, broad-based, and fair. Rules and disciplinary procedures are developed collaboratively by representatives of the total educational community and are communicated clearly to all parties and, as the guide emphasizes, *are followed consistently by everyone.* Schools that are most effective:

1. Develop a schoolwide disciplinary policy that includes a code of conduct with specific rules and consequences (including antiharassment and antiviolence policies and due process rights). The code should be able to accommodate student differences on a case-by-case basis as necessary.
2. Ensure that the cultural values and educational goals of the community are reflected in the rules, which should include a statement expressing the values that underlie the schoolwide disciplinary policy.
3. Include school staff, students, and families in the development, discussion, and implementation of the rules, which should be perceived as fair.
4. Make sure that consequences are commensurate with offenses and that rules are written and applied in a nondiscriminatory manner, accommodating cultural diversity.
5. Make sure that negative consequences (such as the withdrawal of privileges) are combined with positive strategies that teach socially appropriate behavior and address external factors that might have caused the behavior.
6. Include a statement of zero tolerance for possession of weapons, alcohol, or drugs. Provide services and support for students who have been suspended or expelled.

In working to improve school discipline, it is important to keep in mind the ultimate goal: to encourage responsible behavior and provide all students with a safe and orderly school experience, and to discourage misconduct. Juvonen (2001) points out that in crafting strategies and policies, choices have to be made between psychological safety and physical safety, proactive strategies and reactive strategies, targeted and whole-school approaches, punitive and instructional methods, incident-based and person-based interventions.

The National Association of School Psychologists (NASP) Center (2002) believes that at the heart of the challenge of disciplining students, particularly those with chronic or serious behavior problems, is the issue of punitive versus supportive disciplinary practices.

> Though increasingly common in recent years, reliance on punitive approaches to discipline, such as "zero tolerance" policies, has proven largely ineffective, even counterproductive. This holds true both for general education students and those with disabilities. Current research and legislation offer alternative "best practice" strategies that support the safe education of all students. (para. 1)

NASP contends that positive discipline strategies improve safety and outcomes for all students. Positive strategies are research-based and focus on increasing desirable behaviors instead of simply decreasing undesirable behaviors through punishment; they emphasize the importance of making positive changes in the child's environment in order to improve the child's behavior. Making changes may entail the use of positive reinforcement, modeling, supportive teacher-student relations, and family support and assistance from a variety of educational and mental health specialists. Results of the Safe and Responsive Schools Project (2000) suggest that schools should make use of a variety of disciplinary alternatives to expulsion and suspension. These alternatives include:

1. *In-school disciplinary alternatives.* Saturday school or in-school suspension keeps students in school while they are disciplined and requires students to continue their academic assignments.
2. *Restitution.* Restitution involves "setting things right" and is typically geared to the nature of the offense. For example, vandals might be expected to clean up the results of their vandalism or participate in a project to improve the physical environment.
3. *Anger management.* Aggressive students often lack self-control in social situations, perceiving the actions of others to be more hostile than they really are. Anger management classes or programs may help these students change their perceptions and learn alternative behaviors to use in conflict situations.
4. *Individual behavior plans.* In functional assessment, school psychologists or special education consultants use interviews, checklists, and observation to better understand the reasons for disruptive

behavior and develop specific plans to address objectionable behaviors.

5. *Alternative disciplinary methods.* To shift the burden of discipline from teachers and administrators, some schools have developed alternative strategies and procedures, such as peer mediation and teen court, for resolving conflict or determining disciplinary consequences.

6. *Alternative settings.* Well-planned and coordinated alternative schools may meet the needs of some students.

7. *Community team approach.* Problems of disruptive and violent youth are often highly complex, cutting across school, family, and community. Interagency approaches such as "wraparound" teams increase the communication and collaboration of child-serving agencies and allow them to develop comprehensive community-based plans for disruptive youth and their families.

To be effective, and likely to be accepted, discipline policies should be developed with as much input as possible from representatives of those who will be affected by them both directly and indirectly. Once developed, the policies must be communicated to staff, students, parents, and the community. But, as Gaustad (1992) warns, a policy on paper is meaningless in itself. "Ongoing administrative support, inservice training in new techniques, continued communication, and periodic evaluation and modification are needed to adapt a school discipline plan to the changing needs of the school community" (para. 22).

Zero Tolerance

The concept of "zero tolerance" raises some controversial issues and needs careful consideration. As Skiba (2004) points out, the term derives from a law enforcement perspective popularized in the Reagan-era war on drugs. Shortly after its adoption, it began to be applied to a widening range of issues and eventually found its way into education as a tough, no-nonsense answer to the safety threats faced by schools. Zero tolerance became part of national policy when Congress passed the federal Gun-Free Schools Act of 1994. Containing a threat of withholding federal education money for noncompliance, the law mandates a one-year calendar expulsion for possession of a firearm, referral of law-violating students to the criminal or juvenile justice systems, and the provision that state law must authorize the chief administrative officer of each local school district to modify the expulsion policy on a case-by-case basis.

The 1994 act does not use the term *zero tolerance* and thus does not define the concept. The National Center for Education Statistics performed a statistical analysis of "zero tolerance" policies in 1998. A follow-up survey defined *zero tolerance* as "any policy that provides a 'known consequence' if a given act is committed—bringing a gun to school, for example—regardless of the severity of the consequence. A 'known consequence' specifying a minor punishment would be as much 'zero tolerance' as long-term suspension from the school" (Ficus, 2000, p. 2).

Skiba (2004) notes that when school policy was expanded beyond weapons possession to drugs, alcohol, and fighting, substantial variation developed in local definitions of zero tolerance. Some school districts adopted a pure zero tolerance policy for punishing major and minor offences fairly equally, while others defined zero tolerance in a more graduated way, scaling the severity of the consequence to the severity of the offense.

Research on the effectiveness of a zero tolerance policy is limited and has produced conflicting results. Wasser (1999) argues that zero tolerance policies are effective when applied consistently as one part of a structured disciplinary program. Other researchers have documented the inequitableness of zero tolerance policy application. A review of the data on suspensions by the U.S. Office of Civil Rights (Ficus, 2000) showed that more than two-thirds of the 3,000 districts studied had higher expulsion rates for black students than for white students. The higher expulsion rates did not appear to be related to either the higher poverty level among African Americans or to a higher level of disruptive behavior by black students.

The conflicting results seem to stem not so much from the concept of zero tolerance, but from the way it is defined and applied. McAndrews (2001) observes, "Perhaps the biggest problem with zero tolerance policies is inconsistent application and interpretation" (section 4, para. 3). This conclusion is reflected in a resolution adopted in 2001 by the American Bar Association opposing "policies that have a discriminatory effect, or mandate either expulsion or referral of students to juvenile or criminal court, without regard to the circumstances or nature of the offense or the student's history" (McAndrews, 2001, section 4, para 4).

Promotion of Tolerance

In 2001, 12% of students ages 12–18 reported that someone at their school had used hate-related words against them, and more than one-third (36%) had seen hate-related graffiti at school (DeVoe and others, 2004). The Safe and Responsive Schools Project (2000) found that bullying is commonly underestimated by school personnel; almost one-third of elementary students and about one-tenth of secondary students reported having been bullied. Bullying, intolerance, and prejudice are the underlying cause of many school conflicts. The question for school leaders is what can be done to increase students' tolerance for those who are different from themselves?

Godwin and others (2001) suggest that schools become proactive in developing tolerance. Simply increasing diversity in the classroom does not guarantee an increase in tolerance. The researchers found that the schools that achieved the highest rates of student tolerance were those schools that supported increased opportunities for students to develop interethnic friendships. Henze (2001) suggests including multicultural or ethnic assemblies, after-school programs and other opportunities for students to mix and interact, conflict resolution training, and innovative teaming of a bilingual class with a traditional class.

The NSPRA (2002) distributes a packet of articles intended to help educators promote tolerance and increase multicultural communication. The overall message is to watch for emerging signs of racial tension among students, staff, and community:

An unfortunate consequence of international terrorism is the potential for some to look for scapegoats to unleash anger and frustration. Some students may target others from particular races, nationalities, and religious groups for aggression. All students and staff need to be reminded that aggression toward these individuals cannot be tolerated. Administrators and teachers need to be particularly sensitive to aggressive student behaviors such as racial slurs, put-downs, threatening notes, defacement of property, and taunting. Let's not have minor infractions escalate into more serious incidents. So the time to address these infractions is now. (Overall Messages section, para. 2)

NSPRA's (2002) suggestions for achieving and maintaining a safe and respectful environment include:

1. Be vigilant for any signs of inappropriate behavior and reprisals against any students based on their faith or country of origin (for example, verbal or physical harassment, including insults, name calling, inappropriate celebratory behavior, intimidation, hate-based graffiti, etc.).
2. Give students a clear message that they are expected to be respectful in all ways.
3. Remind students and staff to report incidents reflecting intolerance immediately to the principal.
4. Encourage students to talk to a teacher or administrator if they have concerns about the behavior of a fellow student or if they know of a student who is being harassed or intimidated. Explain that their cooperation is important for everybody's safety and that the best way they can help a fellow student who is having difficulty is by involving a staff member.
5. Encourage students and staff to refrain from making comments that undermine a positive and respectful environment or that may be hurtful to others.
6. Try not to focus on who is "bad" and who is "good," but rather on how debilitating hate and dissension can be. Emphasize how tragic it is that hate exists and describe the negative impact hate-based activities can have on all of us.
7. Use the tragedy of 9/11 to focus on consequences of hatred and intolerance.

NSPRA emphasizes that in the multicultural environment of most of today's schools, educators must pay attention to warning signs that tension is building and watch for the self-segregation of ethnic groups during lunch and other breaks and at after-school events. Contention over group or team working assignments should be carefully examined to determine the cause. Signs of intolerance or insensitivity on or near ethnic and cultural days of celebration should be noted. Graffiti and vandalism targeted at students or staff may signal that trouble is brewing.

CONFLICT RESOLUTION

Safe and orderly school environments are essential to ensuring that all children have the opportunity to develop to their fullest potential. Some of the conflicts that youths face begin at school, but many are brought into the school from the home or community.

Cultural conflicts are based on differences in national origin or ethnicity, and social conflicts on differences in gender, sexual orientation, class, and physical and mental abilities. Personal and institutional reactions to differences often take the form of prejudice, discrimination, harassment, and even hate crimes. As the *Conflict Resolution Education* guide (Crawford and Bodine, 1996) points out, these conflicts are complex because "they are rooted not only in prejudice and discrimination related to cultural and social differences but also in the resulting structures and relationships in inequality and privilege" (p. 2).

Conflict resolution education offers schools strategies for uncovering the causes of conflict and finding ways to resolve the conflict. Jones (2000) defines conflict resolution education (CRE) as "a spectrum of processes that utilize communication skills and creative and analytic thinking to prevent, manage, and peacefully resolve conflict" (Overview, para. 1). She points out that while CRE has commonalities with violence prevention, there are significant differences. Violence prevention is more limited in scope than CRE, which is concerned with issues and situations beyond violence and focuses on both violent and nonviolent behavior. Violence prevention emphasizes policy changes and tends to look at the environment, analyzing risk factors for violence and looking for ways to reduce or eliminate those factors. CRE emphasizes individual skill building and community education and focuses more on the conflict itself, trying to find alternatives for resolving the conflict and repairing the relationship. CRE overlaps with the promotion of tolerance because prejudice and intolerance are often underlying causes of conflict.

Jones explains that, although there are variations, most CRE efforts include components intended to help develop an understanding of conflict; principles of conflict resolution (win-win, interest-based problem solving); process steps in problem solving (agreeing to negotiate, establishing ground rules for negotiation, gathering information about the conflict, exploring possible solution options, selecting options, and reaching agreement); and skills/abilities required to use each of these steps effectively.

The Conflict Resolution Education Network (Jones, 2000) estimates that at least 12,000 public schools (K–12) in the United States have some form of CRE. The Safe and Responsive Schools Project (2000) found that most of the curricular approaches are integrated into a broader program, some of which have been able to document promising changes in student attitudes and behavior, decreased physical violence, increased student cooperation, and lower suspension and dropout rates. However, the study cautioned that consistency and commitment are highly important; students appear to show favorable outcomes in direct relationship to how often the curriculum is taught.

The Safe and Responsive Schools Project also found that attention to several planning and training issues increased the chances for success. Most important, perhaps, is selecting a curriculum that meets the needs of students in a particular school. Before implementation, staff must understand the time and effort involved and be trained adequately in the proposed curriculum in order to ensure commitment to a level of instruction that will be effective in changing student attitudes and behavior.

School-Based Peer Mediation

Cohen (2003) states that school-based peer mediation is "one of the most popular and arguably the most effective approach to integrating the practice of conflict resolution into schools" (para. 2). Peer mediation is a form of conflict resolution in which trained student leaders help their peers work together to resolve everyday disputes. For the peer mediation process to work, participation must be voluntary and students must possess the skills necessary to be effective mediators. Although these skills are not precisely defined, Vera and others (2004) point out that they are like all social competencies, largely influenced by such individual traits as temperament, family traits including parenting styles, reactions to pressures to adhere to group norms, and cultural factors including gender and ethnic socialization. In the peer mediation process, all matters discussed in mediation sessions remain confidential, with the exception of information that is illegal or life-threatening. Student mediators do not make judgments or offer advice and have no power to force decisions on their peers. However, as Cohen points out "mediation is sensitive to the underlying causes of conflict, [so] the vast majority of peer mediation sessions (85%) result in lasting resolutions" (para. 1).

Cohen warns that successful implementation of a school-based peer mediation program requires the completion of each of the four stages of the process. In the first stage, initiators must generate support and gain a commitment to implement the program. Once administrator, teacher, and student support is ensured, a coordinator must be identified. The coordinator can be drawn from school administrators who are not disciplinarians, counselors, teachers, special staff, or even community volunteers. The coordinator's responsibilities include handling in-school publicity and education of students and staff, overseeing the training of peer mediators, scheduling and supervising mediation sessions, following up on sessions, and keeping records.

In the second, or planning and outreach, stage, the coordinator usually forms advisory committees to help formulate program policies. Important questions to be answered are the following: (1) How will the program be funded? (2) Which students and staff will be trained to mediate? (3) Who will conduct the training? (4) When will the training be scheduled? (5) What issues will be mediated? (6) Where will the mediation sessions be held? (7) When will the sessions be held? (8) What is the program's confidentiality policy? (9) How will the school at large be informed about mediation? (10) What kinds of follow-up training and support will be provided for mediators?

The third stage is the actual training of the mediators. It is essential that peer mediators master the needed knowledge and skills. This training usually requires about 18 to 25 hours for high school students, 12 to 20 hours for middle school students, and 8 to 15 hours for elementary school students. Only after the training is complete should peer mediators begin mediating cases.

Although peer mediation procedures vary, there are several basic steps (Guanci, 2002):

1. *Intake.* The coordinator receives and reviews the referral form, then meets with the students in conflict, answers questions about peer mediation, and asks if the students would like to continue with the process.
2. *Activating the process.* Upon agreement, the coordinator selects mediators and schedules mediation within 24 hours. The motive behind a 24-hour delay is to allow for a cool down period.
3. *Setting the stage.* The mediators describe the process, establish the ground rules, answer questions, and confirm the parties' willingness to participate.
4. *Hearing the story.* All parties are afforded the opportunity to describe their side of the conflict without interruption.
5. *Defining the problem.* Mediators ask questions of the parties to uncover feelings and discern and clarify the area of the conflict. Parties may question each other.
6. *Brainstorming for solutions.* Mediators ask all parties individually what they want to happen to help resolve the conflict. With the mediators' help, the parties then discuss possible solutions to try to arrive at a settlement agreeable to all.
7. *Agreement.* When the parties are able to reach an agreement to resolve their conflict, the mediators write down the terms, ask the parties to sign it, and provide each party with a copy.
8. *Follow-up.* The coordinator/student mediators check with the parties to ensure that the agreement is working and to offer further assistance if necessary.

Cohen (2003) lists three conditions that must be met if a school-based peer mediation program is to be successful. First, there must be enough interpersonal conflict to warrant initiating the program. If mediators do not have the opportunity to mediate cases, few of the benefits associated with peer mediation programs will be realized. Every school must decide what constitutes enough conflict, but experience suggests that there must be at least one case per week for the program to be significantly beneficial. Second, there must be administrative support. Administrators must work aggressively to overcome attitudinal and structural resistance; in particular, administrators in charge of discipline must be willing to make referrals and to support student mediators' efforts. Third, there must be a peer mediation coordinator who oversees all aspects of the program. The more resources this school-based adult has in terms of skill, commitment, and time during the school day, the more successful the program is likely to be.

School Crisis Plan

Unfortunately for many school leaders, the question is not *if* crises will occur but when, and what should be done? Gallagher and others (2005) define *crisis* as "an unstable or crucial time or state of affairs in which a decisive change is pending" (p. 160). According to the U.S. Department of Education guide, *Practical Information on Crisis Planning* (2003), "a crisis is a situation where schools could be faced with inadequate information, not enough time and sufficient resources, but in which leaders must make one or many crucial decisions" (p. 10). Crises can happen before, during, or after school and on or off school campuses. They can arise from some physical or fiscal impropriety, as well as something violent, and can range in scope and intensity from incidents that directly affect a single student to those that have an impact on the entire community. Even what a school defines as a crisis may vary with the unique needs, resources, and assets of a particular school and its community.

Gallagher and others (2005) emphasize that a crisis plan is essential because "every crisis can prompt panic-like reactions" (p. 160). Schonfeld and Newgass (2003) stress that a school crisis plan should address three general areas: safety and security; dissemination of accurate information to the crisis response team, school staff, students, parents, and the general public when it is appropriate; and the emotional and psychological needs of all parties. The authors state that all three of these areas must be addressed concurrently or none will be addressed effectively.

The development of a crisis response plan should be a collaborative effort involving all members of the school community—teachers and support staff, school administrators, law enforcement, the fire department, mental health agencies, parent-teacher groups, and other community partners. *Practical Information on Crisis Planning* (U.S. Department of Education, 2003) suggests planning four phases of crisis management:

1. *Mitigation/prevention:* addresses what schools and districts can do to reduce or even eliminate risks to life and property.

2. *Preparedness:* focuses on the process of planning for a worst-case scenario.
3. *Response:* identifies actions to take during a crisis.
4. *Recovery:* deals with restoring the learning and teaching environment after a crisis.

According to Paine and Sprague (2000), "school leaders must make crisis response an ongoing, integral part of school-improvement planning" (para. 2). The authors suggest that preparation for a possible crisis should be a four-step process.

Step 1. Form a crisis-response team within the school. A group of individuals should be identified who can serve as members of a team whose primary goal is to assist a school in responding during and after a crisis. A team approach is suggested because it can help reduce the fear and anxiety that accompany a crisis, educate students and staff in the dynamics of grief and prepare them for what they might experience, and give members of the school community an opportunity to express their feelings in an accepting environment.

Step 2. Develop a written crisis- or emergency-response plan. A written crisis-response plan should be developed that describes intervention procedures and the responsibilities of the team members. The plan should address topics such as the duties of specific crisis team members, phone-tree directions, activities to help students deal with loss, media and other communications guidelines, tips for handling special situations, grief and loss reactions in children and adults, and long-term follow-up.

Step 3. Coordinate the plan with community emergency personnel. After a draft of the plan is developed, police, fire, hospital, and mental health services personnel should be asked to review it. Strategies should be developed to coordinate the efforts of these agencies in case of a large-scale crisis. Maps of school buildings should be provided to law enforcement, fire department, and emergency personnel, including the location of important switches and valves. Mock emergency drills including both lockdown and evacuation procedures should be conducted to test the plan.

Step 4. Conduct training for staff, including detailed information on the elements of the plan. This training is necessary to ensure rapid and sensitive response during an actual crisis.

Crisis-response teams vary in size. Schonfeld and Newgass (2003) suggest that the personnel include a team chair, assistant chair, counseling coordinator, staff notification coordinator, communications coordinator, media coordinator, and crowd management coordinator. A team member might hold more than one position or several team members might share a position. What is important is that team members receive training for their positions and that they develop an appreciation of and respect for other team members' responsibilities.

The National Strategy Forum (2004) believes that most crisis plans are too general. A comprehensive plan should spell out detailed responses to fires, explosions, bomb threats; power outages; tornadoes, storms, and other natural disasters; intruders/hostages; civil disruptions; and chemical or biological attacks. It should also address the mental health of students and faculty, including such special-needs populations as the non-English speaking, nonambulatory, and visually and hearing impaired. The crisis plan should include strategies for monitoring news media reports and handling relations with the news media.

According to Gallagher and others (2005), most school crisis plans include:

1. Reasons for the plan.
2. Types of crises covered in the plan, with checklists for responding to each one.
3. Procedures common to all crises.
4. Necessary equipment and supplies, including distribution of master keys to emergency responders; phones, radios, and other equipment needed when electricity is cut off; and first aid supplies, food, and water for students and staff.
5. Emergency telephone numbers.
6. Detailed maps of each school facility.
7. Procedural information, including guidelines for closing the school, and lockdown or evacuation procedures.
8. Guidelines for effective communication with the media, staff, and community.

9. Sample letters that can be quickly tailored to a particular situation and sent home with students.

The school crisis plan should also cover the follow-up response in the wake of a crisis. The American Academy of Experts in Traumatic Stress (Lerner and others, 2003) points out that the way children react to tragic events depends on such variables as their age, personal history, and personality, plus the severity and proximity of the event, the level of social support available, and the type and quality of interventions.

It is important to realize that most children will recover from the effects of a crisis with appropriate support from family, friends, and school personnel. . . . Effective response to a crisis capitalizes on the resources within the school environment. A Crisis Response Team that identifies and responds to a crisis in a unified and collaborative manner can alter the aftermath of a crisis. (p. 94)

THE OVERALL STATE OF SCHOOL EMERGENCY PREPAREDNESS

A survey by the National Association of School Resource Officers (NASRO) (2005) found wide variation in school emergency preparedness. Key findings of the survey raise concern:

1. School-based police officers continue to report glaring gaps in the schools' emergency preparedness planning.
2. More than half of the officers reported that the school crisis/emergency plans are inadequate.
3. More than two-thirds reported that their school emergency plans are not exercised (with tabletop drills, full-scale drills, etc.) on a regular basis.
4. A significant percentage (more than 43%) of the officers indicated that school officials do not meet formally at least once a year with police, fire, emergency medical services, emergency management agencies, and other public safety officials to review and revise school plans.

5. More than half of the respondents indicated that teachers, administrators, and support staff do not receive ongoing professional development training on school security and emergency preparedness
   issues.
6. Almost two-thirds of the officers stated that school bus drivers and
   transportation personnel have not had any training in the past three
   years related to security measures, emergency planning and
   response, terrorism, and associated topics.
7. More than 70% of the officers indicated that funding for school
   safety in their districts had either decreased or remained the same;
   only 15% reported an increase in funding.
8. Almost 74% of the school-based police officers believe that their
   schools are inadequately prepared to respond to a terrorist attack.
   (Executive Summary section)

Addressing the question of the overall status of school emergency preparedness and readiness, Kenneth Trump, president of the National School
Safety and Security Services (2005) said:

Many schools took a much more serious approach to school security and
crisis preparedness issues following the spate of school shootings nationwide in the late 1990s. As a result of this, many improvements were
made. . . . However, progress has stalled in the past couple of years and
we are seeing increasing indications that we may be losing that progress
nationwide. For example, school safety budgets continue to be slashed. . . .
Pressures for meeting mandated test score standards have pushed school
safety training and planning to the back burner in many districts. Time and
distance from high-profile school violence incidents also breed compla-
cency and fuel denial. Most schools have developed written crisis plans;
however, in our school safety assessments for school districts around the
country, we consistently find questionable content in these plans. We also
find that many plans are sitting on office shelves collecting dust and have
not been exercised for the purpose of seeing if what is on paper would actually work in a real emergency. (p. 48)

When asked about the future, Trump responded:

Schools will always be subject to facing crisis situations, especially those
involving some type of crime or violence. . . . This is simply a fact that is

not subject to debate. The more interesting question, though, is whether the preparedness level for a school crisis will improve. . . . School safety, security, and emergency planning are truly leadership issues. The level of preparedness is directly related to the true importance of these issues to the leaders of our schools. (pp. 52–53)

The America Prepared Campaign (Phinney, 2004) examined the state of preparedness in the 20 largest school districts in the United States and drew the same conclusion. In its canvas of the 20 districts and its interviews with administrators, emergency management personnel, parents, and volunteers, the campaign found several important trends. "Money was almost always a problem, as was size—no matter how rich or large the district was. Parents played a significant role in getting a district prepared. But the biggest factor was the resolve of each school system's administrators" (p. 56).

REFERENCES

Center for the Study and Prevention of Violence. (no date). *A blueprint for safe schools.* Retrieved September 22, 2005, from http://www.colorado.edu/cspv/publications/factsheets/safeschools/FS-SC02.html

Cohen, R. (2003). *Implementing a peer mediation program.* Retrieved September 20, 2005, from http://acrnet.org/acrlibrary/more.php?id = 6_0_1_0_M

Crawford, D., and Bodine, R. (1996). *Conflict resolution education: A guide to implementing programs in schools, youth-serving organizations, and community and juvenile justice settings.* Retrieved September 27, 2005, from http://www.ncjrs.gov/pdffiles/conflic.pdf

DeVoe, J., and others. (2004). *Indicators of school crime and safety: 2004.* Washington, DC: National Center for Education Statistics, Bureau of Justice Statistics.

Dwyer, K., and Osher, D. (2000). *Safeguarding our children: An action guide.* Washington, DC: U.S. Departments of Education and Justice, American Institutes for Research. Retrieved September 20, 2005, from http://cecp.air.org/aifr5_01.pdf

Dwyer, K., Osher, D., and Warger, C. (1998). *Early warning, timely response: A guide to safe schools.* Washington, DC: U.S. Departments of Education and Justice, American Institutes for Research. Retrieved September 20, 2005, from http://.cecp.air.org/cecp/guide/

Ficus, J. W. (2000). Zero tolerance: Effective policy or display of administrative machismo? *The Safety Zone, 2*(1), 1–2, 7. Retrieved September 21, 2005, from http://safetyzone.org/pdf/newsletters/newsletter_spring_00.pdf

Furlong, M. J., and Morrison, G. (2000). The school in school violence: Definitions and facts. *Journal of Emotional and Behavioral Disorders, 8*(2). Retrieved September 21, 2005, from http://www.questia.com/PM.qst?a = o& d = 5001750209

Gallagher, D. R., Bagin, D., and Moore, E. H. (2005). *The school and community relations.* Boston, MA: Pearson Education, Inc.

Gaustad, J. (1992). *School discipline.* ERIC Digest 78. Retrieved September 26, 2005, from http://eric.uoregon.edu/publications/digests/digest078.html

Godwin, K., Ausbrooks, C., and Martinez, V. (2001). Teaching tolerance in public and private schools. *Phi Delta Kappan, 82,* 7.

Guanci, J. A. (2002). Peer mediation: A winning solution to conflict resolution. *The Education Digest, 67,* 6.

Henze, R. (2001). Segregated classroom, integrated intent. *Journal of Education for Students Placed at Risk, 6,* 1–2.

Hurst, M. D. (2005). Safety check: High-profile attacks raise concerns, but statistics show school violence is down. *Education Week,* April 27. Retrieved October 10, 2005, from http://www.edweek.org/ew/articles/2005/04/27/33youth violence.h24.html

Jones, T. S. (2000). *Conflict resolution education: Goals, models, benefits and implementation.* Retrieved September 27, 2005, from http://www.directionser vice.ore/cadre/pfriendly.cfm?id = 715

Juvonen, J. (2001). *School violence: Prevalence, fears, and prevention.* Rand Education. Retrieved September 27, 2005, from http://www.rand.org/publica tions/IP/IP219/

Lerner, M. D., Lindell, B., and Volpe, J. S. (2003). Practical suggestions for assisting children in the aftermath of a tragedy. *A practical guide for crisis response in our schools.* New York: American Academy of Experts in Traumatic Stress. Retrieved October 13, 2005, from http://www.schoolcrisisre sponse.com/download.htm

Lumsden, L. (Ed). (2001). *Trends & issues: School safety.* Eugene, OR: University of Oregon, Clearinghouse on Educational Management. Retrieved September 22, 2005, from http://eric.uoregon.edu/trends_issues/safety/index

McAndrews, T. (2001). *Zero tolerance policies.* ERIC Digest 146. ED451579. Retrieved September 22, 2005, from http://www.eric.ed.gov.html

Muller, J., and Mihalic, S. (1999). *Blueprints: A violence prevention initiative.* OJPDP Fact Sheet 110. Retrieved September 22, 2005, from http://www.ncjrs .org/pdffiles1/fs99110.pdf

National Association of School Psychologists Center. (2002). *Fair and effective discipline for all students: Best practice strategies for educators.* Retrieved September 26, 2005, from http://www.naspcenter.org/factsheets/effdiscip_fs.html

National Association of School Resource Officers. (2005). *School safety left behind? School safety threats grow as preparedness stalls and funding decreases.* Retrieved September 23, 2005, from http://www.nasro.org

National Center for Education Statistics. (2002). *Collecting and using crime, violence, and discipline incident data to make a difference in schools.* Retrieved September 26, 2005, from http://nces.ed.gov/pubs2002/safety/introduction.asp

National Criminal Justice Reference Service. (2002). *In the spotlight: School safety.* Retrieved September 20, 2005, from http://www.ncjrs.gov/spotlight/school_safety

National Governors Association Center for Best Practices. (1999). *Issue brief: Making schools safe.* Retrieved September 23, 2005, from http://www.nga.org/cda/files/19990823SAFESCHOOLS.pdf

National School Public Relations Association. (2002). *Public relations: Information on promoting tolerance in an age of global terrorism.* Retrieved September 22, 2005, from http://www.nspra.org/main_prarticles.htm

National Strategy Forum. (2004). *School safety in the 21st century: Adapting to new security challenges post-9/11.* Retrieved September 22, 2005, from http://www.schoolsecurity.org/School_Terrorism_NSf.pdf

National Threat Assessment Center, U.S. Secret Service. (no date). *Secret Service Safe School Initiative.* Retrieved May 3, 2006, from http://www.secretservice.gov/ntac_ssi.shtml

Paine, C., and Sprague, J. (2000). *Crisis prevention and response: Is your school prepared?* Eugene, OR: University of Oregon, Clearinghouse on Educational Management. Retrieved September 22, 2005, from http://eric.uoregon.edu/trends_issues/safety/bulletin

Phinney, A. (2004). *Preparedness in America's schools: A comprehensive look at terrorism preparedness in America's twenty largest school districts.* America Prepared Campaign, Inc. Retrieved October 10, 2005, from http://www.americaprepared.org/pdf/0904_SchoolsAssessment.pdf

Public Agenda. (2004). *Teaching interrupted: Do discipline policies in today's public schools foster the common good?* Retrieved September 26, 2005, from http://www.publicagenda.org

Riley, P. L. (2000). *How to establish and maintain safe, orderly, and caring schools.* Raleigh, NC: Center for the Prevention of School Violence. Retrieved October 10, 2005, from http://www.ncdjdp.org/cpsv/Acrobatfiles/SOC_1pager.pdf

Safe and Responsive Schools Project. (2000). *Facts about school violence.* Indiana Education Policy Center. Retrieved September 23, 2005, from http://www.indiana.edu/%7Esafeschl//facts.html

Schonfeld, D. J., and Newgass, S. (2003). *School crisis response initiative.* U.S. Department of Justice, Office of Victims of Crime Bulletin. Retrieved September 23, 2005, from http://www.ojp.gov/OVC/publications/bulletin/Schoolcris i/NCJ197832.pdf

Skiba, R. (2004). Zero tolerance: The assumptions and the facts. *Education Policy Briefs 2,* 1. Retrieved September 23, 2005, from http://www.ceep.indiana .edu/projectsPDF/PB_V2N1_Zero_Tolerance.pdf

Stephens, R. D. (2005). *Safe school planning: The art of the possible.* Retrieved October 10, 2005, from http://www.nsscl.org/message

Trump, K. (2005). Revisiting communication during a crisis: Insights from Kenneth Trump. *Journal of School Public Relations, 26,* 1.

U.S. Department of Education. (2004). *Violent crime rate against students drops, new report says.* Retrieved September 26, 2005, from http://www.ed.gov/news/pressreleases/2004/11/11292004.html

U.S. Departments of Education and Justice. (1999). *Annual report on school safety.* Retrieved June 22, 2005, from http://www.ed.gov/pubs/School Safety/

U.S. Department of Education, Office of Safe and Drug-Free Schools. (2003). *Practical information on crisis planning: A guide for schools and communities.* Washington, DC.

Vera, E. M., Shin, R. Q., and Montgomery, G. P. (2004). Conflict resolution styles, self-efficacy, self-control, and future orientation of urban adolescents. *Professional School Counseling, 8.* Retrieved August 21, 2006, from http://www.findarticles.com/p/articles/mi_m0KOC/is_1_8/ai_n6335445

Wasser, J. (1999, Fall). Note: Zeroing in on zero tolerance. *Journal of Law and Politics, 15*(4).

Websites for More Information and Links to Other Relevant Sites

Center for the Prevention of School Violence, http://www.colorado.edu/cspv/

Hamilton Fish Institute on School and Community Violence, http://www.hamfish.org

Keep Schools Safe.Org, http://www.keepschoolssafe.org/index.htm

Knowledge Path, http://mchlibrary.info/KnowledgePaths/kp_adolvio.html

National Criminal Justice Reference Service, http://www.ncjrs.org/viewall.html
National School Safety and Security Services, http://www.schoolsecurity.org
National School Safety Center, http://www.nssc1.org
National Youth Violence Prevention Resource Centers, http://www.safeyouth
   .org

Chapter Ten

Planning and Evaluating a Comprehensive Educational Partnership Plan

Some schools enjoy broad family and community support, but many do not. The difference may be in the careful planning of meaningful involvement activities, not just for family members but also for all educational stakeholders. Support is gained when involvement opportunities reflect the reality that today's families are often overloaded with employment obligations, household chores, complicated family schedules, and the absence of extended-family members to help with childcare and other responsibilities. Community agencies, institutions, and businesses are similarly burdened with multiple demands for their time and resources. Ellis and Hughes (2002) believe that educational partners must be convinced that their participation will directly benefit students:

> All partners need to know there will be a bottom line benefit before committing themselves to being involved in school-family-community partnerships. To them, meaningful involvement is participating in a broad, academically significant array of activities that allow partners to help children learn, have a direct impact on student achievement and help solve real school problems. (p. 5)

As the percentage of households with school-age children continues to decline, the success of a school system's educational efforts is likely to depend directly on its ability to communicate with the total community.

Its public image is almost certain to affect the community's willingness to provide support. In the past, an educational partnership program might have succeeded simply by assuring the community that the schools were doing a good job. Today, an increasingly skeptical public is concerned about both fiscal and academic accountability and demands accurate, credible, and detailed information from the schools it is asked to support. To win that support, public schools must carefully plan an educational partnership program and have in place an evaluation process that allows for adjustments as changes occur in the community and in the society as a whole.

Wegner and Jarvi (2005) believe that an organization, regardless of its size or focus, should engage in four types of planning. *Strategic planning* develops an organization's vision and mission and then its goals and objectives, with an action plan. *Comprehensive planning* builds on the vision to provide specific long- and short-term directions and continuity for present and future organizational development. *Community planning* puts the organization in the context of the total community, involving all sectors. *Internal systems planning* integrates the components of the organization's operational systems.

STRATEGIC PLANNING

In their attempts to reform public education, educators have sought out "best practices" and tried to incorporate them into specific schools or situations. One crucial lesson learned from the failure of many change efforts is that a best practice cannot simply be pasted onto a school's operation, ignoring the uniqueness of a specific community or school system. Strategic planning gives direction and meaning to the day-to-day activities of an organization. According to the National Center for Continuing Education (2006), "A strategic plan must integrate the values and goals of your organization, reflect the wisdom and collective experience of all levels of staff, be 'owned' by everyone, and [be] used day-to-day as a guide in decision-making" (para. 3). Allison and Kaye (2005) add the reminder that strategic planning is not linear and does not predict the future.

Too often, organizational strategic planning is seen as an end product, usually a document, produced at the request of an authority and, when completed, left to gather dust on a shelf or in a drawer. Halfacre and others (2006) suggest that, historically, school strategic plans have not been living documents because the planning effort itself has not been an exciting and dynamic process. They propose that successful strategic planning for schools be grounded in the following premises:

1. *The planning process may be more important in effecting positive change than the planning product.* The plan should evoke energy, commitment, and positive action. The selection of who is brought to the table and who is believed to "own" the plan in the development process is very important.

2. *The rationale for the plan's content must be clearly understood and accepted.* The people who will eventually implement the plan must be able to verbalize the key elements simply and clearly.

3. *Successful strategic plans follow three R's: repeat it, recognize it, reinforce it.* Goals should be few, clear, and repeated often. Leaders should recognize the relationship between activities and events that are consistent with the goals, and then reinforce the message with encouragement, necessary resources, and support.

4. *A small group of staff members should accept the role of monitoring the plan's implementation.* An oversight team should be created to monitor the implementation and effectiveness of the activities stated in the plan, connect them with the day-to-day reality of the classroom, and communicate the plan's programs and practices to all stakeholders.

5. *The plan must be built upon pre-existing values that reflect the desired culture of the school.* The plan should be consistent with the already agreed-upon expectations of effective classroom instructional practices, student behavior, staff relationships, and parent communication.

6. *Strategic planning is not an isolated event, but rather one component of a reflective school culture that continually questions its purpose and effectiveness.* A successful planning process will involve all stakeholders, including the students, in asking four questions: Where am I going? How will I get there? How will I know I've arrived? What will I do if I don't arrive?

7. *The plan should be considered, not as a rigid mandate, but as a path*

that can be modified by changing events, values, and learnings. The plan should be flexible and evolving, based on common sense combined with data-driven decision making, to help ensure the maximum positive impact upon student learning.

8. *The strategic plan is "the" plan for the school.* The strategic plan is the umbrella for all other planning activities undertaken by school personnel.

9. *A high-quality, formal strategic plan is a positive byproduct of an already effective school organization.* A dynamic strategic plan is usually the product of a dynamic and enthusiastic staff. It will not by itself result in a high-quality school. (para. 5)

Before the strategic planning process begins, the stakeholders of the organization must be identified and decisions made about how they should be involved. Stakeholders are the individuals and groups, internally and externally, who have an interest in the work of the school. They include employees, students, parents, PTA and advisory councils, regulatory bodies, potential partners in the community, volunteers, and a host of others. Although stakeholders are by definition important to the organization, Logan (2005) points out that it is neither practical nor necessary to include all stakeholders in the planning sessions even though their input is important. Focus groups, facilitated meetings, written questionnaires with open- and close-ended questions, telephone interviews, and one-on-one personal interviews are among the methods that can be used to gain the perspectives and ideas of a broad range of stakeholders.

Logan emphasizes that consulting with stakeholders is an important factor in achieving success. However, she cautions, "Above all, don't consult stakeholders just to say you did. If you include them, it must be because you are willing to include their point of view and you intend consultation to result in change or a new direction" (para. 4). She enumerates several important benefits of reaching out to stakeholders:

1. Quality input leads to quality decision making. A broader perspective reduces "group think," challenges traditional thinking, and sparks creativity.

2. Greater stakeholder satisfaction with the final planning product comes from their involvement in shaping it.

3. The chances of successful implementation increase as more stakeholders feel committed to the plan and take ownership of the plan's design.
4. Good governance, transparency, and open communication are served when an organization communicates and receives feedback from stakeholders, instead of being guided by internal agendas. (para. 3)

Allison and Kaye (2005) describe strategic planning as a means rather than an end and emphasize that only implementation of the plan will produce results. They point out that if a plan is well developed, there is a much better chance that the day-to-day activities of the organization will lead to successful results because all parties will be focused on priorities and will work together to pursue them. Romney (1996) describes strategic planning as:

[A] practical process for dealing with the ambiguities of the environment. Its purpose is to move the organization from being a pawn of changing events to being a proactive participant, making decisions about, and acting to create, its own future. It requires organizational flexibility to adapt and revise as conditions change and a willingness to move beyond obsolete paradigms. (p. 14)

According to the Alliance for Non-Profit Management (2003), there are five steps in the strategic planning process. Although these steps are not intended as a rigid prescription, they do give a general guideline to the work to be done when creating a written strategic plan.

1. *Assessing readiness and preparing.* If the organization is undergoing great change or turbulence it probably is not the right time to embark on a strategic planning effort. Those who judge themselves ready should identify specific issues or choices that the planning process should address, decide who will do what in the process, create a planning committee, develop an organizational description/profile, and identify the information that must be collected. All of this information should be gathered into a work plan.
2. *Developing a mission and vision.* A mission statement must com-

municate the essence of an organization to the reader. An organization's ability to articulate its mission indicates its focus and purposefulness. While the mission statement explains the how and why of an organization's work, its vision statement presents an image of what success will look like.

3. *Assessing the situation.* Information should be gathered about the organization's strengths, weaknesses, and performance in order to choose the most important issues to address. There should be no more than 10 critical issues within the strategic plan.

4. *Developing strategies, goals, and objectives.* When the mission and vision have been created and the issues identified, the broad approaches to be taken (strategies), and the general and specific results to be sought (goals and objectives) are created.

5. *Completing the written plan.* The final planning document is drafted and submitted for review by all key decision makers. The written part of the plan is completed.

Humphries (2004) recommends that the first step in the strategic planning process be environmental scanning (ES)—an assessment of the external and internal environments of the organization. ES involves gathering information about events, trends, and relationships in an organization's surroundings and using that knowledge to plan for the organization's future and to help with organizational decision making. Usually, ES involves three main activities: the gathering of information related to the organization's internal and external environments, the analysis and interpretation of that information, and the application of these findings to decision making.

As a written document, the plan is essentially useless unless it is actively accepted in the organization as a workable guideline for action. Robinson (2003) suggests three steps for ensuring that the vision articulated in the strategic plan is actually implemented:

1. *Develop strategic priorities.* Strategic priorities are the focus or goals of the organization. They are broad statements of what is to be achieved. There should be only three to five priorities, all chosen to match available resources.

2. *Determine objectives.* A limited number of objectives should be

developed for each strategy. The objectives are short, realistic, time-limited, and measurable. They provide a basis for evaluating the organization's success in meeting its strategic priorities.

3. *Establish action steps.* Action steps are taken by individuals within the organization to achieve the objectives within the strategic priorities. They answer the questions: What will be done? Who will do it? When will it be done? One individual should be assigned responsibility for each action item and a specific date for completing it. (Sections 2, 3, 4)

Wegner and Jarvi (2005) emphasize that, beyond the obvious outcomes of the planning process, important additional benefits can be expected because the planning process itself:

1. Helps articulate questions that ordinarily would not be addressed about the function and direction of the organization.
2. Helps identify constituent groups that have a need to be served and that may otherwise be overlooked.
3. Creates new partnerships.
4. Generates new and constructive ideas from all levels within the organization.
5. Helps prioritize resources to ensure efficiency of effort.
6. Helps eliminate programs and services that are no longer viable.
7. Encourages ownership and commitment by all stakeholders.
8. Creates benchmarks for assessing the performance of the organization itself, as well as of individual managers within the organization.
9. Develops tremendous power within the organization as all elements focus on commonly held strategies, unleashing formerly unidentified synergism.

Logan (2005) emphasizes that the strategic plan should be a living document that is monitored and evaluated on a regular basis. External and internal events around the school may prompt a good deal of fine tuning. Day-to-day decisions can be measured against their compatibility with the mission and vision laid out in the plan.

COMPREHENSIVE PLANNING

Comprehensive planning is based on the strategic plan. It identifies the specific steps that need to be taken to implement the mission and vision. It is both an inventory of existing conditions and a list of recommendations for future programs and services, the acquisition and development of areas and facilities, and administration. It provides specific long- and short-term direction and continuity for both present and future programs, services, and physical resource development. The comprehensive plan has two distinct but related dimensions—a program/services plan and a physical resources plan and is the operational blueprint for the administrator, as well as a valuable tool for ongoing decision making (Wegner and Jarvi, 2005).

COMMUNITY PLANNING

Community planning is a collaborative effort by representatives of agencies and organizations to consider jointly the needs, resources, and objectives of each, and to develop plans for integrating each agency and organization into the community as a whole. It may involve social planning or physical resource planning or both. It includes assessing what is happening in legislatures and other regulatory bodies, as well as population shifts and changing social and economic conditions. Community planning has the benefit of helping agencies and organizations understand each other and the direction being taken by each and of mitigating potential turf issues (Wegner and Jarvi, 2005).

INTERNAL SYSTEMS PLANNING

Internal systems planning is essential for effective operational management. It integrates the various components of an organization: typically, the plans for maintenance, information technology, public relations and marketing, human resources, financial management and budgeting, risk management, law enforcement and security, and evaluation (Wegner and Jarvi, 2005).

FRAMEWORK FOR A COMPREHENSIVE
EDUCATIONAL PARTNERSHIP PLAN

Effective educational partnership programs do not just happen. Schools should formulate a written partnership plan that provides guidelines and a road map for what can be expected from a partnership. Ellis and Hughes (2002) recommend that a partnership plan define immediate and future goals and outcomes, and how they will be attained; outline the roles each partner will play in reaching the goals; anticipate potential barriers to collaboration and recommend methods for overcoming them; and identify strategies to evaluate whether the partnership has actually met its goals, along with a method for communicating this information.

The Educational Broadcasting Corporation (2004) offers the following steps to guide the development of an effective school-community partnership program:

Step 1. Create an Action Team for Partnerships (ATP) consisting of at least two or three teachers at different grade levels, two or three parents with children in different grades, and at least one administrator. There should also be representation from the PTA, one or more business or community partners, other school personnel, and perhaps one or two students if the plan is at the middle or high school level.

Step 2. Obtain funds to support the costs of planned partnership activities each year. This may be accomplished by applying for funds from local, state, and federal program budgets that already mandate or recommend family involvement or from other sources such as local businesses or community and civic organizations.

Step 3. The ATP should evaluate existing strengths in parental and community involvement programs and collect information about the experiences and needs of students, teachers, administrators, and parents. The team should consider what changes are needed and how the community can be involved. All of the information collected should be linked to the goals of the partnership program.

Step 4. The team should develop a three-year outline with broad goals and a detailed one-year action plan that specifies the responsibilities of committees. The action plan is the basis for end-of-year evaluations to determine what is working and what should be continued.

Step 5. The team must implement the one-year action plan every year. Additionally, the three-year outline should be updated each year, and specific plans for the coming year should be discussed in detail.

The National Coalition for Parent Involvement in Education (no date) recommends using the following concepts as a framework upon which to build specific programs. The coalition emphasizes that a comprehensive and meaningful educational partnership plan incorporates each concept in ways that are unique to a particular school community.

1. *Supporting communication.* Communication is the foundation of effective partnerships. Families and schools should communicate regularly and clearly with each other about information that is important to student success. This communication includes informing families about standards and how they relate to curriculum, learning objectives, methods of assessment, school programs, discipline codes, and children's progress. Schools should also form partnerships with community- and faith-based organizations to engage families who do not feel comfortable in schools.

2. *Supporting school activities.* Families and community members can support schools and children's learning in many ways. The school environment is critical to making families and other community members feel welcome and needed. Signs at the school door, central office, and classroom should convey a warm greeting and be in languages spoken by the community. A school-based family resource center that provides information, links to social services, and opportunities for informal meetings with staff and other families contributes to a family-friendly atmosphere.

3. *Supporting the student learning environment.* Families support children's education at home by helping their children develop good study habits, supervising homework, monitoring TV viewing and after-school activities, and encouraging regular bedtimes and school attendance. Teachers can suggest family/child activities that are coordinated with the curriculum. Community members can serve as tutors and mentors.

4. *Supporting lifelong learning.* Families and community members can be encouraged to participate in programs to develop their knowl-

edge and skills. To support these programs, schools can offer the use of facilities and other resources. Schools can provide staff development in cultural and community values and customs, and in ways of working with all families.

5. *Promoting advocacy and shared governance.* When parents and community members are members of school advisory or site-based management councils, Title I, parent organizations such as PTAs, and other groups, they can advocate for change, help develop family and community involvement and school improvement plans, participate in the development of school policy and governance procedures, and provide community representation and support. Leadership training should be provided for educators, staff, families, and other community members interested in participating in school governance.

6. *Collaborating with community agencies and organizations.* Schools support families and students by forming collaborative relationships with public and private agencies that provide family support services. These relationships may include partnerships with public health and human service agencies, local businesses, institutions of higher education, youth-serving organizations, and religious, civic, and other community-based organizations. Linking families to services and community organizations can strengthen home environments and student learning. These partnerships create shared responsibility for the well-being of children, families, and schools by all members of the community. (A Framework for Family Investment, sections 1–6)

EVALUATION: AN OUTCOMES ORIENTATION

A comprehensive educational partnership plan should be viewed as an integrated whole—each step influencing and being influenced by every other step in the process. Evaluation should, therefore, be a continuous process throughout the development of the plan. New information or changes at any point in the process may prompt reevaluation of the preceding steps and a rethinking of the organization's future. The final, formal evaluation step then becomes a fine tuning of the plan to fit the realities of actual day-to-day implementation.

The Northwest Regional Educational Laboratory (2001) describes two types of program evaluation. *Formative evaluation* relies on gathering information during the early stages of the program to find out whether the plan is unfolding as expected, what obstacles are being encountered, and whether any unexpected opportunities have presented themselves. Adjustments can be made at this stage depending on the findings. Successful *summative evaluation* depends on good data collection based on the specific measures identified in the plan. Summative evaluation involves the creation of a report that details the impact of the program on the participants, lists the specific gains made, and identifies program costs and benefits. There is no clear demarcation between formative and summative evaluation. Often material gathered at the formative stage can be used in the summative report.

OUTCOMES AND ACCOUNTABILITY IN EDUCATIONAL PARTNERSHIPS

Almost everyone—educators as well as the general public—agrees that the goal of improved academic success for all children cannot be achieved if conditions that are prerequisites to learning, such as good health, appropriate behavior, and a stable home environment, are ignored. Gardner (2001) discusses the relative importance of nonacademic outcomes in partnership initiatives:

> At its inception, every [educational] partnership must reach a consensus on the relative importance of non-educational outcomes. . . . When there is consensus that the [partnership's] focus on non-academic outcomes should either be co-equal or proportional to academic outcomes, the relative importance of classroom performance and interventions aimed at the external causes of classroom achievement gaps must be negotiated. In that discussion, schools are correct to emphasize the academic outcomes, but the school's partners are also correct to emphasize how their efforts can make a major contribution to academic performance and other goals in the lives of the students and their [families]. An overarching concern must be identifying where overlapping goals can form the glue that cements the partner-

ship. . . . At this point, the partners must establish accountability by negotiations toward a consensus on what outcomes should determine success and what levels of attainment indicate a project should be replicated. . . . Partners can then determine what outcomes indicators will be used as fair measures of progress and how data will be collected and reported. (p. 10)

Gardner suggests that the relationships between the types of outcomes sought by most educational partnership programs be conceptualized as three concentric circles. The *innermost* circle represents the core school-based outcomes: achievement (test scores), attendance, and graduation rates. The *middle* circle represents outcomes that are achievement-related but are not restricted to what happens in the classroom: family involvement, help with homework, reading to children, family engagement with teachers in response to classroom problems, etc. The *outermost* circle represents community building and youth development and includes such outcomes as the school's success in attracting community volunteers, improved human services delivery in the community, and the effects of programs to improve school readiness. He points out that the circles suggest a range of options for educational partnerships and adds: "Circumstances—such as strong or strained relations with families and the community—will dictate the extent to which the outer circles of outcomes can be goals of the partnership; academic achievement may be all the partnership can handle" (p. 10).

Many factors in today's educational environment, including the No Child Left Behind Act of 2001, focus attention on accountability. When examining educational partnerships, Gardner explains that accountability issues are driven by (1) the types of agencies involved and their appropriate goals, (2) the collaborative's capacity to evolve from lower to higher stages of cooperation, and (3) the willingness of partners to negotiate the goal of academic achievement as opposed to other goals.

Gardner differentiates four different kinds of partners, each with a different approach to working with schools and a particular set of funding sources, and therefore with different accountability issues:

1. *Public city, county, and regional agencies.* An example is child protective services agencies. These agencies receive institutionalized,

recurring funding. They are accountable to legislatures, resulting in a compliance mentality that emphasizes spending rules.

2. *Major not-for-profit agencies.* Examples are Boys and Girls Clubs and children's hospitals. These agencies rely on United Way, contracts with public agencies, and sometimes fee income. Some have developed detailed outcomes measures.

3. *Community-based agencies.* These agencies are more informally funded than the not-for-profits. They range widely in accountability, from those that use specific outcomes to a larger group that measures success by the number of clients contacted.

4. *Organizations that represent families.* Frequently this type of partner has no formal budget and typically no explicit outcomes framework.

Gardner points out that accountability issues are also affected by the stage of a collaboration.

A four-part approach to the stages of collaboration distinguishes between the initial stages of *information exchange* and *joint projects,* and the third and fourth stages of *changing the rules* and *changing the system.* As long as it is working at the level of a project, a [collaborative] can get along without emphasizing accountability. When the collaborative begins to change the rule of service—because of changes in its shared outcome or as it attempts to scale up the operation—accountability issues become more important. That is because changing the rules should not be done for convenience but to achieve different or better outcomes than the old rules permit.

When the collaborative is working on changing the rules and moving from the project level of collaborative operations to going to scale, both client and systems outcomes matter. Assessing the relations among the partners may be as important as assessing the impact on students and families. Tracking the efforts made by [home-school-community] partnerships to change the rules, enabling agencies to work together more effectively, can help ensure that fixing the kids does not always become the sole focus, with fixing the institutions being ignored. (p. 12)

TECHNIQUES AND TOOLS IN EVALUATION

A variety of techniques and tools can be used to evaluate an educational partnership program. One technique is an audit. An audit can pinpoint both strengths and weaknesses, uncover needs, and provide a rationale for greater effort.

The NSPRA (1999) recommends doing a communications audit, described as a snapshot of the school's or school district's needs, policies, capabilities, activities, and programs. An audit assesses the effectiveness and credibility of current publications and other communications and marketing activities. It involves a review of PR and communications policies, and examines budget, current plans, and staffing patterns. It looks at demographic data, long-range plans, and past surveys of family/staff/community attitudes and reviews coverage by the local newspaper, radio, and television media. NSPRA recommends using focus groups of 8 to 10 people representing citizens, parents, business people, administrators, teachers, support staff, and other key audiences whose support is needed to improve communications in the district or the community.

NSPRA suggests five major steps in a comprehensive communications audit:

1. *Make the decision to do it.* Nothing is more important in building trust and support between your organization and the public you serve than the quality of your communications effort. Are you addressing the community's concerns? Are you communicating effectively? Does your staff understand and support what you are trying to do?

2. *Analyze the current program.* It is important to review your existing policies, publications, strategies, media relationships—every aspect of your internal and external communications effort.

3. *Listen to your audiences.* The core of the audit is focus groups that are representative of your internal and external audiences. They can generate more useful information than most surveys because a trained facilitator can probe the feelings behind their opinions. The number and composition of focus groups may vary, depending on the main purpose of a particular aspect of the audit.

4. *Develop constructive recommendations for improving your communications program.* Based on an analysis of your current program and the input from the focus groups, make recommendations for improvement.

5. *Get implementation assistance when appropriate.* Once the decision

is made to take steps to improve or update aspects of your public relations/communications programs, it may be necessary to examine sample materials and policies. Colleagues who have successfully dealt with similar situations can be contacted and/or experts can be consulted. (section 4)

Several other evaluation tools may be effective in assessing the progress of an educational partnership plan. Gretz (2003) suggests that portfolios highlighting the successes and progress of the partnership be compiled and used to communicate with parents and community members. They can be displayed for visitors at the school and sent electronically through the Internet. Murals created by students can be used to express the goals and activities of the partnership. Satisfaction surveys can be mailed to school and community groups. Gretz also emphasizes the importance of ongoing data collection based on the measurable goals of the partnership and suggests a variety of collection methods including observations, interviews, self-reports, and focus groups.

How Customer Friendly Is Your School? (Chambers, 1998) focuses on a visitor's or caller's first impressions. It asks yes or no questions about the school environment and telephone services to find out how people perceive the school. Table 10.1 is an example.

The Coalition for Community Schools has an assessment tool with three checklists intended to help school and community leaders create or strengthen community-school partnerships. The first checklist helps to assess the development of the community-school partnership; the second helps to take inventory of existing programs and services; and the third helps to catalog the funding sources that support these programs and services. Blank and Langford (2000) explain the rationale for the three checklists:

To be effective, partnerships need to engage in a thoughtful process to define a vision and clear goals. Partnerships need to have effective governance and management structures to ensure that programs operate efficiently and the partnership is responsive to community needs. Community school partnerships also need to draw from a broad range of perspectives and expertise—from inside the school as well as from other organizations and individuals within the community. Finally, community school partner-

Table 10.1.   How Customer Friendly Is Your School?

Answer each question yes or no.

Environment
Grounds
___ Are the grounds attractively landscaped?
___ Are they clean and well maintained?
___ Is there adequate visitor parking?
___ Is there easy access from visitor parking to the main entrance?

Entrance
___ Is the main entry clearly marked (including directions for visitor parking)?
___ Do entry signs welcome visitors and give directions to the main office?
___ Does the main entrance set a good tone for the school?
___ Does it feel warm and welcoming?
___ Is it clean and in good repair?
___ Does it highlight student, teacher, and school accomplishments (pictures, awards, student projects, artwork, etc.)?
___ Does it provide a positive image?
___ Is it free of unpleasant noises or unfriendly written rules or directions?

Interior
___ Are halls and rooms clean, well decorated, and in good repair?
___ Are rooms and common areas such as the library clearly marked?
___ Are students' work and accomplishments highlighted on the walls or in display cases?
___ Is the lighting bright and the temperature comfortable?
___ Are announcement and bell systems set at a comfortable decibel level?

Main Office
___ Can the sign for the main office be clearly seen from a distance?
___ Can office personnel easily see visitors when they enter?
___ Is the decor of the office inviting?
___ Are desks and other areas in view of visitors kept organized and clean?
___ Is there a nameplate identifying the person responsible for greeting visitors?
___ Do office personnel greet visitors within a few seconds of their entry, letting them know they'll be right with them if they can't help them immediately?
___ Are all office personnel welcoming and helpful?
___ Is there a comfortable place for visitors to sit while waiting for appointments?
___ Is the noise level comfortable and the area free of unpleasant odors?
___ Do office staff avoid personal conversations in public areas?

Telephone Etiquette
___ Are all employees, not just secretaries, informed about proper etiquette for answering calls and taking messages?
___ Do they answer by immediately identifying the school or department and themselves?
___ Do they answer in a pleasant tone of voice, making callers feel they are happy to be of assistance?
___ Are they helpful to callers? When unable to answer a question, do they try to find the answer themselves to avoid routing the call to another person?

Automated Answering Services and Voice Mail
___ Is the automated answering service easy to understand and follow, giving the caller an option to speak to a person if desired?
___ Does it give office hours and let callers know when school is not in session?
___ Does it provide callers with directions to the school?

ships need to connect, coordinate, and leverage resources from a variety of sources to support and continue their work. (p. 2)

The first checklist, Community School Partnership Assessment (Blank & Langford, 2000), focuses on the *process* of bringing partners together and working to achieve desired results. It is designed to help partnerships focus on, assess, and improve the quality of their collaborative efforts. The checklist is a series of nine statements. Respondents are directed to rank the statements on a scale of 1 (disagree) to 5 (agree):

1. Our partnership has developed a clear vision.
2. Our partnership has collaboratively identified the result we want to achieve for children, youth, families, and our community.
3. Our partnership has successfully engaged a broad base of partners from a range of individuals and organizations representing the school and the community.
4. Our partnership has developed strategies for coordinating and linking the array of supports and opportunities for children, youth, families, and community members that are available at or connected to the school.
5. Our partnership has established a clear organizational structure. Our partnership has agreed upon the roles that individual partners will play, and ensured that all partners understand and accept the responsibilities of those roles.
6. All partners involved in our community school have an understanding of who the other partners are, what organizations they come from, and what those organizations do.
7. Our partnership regularly communicates with all partners to keep them informed about its work.
8. Our partnership engages in activities to create awareness about and increase support for the work of the partnership.
9. Our partnership has identified and mobilized resources (financial and others) from partner organizations and other entities throughout the community. (p. 3)

THE ROLE OF SCHOOL LEADERS

School leaders are responsible not just for initiating educational partnership programs with families and community members, but also for planning the ongoing support and enhancement of these programs to ensure their success. Epstein and Jansorn (2004) recommend that school leaders represent their school as a partnership school to staff, parents, and community, and communicate to students how important home-school-community partnerships are for student support and success. Communication at faculty meetings, especially at the start of the school year, should emphasize the importance of partnerships and teamwork. A plan should be in place for helping teachers communicate successfully with parents. Teachers should be encouraged to participate in involvement activities. When planning the budget for each year, school leaders should set aside funds for partnership activities, including publicity for involvement events. A recognition program should be designed to reward teachers, families, and community members for their contribution to school partnerships. School leaders should make periodic reports about partnership plans to the faculty, parent organizations, local media, and key community groups.

THE NEED FOR DOCUMENTATION

Wang (2001) points out that, in spite of the criticism over the past decade of a wide variety of educational partnerships to improve educational and social outcomes for children and families, there is a general lack of evidence about the effects of these partnerships on school improvement efforts.

Wang stresses the need to place a sharp focus on documentation. She cites a variety of forces that are shaping current school reform initiatives:

1. Advocates of standards-based education reform and accountability recognize that students learn both inside and outside of school and that communities have a responsibility for students' academic success and for ensuring that all students are ready to learn.
2. Emergent brain research is creating greater clarity about the effect of early childhood development on later success in school and life.
3. Chilling episodes of school violence have brought home the understanding that students' "connectedness" inside and outside of school is everyone's concern.
4. The devolution of federal responsibility for welfare and workforce-development programs has heightened local partners' awareness of

their critical role in fostering economic self-sufficiency for poor families. (p. 1)

Wang observes:

[A] major question still remains about what difference [partnerships] make. Neither the participants in these partnerships nor the policymakers who often compel them to take on these important social issues can answer this basic question. . . . [F]or a myriad of political, philosophical, and policy reasons, forging a common vision about what outcomes matter and how best to measure them remains one of the most vexing stumbling blocks in this field. (p. 1)

Gardner (2001) suggests that "if communities opt for cooperative reforms, which currently offer the best hope for reducing the barriers to learning for our most severely disadvantaged students," each educational partnership must negotiate a series of issues to reach a consensus on general goals, specific outcomes, and the measures of accountability that define progress, both for the school and for external agencies" (p. 12). In his opinion, schools need a "tagging" capacity for student files so they can report on how educational partnerships are affecting academic performance, attendance, and behavior. This kind of monitoring would allow both the school and its partners to get regular feedback on the impact of their program.

Fortunately, there is growing, research-based evidence of a connection between family and community involvement programs and student achievement and success. Epstein (2005) examined studies conducted over the last five years by the National Network of Partnership Schools regarding the impact of family involvement on student outcomes. The studies show that family involvement contributes to higher achievement, better attendance, more course credits, and better preparation for class. The studies also examined the impact of family and community involvement in activities that focused on student behavior, and reported a decrease in the number of disciplinary actions. Other studies examined the impact of family involvement on homework completion and found significant improvements in science report card grades and homework completion.

THE BOTTOM LINE

Despite the fact that current data present tenuous estimates of their overall impact, educational partnerships are widely believed to be having a positive effect on educational quality. The most effective appear to have common characteristics: they are carefully planned, data driven, and based on measurable objectives. Because the involvement of stakeholders from the very beginning is one of the keys to success, school leaders must make partnership planning a priority. They can help ensure the success of the plan by communicating its importance to teachers, family members, and the community; budgeting resources to support the plan; recognizing the achievements of the participants; and putting in place an evaluation process.

REFERENCES

Alliance for Non-Profit Management. (2003). *What are the basic steps in the strategic planning process?* Retrieved March 9, 2006, from http://www .allianceonline.org/FAQ/strategic_planning/what_are_basic_steps.faq

Allison, M., and Kaye, J. (2005). *Strategic planning for non-profit organizations: A practical guide and workbook.* New York: Wiley & Sons.

Blank, M. J., and Langford, B. H. (2000). *Strengthening partnerships: Community school assessment checklist.* Coalition for Community Schools. Retrieved March 10, 2006, from http://www.financeproject.org/publications/csassessment.pdf

Chambers, L. (1998). How customer friendly is your school? *Educational Leadership, 56, 2.*

Educational Broadcasting Corporation. (2004). *Making family and community connections: Step-by-step planning.* Retrieved March 8, 2006, from http://www .thirteen.org/edonline/concept2class/familycommunity/implement_sub1.html

Ellis, D., and Hughes, K. (2002). *Connecting school, families and communities for youth success.* Retrieved March 15, 2006, from http://www.nwrel.org/part nerships/cloak/booklet2.pdf

Epstein, J. L. (2005). *Developing and sustaining research-based programs for family and community partnerships. Summary of five years of NNPS research.* Retrieved March 8, 2006, from http://www.csos.jhu.edu/p2000/Research%20 Summary.pdf

Epstein, J. L., and Jansorn, N. R. (2004). *Developing successful partnership pro-*

grams. Retrieved March 8, 2006, from http://www.naesp.org/ContentLoad.do ?contentId = 1121

Gardner, S. (2001). Outcomes and accountability in school-community partnerships. *CEIC Review, 10*, 1. Retrieved March 10, 2006, from http://www .temple.edu/lss/pdf/ceicreviews/CEICVol10No1.pdf

Gretz, P. (2003). School and community partnerships: Cultivating friends. *Principal Leadership* (High School Ed.) *3, 5.*

Halfacre, J. D., Lindsay, S. R., and Welch, F. C. (2006). *Planning for strategic planning*. Retrieved March 8, 2006, from http://www.naesp.org/ContentLoad .do?contentId = 1544

Humphries, C. (2004). *Look out: Environmental scanning for associations*. Retrieved February 16, 2006, from http://www.axi.ca/tca/may2004/associate article_1.shtml

Logan, J. (2005). *Stakeholder consultations*. Retrieved February 16, 2006, from http://www.charityvillage.com/cv/research/rstrat33.html

National Center for Continuing Education. (2006). *Strategic planning*. Retrieved March 2, 2006, from http://www.nccetraining.com/sp.cfm

National Coalition for Parent Involvement in Education. (no date). *A framework for family involvement*. Retrieved March 10, 2006, from http://www.ncpie.org/ DevelopingPartnerships/

National School Public Relations Association. (1999). *Communications audit*. Retrieved March 10, 2006, from http://www.nspra.org/main_audit.htm

Northwest Regional Education Laboratory. (2001). *Summative evaluation: Measurement and documentation of program impact*. Retrieved March 8, 2006, from http://www.nwrel.org/evaluation/summative.shtml

Robinson, R. (2001). *Who should be involved in the strategic planning process?* Retrieved March 10, 2006, from http://www.charityvillage.com/cv/research/ rstrat4.html

Robinson, R. (2003). *Translating vision into action*. Retrieved March 10, 2006, from http://www.charityvillage.com/cv/research/rstrat16.html

Romney, V. A. (1996). *Strategic planning and needs assessment for schools and communities*. Fairfax, VA: National Community Education Association (ERIC Document Reproduction Service Ed 392 135).

Wang, M. C. (2001). Pathways to school/community/family partnership results: Measures of success and student learning. *CEIC Review, 10*, 1. Retrieved March 10, 2006, from http://www.temple.edu/LLs/pdf/ceicreviews/CEIC V0110N01.pdf

Wegner, D., and Jarvi, C. K. (2005). Planning for strategic management. In B. van der Smissen and M. Moiseichik (Eds.), *Management of park and recreation agencies*. Ashburn, VA: National Recreation and Park Association.

Chapter Eleven

Making Friends before You Need Them

President Lyndon Johnson is among those credited with having said, "The best time to make friends is before you need them." It is good advice, and educational leaders would do well to follow it.

Henig (2002) points out that the American tradition of finding common objectives is deeply embedded in the way we think about our schools, and much of our educational literature depicts education as an apple pie issue about which everyone agrees. If this were correct—if everyone agreed that public education is vitally important—the failure of public schools to institute educational reform to close obvious achievement gaps "could be attributable to lack of understanding about what to do, or lack of coordination in going about it, or self-interested behavior by bad guys elevating their own interests above those of the common good" (p. 30). Obviously everyone does not hold the same belief.

Johnson and Friedman (2006) put it this way: "While there are tantalizing indications of progress in many quarters, there also are signs that the pace of change—and the natural rivalry between different groups with different ideas about what works best—is causing confusion, tension, miscommunication, and outright division among those who need to work together" (para. 3). They point out that Public Agenda surveys show that the views of parents, students, teachers, superintendents, principals, employers, college professors, and others indicate that different groups often operate on surprisingly different wavelengths. Their studies show that several gaps in agreement are serious enough to stall progress:

1. *Parents may not be ready for change.* Research shows that few parents know how their child's skills compared with other students in

their own state, let alone nationally or internationally. If parents do not understand the challenge of preparing students for future success and do not recognize the need for change, they may resist, opting to cling to what is familiar.

2. *Communication within schools and districts could be better.* Seven teachers in ten say that rank-and-file teachers are left "out of the loop" when it comes to district decision making. Less than 50% say administrators listen to and take into account the issues teachers care about. In focus groups, teachers express confusion about exactly how reforms and changes will play out. Many say their concerns about lack of parental involvement and poor student behavior do not get the attention they deserve.

3. *Districts and communities need to agree about where to put their money and what to do first.* In a recent Public Agenda survey, 90% of school administrators agreed that it is essential to "stick to a few core goals and avoid getting sidetracked by peripheral initiatives."

Boston (2005) believes there is disagreement even on the mission of public education. He points to a "disturbing imbalance in the mission of public education" and believes that "the recent preoccupation of the nation with reshaping academics and raising academic performance has all but overpowered a task of equally vital importance—educating our young people to become engaged members of their communities as citizens" (p. 7).

Stevenson (2006) examines eight educational and societal trends and related issues that are expected to significantly impact public education and schools in a changing 21st-century America and addresses the question: "What can we expect regarding education and the place we call school over the next ten to twenty years?" The issues surrounding these trends indicate the wide range of educational decisions that must be made and the difficulty of coming to consensus on those decisions.

Trend 1: The "baby boomers" versus the "new majority." The changing demographics will make educating youth more difficult than any time in our history. The baby boomers will have the numbers and the wealth to exercise great control over the political process. At the same time, the historically minority school populations, Hispanic and African American, in combination, will constitute the major of American youth. Demographics indicate that this new majority will come to school with the chances of living in poverty greater, parents less likely to be well educated, limited access to school readiness experiences, and insufficient health care. *The issues:* An aging population will tend to resist being taxed without seeing an obvious direct benefit. The children coming from increasingly diverse backgrounds are likely to require more assistance from the educational system than ever before. If an aging population is to be expected to continue to pay for school facilities for coming generations of children, educators and policymakers need to explore ways to reconceptualize schools as a place that any member of the community, regardless of age, can come most anytime for personal development, human services support, and human interaction.

Trend 2: The struggle for control of American education. A critical factor related to what is taught and the physical appearance of schools themselves has to do with who, if anyone, will govern education in America. There are five different perceptions of how education should be governed: (1) some argue that the public education system is basically satisfactory, but needs periodic tuning up; (2) others want to keep the present form, but suggest it needs a major overhaul; (3) others suggest that education is a public responsibility but one that needs to be met in a different way; (4) others contend that the only way to ensure quality education is to move to a new delivery system; and (5) still others argue that education is a commodity that consumers need to purchase themselves, and thus the "public" in education should be removed, including taxpayer support. *The issues:* On one hand, significant political efforts are being made to strengthen public education within the context in which it has long operated. At the same time, powerful political efforts are being made to convince the American public and federal and state officials to open up the education enterprise to the free market with vouchers and tax credits.

Trend 3: Defining what school will teach. Some educators have accepted—whether they agree or not—educational accountability as measured by prescribed indicators of academic success (standardized test scores) as the primary driving force in schooling for the foreseeable future. Others continue to fight for a broader definition of what schools should teach and what teachers should be accountable for in the educational process. *The issues:* A basic question is "What do Americans actually want students to learn and know as a result of taking courses and attending classes?" Some argue the responsibilities of schools have been too broadly defined, making the job of educators nearly impossible. Others argue that education has usurped the responsibilities of home, church, and community. Others contend that schools should not use limited resources to teach morals, promote respect for diversity, or present theoretical positions that are in conflict with religious beliefs.

Trend 4: Instructional delivery—people versus machines. A significant debate is occurring about how students should be instructed. There is an increasing shortage of qualified teachers, especially in math and science, and many of today's teachers are baby boomers retiring in the next 5 to 10 years. Some suggest having "master teachers" and technology experts develop a complete curriculum that could be delivered through computer and telecommunications technology. Learning would be largely technology driven and support personnel would be likely to have a two-year technological degree in instructional management. *The issues:* Providing effective teachers for classrooms will shortly reach crisis proportions. Educators and citizens will have to find a way to balance the need for providing quality teaching for an increasingly diverse, at-risk student population with an aging population's need to protect a limited or fixed income.

Trend 5: Smaller, neighborhood schools. The concept that "bigger is better" is being rejected by more and more parents, educators, and policymakers. School districts are considering "deconsolidation," returning to smaller schools within defined neighborhoods and communities. *The issues:* On the positive side, when smaller schools are located in readily identifiable neighborhoods, parents and community members tend to take a more personal interest in them. On the negative side, studies conclude that the effect of school size may vary with the type of student. Evidence suggests that at-risk students may perform better in smaller schools while students at a higher socioeconomic level may benefit from a larger school's more diverse curriculum and faculty expertise. There is also concern that the movement to smaller schools may be an unwise use of limited tax dollars, leading to a further fragmentation of American society, and exacerbating the already critical teacher shortage.

Trend 6: Small class size versus technology. Research on the impact of teacher/pupil ratios on student outcomes is the basis for a national movement to reduce class size. In the rush to reduce teacher/pupil ratios, many schools, districts, and states and the federal government have placed unprepared or ill-prepared teachers in spaces not suited to be classrooms. *The issues:* While few deny the potential effect of reducing the teacher/pupil ratio, a growing number of researchers and policymakers argue that unless educators change how students are now taught, smaller class size will not automatically improve student outcomes. Others contend that while student performance may improve, there may be more efficient, less expensive ways to achieve the same results, for example enhanced quality of teaching and use of technology. There is also concern about the reality of having sufficient resources available to fully implement class size reduction.

Trend 7: Grade span reconfiguration. As educators and policymakers work to optimize student learning, every aspect of how education is delivered requires scrutiny. To date, what grade levels are grouped in a school setting has been haphazard and a myriad of grade spans are used across the county. *The issues:* Some research is emerging on what grade spans make schools more or less successful. Findings indicate that while grade spans are not likely the primary determinant on school productivity, they play a part in how much students learn and how much they retain. There is also the view that even if there is not an optimal grade pattern for maximizing student achievement measured by standardized tests, other benefits (such as increased self-esteem and tolerance) may be gained by reconfiguring grade spans. Further research is needed to determine if implementing a new grade span pattern is worth the cost or if the same amount of money spent another way (new technology, teacher development, etc.) produces greater results.

Trend 8: The physical environment in schools and optimizing learning. Research has shown that the quality of the school facility affects teacher retention, student achievement, student behavior, and even the basic health of both students and teachers. *The issues:* The reality is that some schools are not performing adequately, not because of lack of effort, but because the physical environment is either not conducive to attracting top-notch personnel and clients, or it hinders the teaching and learning experience by requiring teachers and students to expend physical and emotional energy to overcome rooms that are too hot, deal with inordinate glare, and/or read without sufficient lighting to view assignments accurately. A national analysis of the physical condition of America's schools indicates that 75% of them need repairs, renovations, and modernizations and that, on average, the estimated cost to bring each school up to standard is $2.2 million.

WOOING THE PUBLIC

Johnson and Friedman (2006) acknowledge that gaining a workable public consensus on a core of common educational goals and drafting reform initiatives to achieve them is one of the greatest communications and engagement challenges schools face.

> There are so many expectations, so many possible avenues for change, so many demands on scarce resources, and so many groups that want to be at the table. The energy aimed at improving student learning, the renewed commitment to closing the achievement gaps, the wellspring of new ideas— are assets. But at some point, school leaders have to decide what to do first . . . [and] create the educational partnerships to make progress toward common goals. (Worrisome Situations section, concluding para.)

A study conducted by the Coalition of Community Schools (Blank and others, 2005) examines leadership strategies that have worked to bring school and community together to create and sustain educational partnerships. The strategies identified include:

1. Leaders understand that the whole community must work together if children are to succeed in school and life, and they advocate expanded supports, realizing that young people who are successful in one area of their development are more likely to be successful in other areas.

2. Leaders take their commitment to the public and make opportunities to talk about how important public schools are to the community.
3. Leaders work to build political support, recognizing that commitment from elected officials, including legislators, mayors, county commissioners, and school board members is key to securing community support.
4. Leaders prepare for—and manage—transitions in leadership.
5. Leaders seek better use of existing resources, rethinking the ways they are being used.
6. Leaders seek innovative strategies to ensure sustainability, seeking solutions that can provide long-term support for direct services and critical resources for coordination.

The influence of the family and the community on what happens inside the school has been well documented. It is equally true that what happens inside the school affects the community. Rich (1998) suggests that educators address the public's need for a new set of R's: *respect, reassurance,* and *recognition.* These three R's, like the old three R's of reading, 'riting, and 'rithmetic, are intimately connected with academic achievement, especially when the goal is to build a sense of investment for everyone in the community.

Rich asserts that educators who want the public to care about local schools should develop school and district plans that:

1. *Build respect.* Set educational responsibilities for the family. Send messages and establish climates that communicate the twin ideas that families are important partners in the educational process, and that every family has strengths that can be mobilized on behalf of children. Make school schedules convenient for families. Overcome the problems caused by conflicting schedules of working parents and teachers by changing the time and place of parent-teacher conferences or restructuring teacher time. Undertake collaborative efforts to reach families. A network of agencies, community groups, businesses, and media can help provide a variety of supports, including mentoring and apprenticeships. Use school for community needs. By increasing the use of school facilities to serve community needs, schools can position themselves to be more than just

suppliers of services; they can be facilitators of learning for the community.

2. *Supply reassurance.* Provide practical information families need about how to help their children before there are problems. Offer a realistic picture of what school can accomplish. Build public awareness of the many roles and services the school provides, its basic strengths, and the challenges and problems encountered by families and schools today. Create a strong understanding of what even the best schools cannot do. Encourage family involvement at all levels of schooling and at every age. School efforts focusing on parent-child communication can allay the fear of teens that no one cares about them and that their schooling lacks meaning. Provide an active role for fathers to be involved directly at home and at school and use messages that support the image of men as caregivers, not just providers. Provide training for teachers on how to integrate what is learned outside the classroom with what is learned inside, and how to work with adults as well as children.

3. *Provide recognition.* Start early, before children come to school. Provide information to parents about their educational role, starting with a child's birth with in-hospital programs sponsored by schools. Establish connections with family daycare and consider offering training about education for daycare providers through a variety of media, from print to local cable channels. Create helpful roles for the private sector. Provide businesses with information on how they can support family-school relationships and engage in educational partnerships. Let people, especially parents, know their involvement is appreciated and valued. Share news about school, student, and family accomplishments widely through a variety of media and at local civic and community group meetings, portraying successes as community accomplishments so everyone can take pride in them.

TAPPING THE POTENTIAL

Johnson and Friedman (2006) stress that school leadership alone cannot secure a broad and lasting base of support for public schools. They point out that Public Agenda's experience in different kinds of districts and in diverse communities provides documentation that genuine public engagement can help build a broader base for change, and "as importantly, it can help avoid the miscommunication that sometimes forestalls progress" (Worrisome Situations section, para. 1). They assert that traditional approaches to public engagement in education have not been particularly successful. In the traditional model, decision making is an expert-driven process where the wider community is rarely seen as a vital resource in the planning stage and sometimes is viewed as a problem to be managed. From this perspective, planning and implementing school improvement are confined to "a small circle of people in order to progress quickly and minimize static . . . [with] a minor nod toward gaining 'input' from 'customers' or 'end users'" (Authentic Alternatives, para. 2).

> By contrast, authentic engagement involves substantive give and take with those who have a vested interest in the decisions being made. If done well, it prompts deliberation, dialogue, shared responsibility, and cooperative action. Such engagement presupposes a more collaborative relationship among school leaders and various stakeholders, including the community, than is often the case. Top-down, one-way communication is replaced by a joint process of figuring out how to define and make progress on core challenges such as closing achievement gaps. . . . Traditional school leadership and professional expertise still count. . . . What it does mean is that leaders consult with a broad swath of the community to set overall goals and establish priorities for change. And because of this, authentic engagement offers a broader base for change and increases the chances that progress will continue even in the face of special interest politics or changes in school leadership. (Authentic Alternatives section, para. 3–5)

Johnson and Friedman stress that three components are indispensable:

1. *Taking time to plan an effective process.* Poorly designed, half-hearted engagement reaps poor results and can even backfire, frustrating and alienating people rather than bringing them together.
2. *Reaching beyond the usual suspects.* Public engagement is most informative and productive if it involves a broad cross section of stakeholders and community members, including a good number of parents, taxpayers, and community leaders who are not already strongly involved in school activities.

3. *Including choice work.* Giving people alternatives to consider is an effective spur to deliberation and dialogue. It is also one of the most efficient ways to help people become more knowledgeable and subtle in their thinking about how to set priorities and use limited resources.

In response to concerns over decreasing levels of participation, the League of Women Voters of Chicago (2004) undertook a civic engagement study to examine the factors that influence Americans' attitudes toward voting and political participation. The findings apply to achieving authentic public engagement in general:

1. The problem of nonengagement is most dire among the generation under 25, at a phase of life when people form lifelong habits of political behavior.
2. Engagement exists on a continuum of behavior that can and should be addressed at every point, from the totally "disengaged" to people who have some level of exposure and awareness of issues, through those who sometimes participate in community activities, and finally to those few who consistently express high levels of interest, awareness, and activism.
3. Cultural and social factors not directly related to politics have a significant effect on the degree of connection (if any) they feel with education and community issues.
4. People (even if interested) cannot and will not increase their levels of engagement unless they have access to reliable information relevant to their interests and are aware of how to interpret and act on that information.
5. Significant institutional barriers still deter engagement by the general public.
6. Many organizational efforts to encourage engagement have suffered from an "ad hoc" sensibility; they focus narrowly and/or in the short term, but lack the elements that could connect people to personally meaningful actions and inspire them to pursue higher levels of engagement over the long term.

Based on its findings, the project task force recommends a number of strategies to help people link their interests to action, both individually and in concert with fellow citizens. The strategies should:

1. Start with outreach toward those who demonstrate at least partial engagement as defined by the continuum, encouraging those individuals to reach those at lower levels of engagement via peer-to-peer networking.
2. Create a "brand" that represents ideas and values that appeal to this target audience, and promote that brand via a media-savvy social marketing campaign, integrating the Internet as an essential—but not exclusive—tool.
3. Identify, recruit, and train people to develop leadership, providing an access point for individuals to connect with each other and with organizations active on issues of concern.
4. Seek to build partnerships with other social institutions, businesses, and community organizations concerned with civic and public engagement.
5. Address politicians themselves as a secondary audience, incorporating them in a positive feedback loop demonstrating the mutual rewards of civic and public engagement.
6. Collect empirical baseline and outcome data on the effectiveness of the engagement initiative and address any shortcomings that are revealed.

Henig (2002) examined the issues of race and class in school politics and educational reform efforts in 11 cities, 4 black-led and 7 not predominately black-led. The findings reflect some interesting conclusions applicable to other efforts to secure effective public engagement.

[M]any of the cleavages did not reflect race in a direct or obvious way. On the other hand, . . . race still was—and is—a powerful force as a perceptual filter. It is a baseline definer of patterns of trust; a reservoir of potent symbols that can be divisive or unifying or both at the same time but that have tended to complicate rather than simplify the challenge of school reform. . . . [In all of the cities studied], there were numerous examples of systemic reform endeavors in which the business community and community leaders came together to elect a reform board, or agreed in other ways. But in all cases, these efforts were sporadic and ephemeral, and had limited measurable long-term gains. I would therefore argue that the primary challenge is to build a constituency that can sustain school reform, not simply initiate it. (p. 32)

SUCCESSFUL EDUCATIONAL PARTNERSHIP
INITIATIVES

Flaxman and others (1998) stress that the most successful education reform initiatives are collaborations within the context of the surrounding community. "Since schools alone cannot solve the problems imported into them from society, some projects reach beyond the schools; they draw upon the power of community . . . to improve schools and aspects of life in the community that impact education."

The authors outline these general characteristics of successful collaboratives:

1. They view the school and community as part of a social ecology that is interdependent and must be understood as a whole in order to identify problems and develop solutions.
2. They build relationships based on common concerns and mutual self-interest to foster increased involvement; create resources such as trust, information channels, and shared norms among people; and promote constructive action for change.
3. They acknowledge the role of power, or *the ability to act,* in school-community relationships in order to help families and educators recognize the self-interests of different groups and individuals in a particular education bureaucracy and the relative power that each has over educational policy and practices, and then to constructively influence these various groups to make decisions beneficial to students.
4. They foster the collaborative leadership of principals, with the goals of creating an environment where teachers and families feel safe enough to take risks, and even to fail, in an effort to create positive change; and of enabling principals to share the responsibilities of leadership with teachers, parents, and community members who have been identified as leaders.
5. They develop and train parents and educators as leaders so they can build networks of relationships and motivate and recruit people to accomplish tasks and develop the skills needed to reform education and resolve conflicts.
6. They monitor and evaluate progress, track the impact of reform

efforts on outcomes, and ensure accountability for educational improvement. (p. 43)

SUMMING UP

Making friends before you need them requires proactive educational leaders. Strengthening connections requires reaching out to families and community members and achieving an accurate understanding of the kind of family-school-community collaboration needed to achieve the goal of academic success for all children. If educators want family and community support, they must ask for it, regularly and often. One key to whether support is forthcoming is the way people are asked; the more personal the approach, the more likely the desired response.

The most effective and inclusive styles of educational leadership combine both bottom-up and top-down approaches. Educational leaders must share power and delegate decision-making authority to representative teams of teachers, parents, business leaders, senior citizens, and others. Understanding and giving voice to the multiple interests and expectations of diverse stakeholders are crucial to building a common vision. A sustained, inclusive dialogue will identify priorities, target strengths, and ensure that even the softest voice is heard.

Duffy (2005) emphasizes that both educators and the community at large need to understand that, given the complex and unstable nature of the school's external environment, planning for the future must be flexible and creative enough to respond to unexpected events.

There must be an understanding that the change path from the present to the future is not a straight line, and that the capacity to anticipate the future and respond quickly to unanticipated events is partially a function of the school's internal climate and partially a function of a redesigned, supportive external system.

Duffy cautions:

Peak performance is an illusion. . . . In the 21st century environment for school districts, there are multiple peaks that evoke images of the Rocky Mountains, where some peaks are higher than others. What if the peak a district sits atop is low compared to others, but people inside the district don't realize it? Wouldn't this lack of perspective create an illusion of success? It is possible, therefore, for a school district to be at what educators perceive as peak performance when it is really sitting on a suboptimal peak? Educators in these districts might cheer themselves silly as they sit atop the suboptimal performance peaks thinking, "We are already good. We don't need to improve." (p. 202)

Most educational reformers agree that engaging families and communities in public education is the pathway to educational success, but they acknowledge that there are many challenges to achieving this engagement. Lashway (2003) points out that the most instinctive response to new challenges is to work harder, and many school leaders have done just that. He emphasizes that at some point working harder reaches a point of diminishing returns and "sooner or later, untamed workloads result in declining morale and dimmed enthusiasm. In addition, just trying harder may not help leaders who are confronting issues for which they have not been trained and for which there are not clear answers" (Responding to Challenges section, para. 1). He would seem to agree with Lyndon Johnson that the best time for educators to make friends is before they need them. In his opinion, they must:

Attend to the learning of all members of the educational community. Together, they explore current practice, beliefs, and assumptions that serve as a basis for posing inquiry questions. These questions are the signposts in the hunt for evidence and the struggle with dissonance. Dissonance is tackled in dialogue, thereby lowering defenses and increasing shared understanding. This journey results in new approaches to student and adult learning, internal school accountability and shared responsibility, and a commitment to the decisions made for school improvement. (Concluding para.)

REFERENCES

Blank, M. J., Jehl, J., and Neary, M. (2005, Summer). Engaging the community: Strategies that work. *Threshold, 7*. A Cable in the Classroom Publication.

Boston, B. O. (2005). *Restoring the balance between academics and civic engagement in public schools.* American Youth Policy Forum and Association for Supervision and Curriculum Development. Retrieved February 28, 2006,

from http://www.aypf.org/publications/Restoring%20the%20Balance%20Report
.pdf

Duffy, F. M. (2005, Summer). Navigating whole-system change in school districts: What school public relations specialists need to know to support the process. *Journal of School Public Relations, 26,* 3.

Flaxman, E., Schwartz, W., Weiler, J., and Lahey, M. (1998). *Trends and issues in urban education.* New York: ERIC Clearinghouse on Urban Education. Retrieved February 28, 2006, from http://iumetc.columbia.edu/eric_archive/
mono//ti20.pdf

Henig, J. (2002). Electoral politics and school finance reform. *Brown v. board: Its impact on education, and what it left undone.* Conference proceedings, The Woodrow Wilson International Center for Scholars. Retrieved February 17, 2006, from http://wwics.si.edu/topics/pubs/ACF23F.pdf

Johnson, J., and Friedman, W. (2006, February). Dear public: Can we talk? *The School Administrator.* Retrieved February 23, 2006, from http://www.aasa.org/
publications/saarticledetail.cfm?ItemNumber=5211&snItemN umber=950&
tnItemNumber=951

Lashway, L. (2003). *The role of the school leader.* Clearinghouse for Educational Policy and Management. Retrieved February 7, 2006, from http://eric.uoregon
.edu/trends_issues/rolelead/index.html

League of Women Voters of Chicago. (2004). Executive Summary. *A time for action: A new vision for participatory democracy.* Retrieved May 4, 2006, from http://www.lwv.org/AM/Template.cfm?Section=Home&section=Voter_
Information1&template=CM/ContentDisplay.cfm&ContentFileID=239

Rich, D. (1998). Respect, reassurance, recognition. *Journal of Educational Relations, 19,* 3.

Stevenson, K. R. (2006). *Educational facilities within the context of a changing 21st century America.* Washington, DC: National Clearinghouse for Educational Facilities. Retrieved May 11, 2006, from http:///www.edfacilities.org/
Ed_Facilities_in_21st_Century.pdf

Index

About the Authors

Larry E. Decker is the Charles Stewart Mott Professor, an Eminent Scholar Chair in Community Education, at Florida Atlantic University, Boca Raton. Formerly, he was director of the Mid-Atlantic Center for Community Education, professor of educational leadership, and associate dean at the Curry School of Education, University of Virginia. He earned his PhD at Michigan State University. A leading spokesperson for the community education/community schools movement, he is the author of numerous publications that address educational reform and strengthening the collaboration of home, school, and community for educational success.

Virginia A. Decker is managing editor of Community Collaborators, Boca Raton, Florida. Formerly, she was the facilitator of the National Community Education Computer Network, an international teleconferencing system, a research assistant with the Bureau of Business and Economic Research at the University of Oregon, and an instructor at Lane Community College in Eugene, Oregon. She earned her MBA from the University of Oregon. She has coauthored a number of publications on grant seeking, family and community involvement, and educational planning and reform.

Pamela M. Brown is a research assistant and the Ernest O. Melby Community Education Fellow completing a PhD in Educational Leadership at Florida Atlantic University. Formerly she was chief of staff to the Fort

Lauderdale City Commission, assistant district administrator for the Florida Department of Children and Families, chairperson of the drama department at Wellacre High School for Boys in England, and external regional examiner for the Certificate of Secondary Education for the North West of England.